BESTSELLING
BOOK SERIES

Buzz Marketing with Blogs For Dummies®

Cheat Sheet

Most blogs have these features.

D0568458

Latest post

Current post category

Buzz Marketing with Blogs - Microsoft Internet Explorer

File   Edit   View   Favorites   Tools   Help

Back ·   ·   Search   Favorites   Links

Address http://www.buzzmarketingwithblogs.com/weblog/blog_most_looked_up_word_of_2004/   Go

Buzz Marketing with Blogs

Blog: Most Looked Up Word of 2004
Posted by S. Gardner on 12/01 at 11:37 AM • Blogging News

Merriam-Webster puts the word "blog" at the top of its list of the 10 most looked-up words of 2004. The count is determined by tracking all online searches of the dictionary and then excluding perennial look-ups. Here's the 2004 list:

1. blog
2. incumbent
3. electoral
4. insurgent
5. hurricane
6. cicada
7. peloton
8. partisan
9. sovereignty
10. defenestration

Here's how Merriam-Webster defines blog: *noun* [short for Weblog] (1999) : a Web site that contains an online personal journal with reflections, comments, and often hyperlinks

ABOUT

This blog is the companion Web site for "Buzz Marketing with Blogs for Dummies," a book for business professionals looking for answers and solutions for business blogging. Available March 2005. > Pre-order the book from Amazon.com now <

SEARCH

[   ] GO

CATEGORIES
- About the Book
- Blogging Events
- Great Blogs

— **Info about blog**

— **Latest timestamp**

— **Post author**

— **Search box**

Link to Trackback URI and references

Link to page containing only this post

Buzz Marketing with Blogs - Microsoft Internet Explorer

File   Edit   View   Favorites   Tools   Help

Back ·   ·   Search   Favorites   Links

Address http://www.buzzmarketingwithblogs.com/weblog/blog_most_looked_up_word_of_2004/   Go

10.   defenestration

Here's how Merriam-Webster defines blog: *noun* [short for Weblog] (1999) : a Web site that contains an online personal journal with reflections, comments, and often hyperlinks provided by the writer

Read about the list in CNN' story "Publisher: 'Blog' No. 1 word of the year". **Visit** Merriam-Webster for definitions of each of the top 10.

Source: Thanks to Robert Scoble for the info.

Comments (1) • Trackbacks (0) • Permalink

CATEGORIES
- About the Book
- Blogging Events
- Great Blogs
- Blogging Tips
- Blogging News
- Blogs and Business
- Buzz Words
- Blogging Tools
- Moblogging

ARCHIVES
- December 2004
- November 2004
- October 2004
- Complete Archives
- Category Archives

RECENT ENTRIES
- Clocks, MP3s, Weather and more from blogbox
- Lattes Are Only the Beginning
- Past Lives Resurface
- Blog: Most Looked Up Word of 2004
- Nominations for 2004 Weblog Awards
- Dave Winer Likes Pho
- Blog Business Summit
- Blogs for Sale
- HP's Linux VP Gets Bloggy
- Moblogging Paranoia
- Book Technical Editor
- Using Expression Engine

— **Post organized by subject categories**

— **Archived posts**

— **Link to add or read categories**

Buzz Marketing with Blogs For Dummies®

Quick HTML Guide for Bloggers

- **Creating bold text:** `This <b>word</b> is bold.`

- **Bolding and italicizing:** `Use <b><i>bold and italics</i></b>.`

- **Indenting a block of text:** `<blockquote>Four score and seven years ago our fathers brought forth on this continent a new nation, conceived in liberty and dedicated to the proposition that all men are created equal.</blockquote>`

- **Creating a link:** `I've got to go to <a href="http://www.google.com">Google</a> and look up basic HTML tags!`

Picking a Blog Solution

Use this table to help you decide whether to go with a hosted or an independent blog solution.

HOSTED	INDEPENDENT
_ I have no technical skills and no time to learn any.	_ I have some technical experience and want to learn more.
_ I don't have a technical person who can help me.	_ I want to fully customize the blog.
_ I have some technical skills, but not much time.	_ I want all the bells and whistles.
_ I can't spend any money on the blog.	_ I want the respect of other bloggers.
_ I have a very small budget.	_ I don't want to be limited by another company's bandwidth and servers.
_ I need to start blogging today.	_ I'm required to keep my data on my own server.

For Dummies: Bestselling Book Series for Beginners

Buzz Marketing with Blogs

FOR

DUMMIES®

Buzz Marketing
with Blogs
FOR
DUMMIES®

by Susannah Gardner

Wiley Publishing, Inc.

Buzz Marketing with Blogs For Dummies®

Published by
Wiley Publishing, Inc.
111 River Street
Hoboken, NJ 07030-5774
www.wiley.com

For general information on our other products and services, please contact our Customer Care Department within the U.S. at 800-762-2974, outside the U.S. at 317-572-3993, or fax 317-572-4002.

For technical support, please visit www.wiley.com/techsupport.

Wiley also publishes its books in a variety of electronic formats. Some content that appears in print may not be available in electronic books.

Library of Congress Control Number: 2005921607

ISBN-13: 978-0-7645-8457-2

ISBN-10: 0-7645-8457-X

Manufactured in the United States of America

10 9 8 7 6 5 4 3 2 1

1O/RR/QT/QV/IN

About the Author

Susannah Gardner is the co-founder and creative director of Hop Studios Internet Consultants [www.hopstudios.com], a Web design company specializing in custom Web solutions for content publishers. Her partner in life, crime and work, is Travis Smith, former editor of Variety.com.

Susannah is also a freelance writer and author; she is the co-author of "Dreamweaver MX 2004 for Dummies," from Wiley Publishing, and "Teach Yourself Visually: Dreamweaver MX 2004," also from Wiley Publishing.

From 1997 to 2003, Susannah was an adjunct professor at the University of Southern California School for Communication, where she taught in the School of Journalism. Her classes in online publishing took students from zero to Web site in a semester.

Prior to running Hop Studios, Susannah worked in the Online Journalism and Communication Program at the University of Southern California, writing curriculum, teaching, and conducting research at the intersection of technology and journalism. She was a senior editor of the Online Journalism Review [www.ojr.org], the media industry's only Internet-focused journalism publication. Susannah also spent four years at *The Los Angeles Times*, one of six editors responsible for launching that newspaper's Web site. During her time at LATimes.com she established the site's multimedia lab, which produced ground-breaking Web audio, video and animation. She also launched and edited MetaHollywood, an online-only publication that covered new Hollywood technology and was LATimes.com's single largest revenue source in 1998.

Susannah earned bachelor's degrees in Print Journalism and American literature at USC. Today she is pursuing a master's degree in Public Art Studies, examining issues that cross the traditional of boundaries of Internet publishing, journalism and art.

To learn more about her Web design company, visit www.hopstudios.com. She keeps a personal blog at www.unfavorablepink.com, and a blog for this book at www.buzzmarketingforblogs.com.

Dedication

This book is for my partner and husband, Travis Smith, who supports me even when I make it impossible for him to do so. Travis, I would not be who I am today without you.

Author's Acknowledgments

I have so many people to thank for making this book possible, and for having patience with me while I wrote it!

First, hugs and thanks to my husband, Travis. His eagle editing eye and voracious appetite for blogs was a huge help and has improved this book to no end. It has fallen on Travis to keep our lives running smoothly when deadlines loomed, and he has done it all with quiet aplomb. Travis is also responsible for signing me up for my very first email account, and quite possibly for everything that followed.

Thanks are also due to Janine Warner, friend and colleague, who invited me to co-author "Dreamweaver MX 2004 For Dummies" with her and started me down this road. Whenever I had questions, no matter how neophyte, Janine shared her expertise with patience and grace — and despite her own book deadlines!

My long-suffering editor Beth Taylor has kept me on time, and fixed all those late-night typos, run-on sentences and general stupidities. This book would never have been possible without the persistence and determination of Melody Layne, acquisitions editor at Wiley (and a blogger!). Thanks also to my technical editor, Paul Chaney of Radiant Marketing, who kept me on the straight-and-narrow. There are many at Wiley Publishing whose names I don't know but who nonetheless played an important role in making this book possible: Thank you to all of you.

I owe much to my friends, family and colleagues, all of whom were wonderfully patient as I shifted work and life around in order to write. Thank you to my parents, Jan and Phil Gardner, my brother Matt, my sister Debbie, my mother-in-law Pat Smith, and my sister-in-law Virginia Smith. Thanks also to Lance Watanabe, Jae and Karin Sung, Elaine Zinngrabe, Zipporah Lax, Jason and Noriko Manikel, Deborah Nathanson, Tracy Dominick, Robin Rauzi, Amy Leach, Dorothy Ingebretsen, Jordan and Michele Raphael, and Martin and Tracy Spedding.

Most of all, I'm grateful to you, the person reading this. An author is not an author without readers.

Publisher's Acknowledgments

We're proud of this book; please send us your comments through our online registration form located at www.dummies.com/register/.

Some of the people who helped bring this book to market include the following:

Acquisitions, Editorial, and Media Development

Project Editor: Beth Taylor

Acquisitions Editor: Melody Layne

Copy Editor: Rebecca Senninger

Technical Editor: Paul Chaney

Editorial Manager: Leah Cameron

Media Development Manager: Laura VanWinkle

Media Development Supervisor: Richard Graves

Editorial Assistant: Amanda Foxworth

Cartoons: Rich Tennant (www.the5thwave.com)

Composition Services

Project Coordinator: Maridee Ennis

Layout and Graphics: Carl Byers, Andrea Dahl, Lauren Goddard, Stephanie D. Jumper, Barry Offringa, Heather Ryan

Proofreaders: Leeann Harney, Carl William Pierce, TECHBOOKS Production Services

Indexer: TECHBOOKS Production Services

Publishing and Editorial for Technology Dummies

 Richard Swadley, Vice President and Executive Group Publisher

 Andy Cummings, Vice President and Publisher

 Mary Bednarek, Executive Acquisitions Director

 Mary C. Corder, Editorial Director

Publishing for Consumer Dummies

 Diane Graves Steele, Vice President and Publisher

 Joyce Pepple, Acquisitions Director

Composition Services

 Gerry Fahey, Vice President of Production Services

 Debbie Stailey, Director of Composition Services

Contents at a Glance

Table of Contents

Introduction

Your time is precious, and you probably bought this book because you have a specific project in mind and need to get it off the ground quickly. *Buzz Marketing with Blogs For Dummies* is designed to take you through the process of starting a business blog from beginning to end, including how to use blogs to generate buzz about your products, services, and business.

This book is useful for you whether you are the head of the marketing department in a huge corporation, the CEO of an Internet startup, or a small business owner, because I focus on what makes a blog work — and how blogs can work for you. Also, I realize that not everyone has the technical skills necessary to start a blog themselves, so I've provided some options for all levels of experience.

This book is useful to you whether you're trying to take part in the conversations in the world of blogs or becoming a blogger yourself. I've covered everything from tech to legal, so you can go forward knowing you have a resource that covers every aspect of this new and exciting medium.

About This Book

Chances are the fact that you bought this book means you have some ideas about starting a blog — and I want to get you started right away! You don't have to memorize this book or even read it in order. Feel free to skip straight to the chapter with the information you need and come back to the beginning later. Each chapter is designed to give you easy answers and guidance, accompanied by step-by-step instructions for specific tasks.

The first part of the book is designed to set the stage by giving you a taste of how blogs can work for your business, how buzz marketing and blogs go hand in hand, and how to go about planning a blog project.

If you need to know whether blogs are the right path for your company, and quickly, the first three chapters help you make that assessment quickly. They also give you a taste of some of the important issues covered in later chapters. Even if you don't read anything else in the book, the first three chapters ensure that you understand just what goes into a successful business blog and how you can get started with one today.

If you want to create a more customized blog or need to know more about the legal issues that have arisen during blogs' short lifespan, you can go directly to the chapter that relates to your situation. Want to find out just how real businesses are using blogs in ways you can be inspired by? I've included case studies of real-life blogs and bloggers. I concentrated on finding blogs that are pushing the boundaries and doing so successfully so that you can benefit from their knowledge.

Blogs, Web logs, blogrolling, RSS — this industry is just packed with jargon, tech terms, and concepts most people never run across. I've worked hard to make sure these terms are clearly defined for you, including examples of best practices (when there are any!). If you run across a term that you don't understand while visiting a blog, check the glossary at the back of the book for help. And if you don't find information there, I created a book blog where I'll keep you abreast of the latest trends in the blogging industry. I hope to see you there soon!

Conventions Used in This Book

Keeping things consistent makes them easier to understand. In this book, those consistent elements are *conventions*. Notice how the word *conventions* is in italics? That's a convention I use frequently. I put new terms in italics and then define them so that you know what they mean.

URLs (Web addresses) or e-mail addresses in text look like this: `www.buzz marketingwithblogs.com`. Sometimes, however, I set URLs off on their own lines, like this:

```
www.buzzmarketingwithblogs.com
```

That's so you can easily spot them on a page if you want to type them into your browser to visit a site. I assume that your Web browser doesn't require the introductory `http://` for Web addresses. Most browsers don't need that anymore, but if you use an older browser, remember to type this before the address.

When I introduce you to a set of features, such as options in a dialog box, I set these items apart with bullets so that you can see that they're related. When I want you to follow instructions, I use numbered steps to walk you through the process.

What You're Not to Read

To make this book work for you, you don't need to sit down and start with Chapter 1. Go right to the information you need most, and get to work. If you are new to blogs, skim through the chapters to get an overview and then go back and read in greater detail what's most relevant to your project. Whether you are building a blog as a rank beginner or working on redesigning an existing blog to make it better, you'll find everything you need in these pages.

Foolish Assumptions

Just because blogs have a funny name doesn't mean they have to be written by funny people — or even humorous ones! If you can write an e-mail, you can write a blog. Have confidence in yourself, and realize that this is an informal medium that forgives mistakes unless you try to hide them. In keeping with the philosophy behind the *For Dummies* series, this book is an easy-to-use guide designed for readers with a wide range of experience. Being interested in blogs and buzz marketing is all that I expect from you.

If you're new to blogs, this book gets you started and walks you step by step through all the skills and elements you need to create a successful business Web log. If you've been reading and using blogs for some time now, *Buzz Marketing with Blogs For Dummies* is an ideal reference that ensures you're doing the best job possible with any blog you start or manage.

How This Book Is Organized

To ease you through the process of building a blog, I organized *Buzz Marketing with Blogs For Dummies* to be a complete reference. This section provides a breakdown of the parts of the book and what you can find in each one. Each chapter walks you through a different element, providing tips and helping you understand the vocabulary of Weblogs.

Part 1: Getting Started with Business Blogs

This part introduces you to the general concepts of using blogs to create buzz and better customer relationships for your business. In Chapter 1, I show you some good business blogs and give you some background about this very young industry. You find out what's involved in creating a blog and take a quick tour of the legal issues they've raised. Best of all, I tell you just what a blog can do for your business — and what it can't.

In Chapter 2, I give you some background in buzz marketing itself, with a special focus on how buzz occurs online. More important, I take a look at just how buzz and blogs work together to form a powerful marketing tool.

While reading Chapter 3, you find out about planning and building a good business blog from the ground up. Discover more about who makes a good blogger, how to name your blog, and some basic HTML tags indispensable for all bloggers. Most importantly, I talk realistically about when it's time to hire a Web designer rather than trying to do everything yourself.

Part II: Setting Up a Business Blog

If Part I is about getting you up to speed on blogging and buzz marketing, Part II is devoted to getting you blogging. In Chapter 4, you make your biggest blogging decision (aside from defining its purpose) by deciding which blogging software solution is right for you and your company. I explain what your options are and how to balance budgets while still getting the functionality you need. In addition, I show you how to register your own domain name so that your blog has a unique identity that people can remember.

Chapter 5 is devoted to getting you started blogging right away using the industry standard blogging tool Blogger — for free! Step by step, I walk you through starting up a blog, creating a post, adding links, and inviting others to contribute to your blog. In addition, I give you information about other blog solutions that get you started quickly and tell you about some common technologies that you may want to include in your blog.

In Chapter 6, I help you take control of your blog by introducing you to some serious blogging software that will let you customize every aspect of your blog. This powerful software can be technically complicated to install and configure, but you gain flexibility, expandability, and even blogosphere cachet when you use one of these solutions. If you have some blog experience and want to take your blog to the next level, this chapter will give you some strategies to pursue.

Part III: Minding Blog Etiquette and Culture

Part III is dedicated to making sure you know how to get the most out of your business blog without committing any serious etiquette breaches. In Chapter 7, you define your audience and find out how to target your blog to reach that group most effectively — and keep them coming back for more. I give you some specifics on tracking your users with traffic software and how to interpret your log files.

In Chapter 8, I introduce you to the blogosphere, the community of bloggers worldwide. They are a talkative group with sharp eyes, but they reward hard work and honesty with respect. You also learn how to participate in the dialogue of others' blogs in a way that conveys your message but doesn't get you branded as a spammer.

Chapter 9 helps you avoid some common business blog pitfalls and traps. I show you how to develop some standards that can help you create a blog that serves your customers without giving away your trade secrets, and I talk about how to handle corrections and mistakes.

Part IV: Positioning Your Blog

In Part IV, you find a series of chapters that help you make the most of your blog. In Chapter 10, I focus on making the most of the informal blog writing style, with some specific tips for making sure your posts are serving the needs of your readers.

Chapter 11 is devoted to developing excitement and buzz around your blog by making sure the public knows about it. I look at some of the technologies that have sprung up to support the trading of links and comments that make the blogosphere such a small world.

In Chapter 12, you find out how to keep things legal and ethical but still interesting. This chapter covers the ways in which blogs might create new legal liabilities for your company, with some strategies for preventing those problems before you can experience them the hard way.

Part V: Making the Most of Your Blog

Part of what makes blogs so exciting is technical innovation. In Chapter 13, I show you just what technologies make your blog the best it can be, and how you can make good use of photos, audio, and RSS feeds.

Chapter 14 puts business tools in your hands, including ways in which advertising services, links, and affiliate programs can make your blog a source of revenue. Find out about the many tools available specifically for bloggers to make some money with their blogs.

In Chapter 15, I look at using blog software for more than it was intended and running intranet Web sites, Web stores, and entire Web sites off powerful blogging software solutions. You may be surprised by how much more than blogs blog software is good for!

Part VI: The Part of Tens

In The Part of Tens, you discover ten ways to break a blog posting dry spell; the ten traits of good bloggers; and best of all, ten outstanding blogs making the most of technology and the Internet.

Part VII: Appendixes

Appendix A is a glossary to all those confusing blog terms that have sprung up in recent years. Appendix B walks you through making the best use of the book blog to get the latest information about blogs, blog technology, and trends.

Use Appendix C during your research into the right blogging software solution for you. Appendix D is a quick refresher on how domain names work so that you can make the most of yours. In Appendix E contains case studies to help you further understand how to create a great blog.

I include a unique feature in *Buzz Marketing with Blogs For Dummies* — case studies of today's best business blogs. I interviewed successful bloggers and gathered information about their experiences. I also asked each of them to give you their best advice for potential business bloggers. You find some invaluable information about what does and doesn't work for a business blog that can help you avoid making the same mistakes.

Icons Used in This Book

This icon reminds you of an important concept or procedure that you'll want to store away in your memory bank for future use.

This icon signals technical stuff that you may find informative and interesting but isn't essential for you to know to develop a blog. Feel free to skip over these sections if you don't like the techy stuff.

This icon indicates a tip or technique that can save you time and money — and a headache.

 This icon warns you of any potential pitfalls — and gives you the all-important information on how to avoid them.

Where to Go from Here

Turn to Chapter 1 to dive in and get started with an intro to business blogs and an overview of what makes a business blog successful and useful. If you just want to get started blogging today, I urge you to skim Chapter 4 and then spend some serious time using the step-by-step instructions. Don't forget to send me your efforts — I can't wait to see your brand-new blog!

Part I

Getting Started with Business Blogs

The 5th Wave   By Rich Tennant

"Just how accurately should my business blog reflect my actual place of business?"

In this part . . .

Part I is all about getting you up to speed on how blogging and buzz marketing are creating exciting new opportunities for businesses. If you're looking to understand the phenomenon that is blogging, and discover a little about the history of their evolution, you'll enjoy Chapter 1. You also get a good overview of the uses to which business blogs are being put today. Chapter 2 gets your creative energies started by giving you a closer look at buzz marketing on the Internet, especially by and in blogs. And in Chapter 3, get a thorough understanding of the issues involved in producing a good blog.

Chapter 1

Checking Out Business Blogs

*T*raditional business marketing is changing. More ads, catchier slogans, louder television commercials, brighter colors . . . everything's been done to catch the consumer's eye. Your company may have a great product that people love, but if you can't make them pick you out of a crowd, you're sunk.

So what's the solution?

Stop talking at consumers, and start talking to them. Begin a conversation with them that encourages them to talk to others about your business or product. That's what buzz marketing with blogs is all about: getting a conversation going between business and consumer.

The term *blog* is a combination of the words *Web* and *log*. Blogs are online chronicles that are updated frequently, sometimes even daily. An *update* (also called an *entry* or a *post*) is usually quite short, perhaps just a few sentences, and readers can often respond to an entry online. People who write blogs are commonly called *bloggers*. Bloggers, tongue in cheek, call themselves and their blogs the *blogosphere*.

Generating Buzz for Your Blog

The power of blogs is *buzz*, or conversations and Web links that bounce from blog to blog and gather mass and impact. Companies that use blogs as buzz-building tools are finding substantial readerships of people who avidly want to know what the blogger has to say and respond with comments to every new posting. The best part is that they often spread that message to others within their sphere of influence through blogs, instant messages, or e-mail.

Word of mouth is one of the strongest marketing tools your company can use. For example, a recommendation for a product or service from a trusted friend is more memorable and convincing than the cleverest television ad — and more likely to be turned into action.

What if you had a tool at your disposal that could reach hundreds of people at once who are actually interested in your products or services and appreciate the fact that you're making information available to them? A Weblog is such a tool. Blogs are all about opening up your knowledge, expertise, processes, and goals to your customers. Done right, they can give back loyalty, goodwill, and valuable feedback.

The blog format is breaking new ground for business by:

- Providing a way to interact with customers
- Being a clearinghouse of information and expertise
- Getting valuable feedback — including criticism — from those who know your products and services best: customers
- Changing public opinion during times of negative attention
- Simplifying and amplifying collaboration between employees

The informal, engaging style and interactive format of blogs make them very attractive for companies looking to change public perception, take part in a dialogue begun in the press, correct a mistake, take a position, and get feedback from customers.

Best of all, blogs are a nearly instantaneous publishing format; the software that runs a blog speeds up, instead of slows down, the publication of news and information to your Web site. They're easy and cheap to set up; from a cost/benefit point of view, blogs are very easy to justify, and results come quickly.

Blogs are a great way to keep employees and customers abreast of the latest news faster and more effectively than a traditional company newsletter. They disseminate announcements more quickly than the most centrally placed bulletin board. And they can get you customer feedback more cheaply than any focus group or survey.

But what makes a blog different from any other corporate Web site? A blog is designed around a particular form of publishing: frequent, short updates often using links, accompanied by a corresponding set of comments from readers. Blogs are an organic process, meant to be written and read regularly — even daily — and simply aren't as "packaged" and controlled as a press release. Their tone is usually informal, almost stream of consciousness. In fact, many bloggers don't bother to use capital letters or spell-checkers!

A typical business blog

A good blog format contains a combination of these elements:

✔ **Name:** You almost always find the name of the blog at the top. It is usually short, catchy, and humorous.

✔ **The latest post:** The date, and occasionally the time, display so that you know which entry is the latest one. Unlike the front page of most business Web sites, a blog home page is usually quite long, because older entries also display on the home page.

✔ **Comment link:** After each entry, most bloggers invite the reader to add a comment.

✔ **A collection of related info:** On the right- or left-hand side of the browser window, this info may consist of e-mail subscription opportunities, explanatory or biographical information, archived entries, and links to other blogs that the blogger reads regularly and recommends.

The following figure is a good example of a standard blog format and layout. Blog Maverick (www.blogmaverick.com) is the blog of Dallas Mavericks owner Mark Cuban.

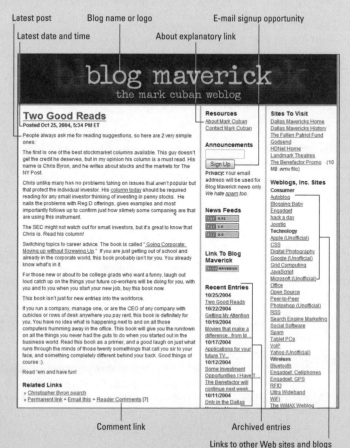

Latest post   Blog name or logo   E-mail signup opportunity

Latest date and time   About explanatory link

Comment link   Archived entries

Links to other Web sites and blogs

Although the writing may be free-form, a blog has some common organizational structures that make understanding and participating in the conversation easy for readers.

Discovering How Businesses Are Using Blogs

Blogs aren't the be-all, end-all solution for marketing, but they go a long way toward establishing rapport, trust, and information exchange — things that are hard to create between companies and the rest of the world. Using blogs effectively is a two-part strategy:

- Being aware of what is being said online about your company. More and more consumers are using blogs to articulate their own thoughts and feelings about a company and its products. Starting a business blog helps you to be a participant in the conversation.

  To find out what's being said about you, simply search for your company name in a search engine, such as Google. In many cases, some of the top returns are blog posts of consumers who've expressed an opinion about your company or products.

- Considering whether your company can benefit from a blog.

In the following sections, I discuss just how businesses are putting blogs to work for them to do a better job reaching and talking with customers, increasing interest in a company or product, setting themselves up as leaders in their industries, and more.

Communicating with customers

Blogs can be used to convey news, events, plans, and customer support information to your customers — and to engage them in dialogue that can be used to improve the way your company functions.

Fast Company, a business publication tracking new business practices, competition, and processes, started the FC Now blog (www.fascompany.com) in order to discuss ideas, business news, and resources with its readers. Shown in Figure 1-1, it encourages readers to suggest topics and to post comments. Several staff members contribute to the blog, each posting on a subject that interests them personally. FC Now is a way for Fast Company to respond quickly to breaking news and to let its readers know about resources and tools. Postings range from asking former customers why they aren't still customers, a link to a Web site that covers technical horror stories, news about the company's *a cappella* music groups, and articles from other publications pertinent to the Fast Company audience.

The effect of the blog is an open, informal interaction between Fast Company and its readers — achieving something that is more free-form, frequent, and organic than the rigid format of a print publication can deliver.

Figure 1-1: FC Now uses its blog to further dialogue with its readers.

Establishing expertise

The law firm of Stark & Stark is promoting the expertise of its lawyers through the Traumatic Brain Injury Law Blog. Lawyer Bruce H. Stern posts regularly to the blog on topics intended to keep his readers fully informed on new case law, news, events, and courtroom strategies. Posts often include information on new medical treatments and research that Stern's clients may find useful.

Postings from October 2004 included information about accident reconstruction experts, pediatric brain injury treatment research, a new online medical journal, and a recent court ruling on the admissibility of computer simulations of car accidents.

The blog is actually part of a larger package of information pertinent to brain injuries that includes articles about brain injury cases, FAQs, and a bulletin board. This strategic positioning is a service for existing clients and makes a strong case to potential clients that Stark & Stark has a great deal of expertise in this area. It's a win–win for the law firm and for Stern, both of which get great exposure and provide a genuine service to clients. Find the blog at www.braininjurylawblog.com and in Figure 1-2.

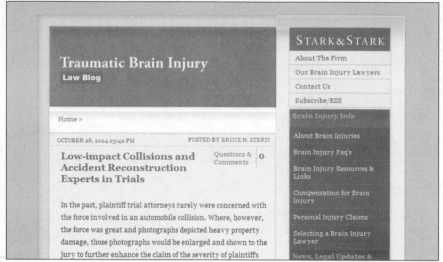

Figure 1-2:
The
Traumatic
Brain Injury
Law Blog.

Generating interest

A deliberately short-lived June 2004 blog called the Art of Speed showcased the work of 15 filmmakers in a 20-day blog collaboration between Gawker Media and Nike. The blog was an experiment in brand blogging, designed to bring together an established and successful brand with a format that reaches the online market.

Posts covered everything from the background of the filmmakers to a speed hiking record, and visitors watched videos of each film online in high or lowresolution. The point? Get the Nike logo in front of an audience that's interested in content, not advertising, while demonstrating Nike's unique company ethos of encouragement and challenge. The blog, which you can still view at www.gawker.com/artofspeed, is shown in Figure 1-3.

Driving action and sales

Buzz Bruggeman, one of the founders of ActiveWords, is a firm believer in the power of blogs — because he experiences their effectiveness every day. ActiveWords (shown in Figure 1-4) is a small company, the maker of software that lets you set keyword shortcuts to any file, folder, or application on your Windows computer. Its target audience is the constant computer user looking for ways to do common tasks faster and with less effort. Buzz says more than 50 percent of the company's trial software downloads are the result of someone blogging about ActiveWords and sending readers to www.activewords.com. A review of ActiveWords on a blog with 500 or 600 readers garners the company more software downloads than a four-star writeup in *USA Today*, which sells more than 2.3 million copies a day.

Figure 1-3:
The Art of
Speed blog
focused
on the
work of 15
filmmakers
and the
concept of
speed.

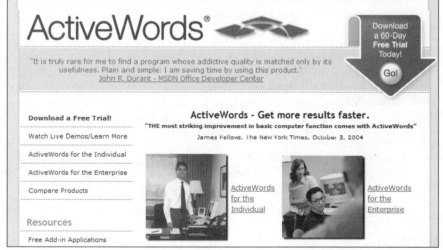

Figure 1-4:
Active
Words co-
founder
Buzz
Bruggeman
uses his
personal
blogs to
give the
company a
human
feeling.

ActiveWords – US™

"In The ClueTrain Manifesto, Doc Searls [and co-authors] writes that 'markets are conversations,'" Bruggeman says. "I say products are also conversations. And if markets and products are conversations, blogs are a terrific way to have that conversation with people."

Part of why ActiveWords has been covered so well is because Bruggeman himself has a blog at buzzmodo.typepad.com/buzzmodo. "I want people to see that behind ActiveWords there are real people with real ideas trying to solve real problems, who will engage in a real conversation, respond, and react," he says.

Fixing what's broke

Thanks to years of monopolistic business practices, Microsoft's reputation in the marketplace has been, shall we say, not the brightest. (A search on Google for the phrase "more evil than Satan" used to return the Microsoft home page. See `en.wikipedia.org/wiki/Googlebomb`.) That feeling has deep roots in much of the technical community, the very group Microsoft relies upon to buy and use its products.

In 2000, Robert Scoble started a blog whose focus was on Microsoft technology. Scoble's smart technical writing attracted a large and dedicated following. Some of the folks at Microsoft admired Scoble's open, honest style so much that the company hired him. He is now a technical evangelist for the company.

Scoble walks a fine line between promoting Microsoft products and being a real resource for technical information, often going so far as to gently criticize what Microsoft is doing. He never hesitates to acknowledge a better competing technology, and he says this straight-shooting attitude has earned him respect in the blogosphere and within the company. Though he is not a spokesperson for the company, Microsoft does not edit his blog.

The overall openness of what Scoble is doing and Microsoft's demonstration of noninterference and trust that Scoble won't misstep have gone a long way toward changing the attitudes of many tech folks — and that's good news for Microsoft. The company has established a culture of blogging and actively encourages its employees to contribute to the knowledge marketplace. The Scobleizer is at `scoble.weblogs.com` and is shown in Figure 1-5.

Figure 1-5:
Scobleizer has helped changed Microsoft's image among technophiles.

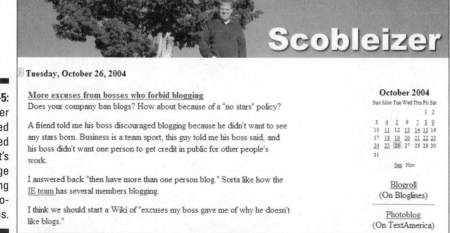

Using internal collaboration, project management, and communication

Entertainment industry magazine *Variety* uses an internal blog to keep staff informed of screenings, position changes, and the competition. The Have You Heard blog is just that — a clearinghouse for "around the water cooler" information sharing. Former Web site editor Travis Smith started the blog as an answer to the common office complaint that employees had no way to keep current on everything happening in the company.

The blog was a moderate success within the main newsroom but got rave reviews from employees in *Variety*'s far-flung offices. Have You Heard lets them experience the newsroom culture of the magazine despite the intervening geography, though they do get frustrated when the blog is used to announce that doughnuts are in the break room.

Any staff member can post to the blog or comment on other posts. Interestingly, *Variety* allows staff to post to the blog anonymously; this is not done to permit gossip, but to allow staff to make critical observations that might not ordinarily be exposed to the light of day. You can't visit the blog yourself, but you can take a peek at it in Figure 1-6.

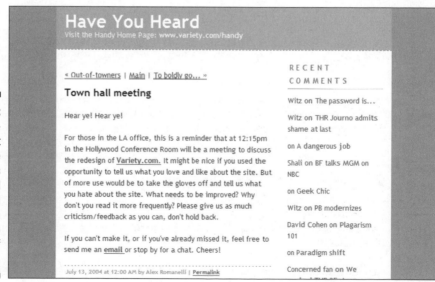

Figure 1-6: Entertainment magazine *Variety* uses an internal blog called Have You Heard to keep staff current.

Finding Out What Makes a Good Business Blog

Many early blogs focused on technology and the ubiquitous "this-is-my-life" blog produced by teens and adults; an intermediate wave focused on news, politics, and the Iraq conflict; more recently, the hottest blogs are business blogs. Why do businesses want to participate in a medium that is commonly perceived to be the stomping ground of narcissists, egomaniacs, and children?

Your company may already have a Web site. (It doesn't? Put this book down, and get yourself a copy of *Creating Web Pages For Dummies,* 7th Edition, by Bud E. Smith and Arthur Bebak. I'll see you in three months.) You may even have some great mechanisms in place for sharing company news or handling customer support. What makes what you're already doing different from a blog? Three words: writing, updating, and dialogue.

Writing

The biggest strength of blogs is in establishing dialogue with readers. For that dialogue to be successful, you need a blogger whose style, personality, and knowledge meet the needs of the audience.

Keeping the writing in your blog short, to the point, and useful. You don't need to finely craft every word; in fact, levity and a casual, friendly style can serve you well.

Blog writing is all about openness, honesty, and information. Blog writing isn't formal, so keep the tone conversational and personal. A blog is not the place for business jargon or marketing propaganda.

Posting new material often

Most blogs are organized reverse-chronologically for a reason — it's so you can't miss the latest post. The blogging format lives and dies on current information.

Current doesn't mean every couple of weeks. Current means posting often, even multiple times daily if you can swing it. Many bloggers post several times a day; most post at least a few times a week.

Posting religiously has its benefits as well:

- Your readers return more often, because they know they're likely to find new information.
- Your blog is more likely to show up more frequently in search engine results lists as well. Quantity is definitely your friend in this medium.

Don't let your quality slip in your quest to post regularly. You may drive readers away.

Gathering feedback through dialogue

Every company can benefit from knowing what its customers want, what they like about its products and services, and what they don't like. Getting that feedback can be a nightmare, though. Focus groups are costly and time consuming, and can be conducted only in areas where you can physically locate a group of appropriate people. Surveys are also time-intensive, nothing to blink at costwise, and are hard to get people to return to.

Blogs can help you gather feedback from your customers more cheaply and faster than almost any other technique. By tracking the feedback you get on your own blog and reading what is said about you on other blogs, you always have a current picture of just how your company is doing in the public's perception.

A blog can also gather responses over time and provide a way to see changes in attitude and perception. If you are doing things right with your blog, your customers will jump at the chance to tell you what they and what they hate about your company, products, and services. These people know what they are talking about; they may even know individual products better than you do. As a Macromedia software developer told me once, although he may be developing the software, he's not a user of it.

So why not use your blog to tap into this rich vein of knowledge? Your organization can benefit at almost every level from knowing whether it's giving customers what they want. A blog is a nonthreatening, nonintrusive, and interactive way to get that information from your customers. Even better, they'll appreciate the opportunity to give it to you!

Fitting Blogs into Your Business

I paint a pretty picture of blogs throughout this chapter, but even the most ardent fan of the format has to admit that blogging isn't always smooth sailing. Business blogs, especially, must fight the traditional culture of control and secrecy to make good use of the blogging format.

Of course, you must consider the technical aspects of setting up, maintaining, and running a blog. The good news is that blogging doesn't cost you an arm and a leg in hardware and software! And finally, where go people, go legal concerns.

Extending corporate culture

Blogging is a great format and can be a dramatically effective tool for many businesses — but not all. The internal culture of some companies simply doesn't lend itself to the openness and honesty the blogging format requires. Does your company maintain rigid walls of secrecy between development groups? Is there a "need-to-know" attitude from upper management? Is your company equipped to handle the additional feedback from customers a blog can produce?

For some companies the answers to these questions is yes. If that's the case for your company, rethink creating a business blog. Be realistic about whether your company is one that suits the blogging format before you jump in, because if you try to hide from customers, even just by spinning information, they won't react well. You're likely to get negative attention and criticism from the blogosphere that can turn into something ugly. Many bloggers are muckrakers who are looking for scandals to expose, especially in business and politics. They pay attention to other blogs because they are fans of the format and they don't take kindly to manipulation of it.

Finding a good blogger

A blogger is your company's Web interface with the public, someone who represents you to readers, conveys new information, makes amends for company mistakes, and generally makes the company more approachable and friendly. Your blogger may serve the role of ombudsman, translating customer needs to the company and rephrasing company positions for the public. Or your blogger might serve a more traditional marketing purpose by letting people know about upcoming events, changes in structure, new ventures, and so on. If your blogger manages this task with humor and flair, this normally dry task becomes a way to establish rapport.

What this really means is that a traditional marketing person is almost definitely not who should be writing your blog. Ideally, it's the company's CEO or someone within the company with real knowledge and expertise who can speak with authority and answer specific questions — maybe even a technician or an engineer.

If the blog is designed to help people use your service or just better understand it, you might be looking for someone who normally handles customer support or someone who is involved in the day-to-day maintenance of the system. In almost every case, you're looking for a blogger whose everyday job is "doing" rather than managing or communicating. Wouldn't you love to have a direct line of communication with someone influential at say, your phone company, rather than talking to a customer service person with no real authority and who perhaps is only peripherally connected to the company?

See Chapter 10 for more information on selecting a good blogger for your company.

Controlling the message

One of the scariest aspects of starting a company blog can be the lack of control over the final message. Even at companies where a blogger's entries are edited before they're posted, the resulting presentation is much more informal than the communication most companies have with the public. This informality is what makes the medium so appealing to readers, so don't succumb to the conservative voice in your head that's thinking, "Well, I'll just run these posts through a blogging committee with a representative from sales, legal, and marketing before I put them online." Nothing kills the spontaneity and genuine feel of a blog faster than giving editing power to a committee.

Use a light hand when editing comments on your blog. Edit for factual accuracy, spelling, and style consistency, but leave in the color that gives your blogger a unique voice and that conveys his or her enthusiasm. Having concerns about propriety of the content is natural, so work with your blogger to establish a set of guidelines for what kinds of material are acceptable for the blog. Take care, also, in choosing your blogger in the first place. If you can't trust the person writing the blog, there's little point in creating it in the first place.

Some companies have even posted their policies online to make it clear to the public that the blogger is speaking on behalf of the company but is not its spokesperson. The home page of Robert Scoble's blog for example, makes clear he is expressing personal, not Microsoft opinions, with a little legal-speak thrown in for good measure: "Robert Scoble works at Microsoft (title: technical evangelist). Everything here, though, is his personal opinion and is not read or approved before it is posted. No warranties or other guarantees will be offered as to the quality of the opinions or anything else offered here."

Dealing with technical concerns

Blogs can be both incredibly easy and quite complex to set up, depending on the software and functionality you use. If you can arrange it, your best bet is to have a programmer or technical person assist you, especially during the setup phase. You may also need the assistance of a graphic designer. Your blog needs to reflect the nature of your business, and few businesses can get away with amateurish or sloppy design, even if the writing is outstanding.

Neither of these things is necessarily a stumbling block, and in fact, if you are willing to accept a few limitations, you may be able to go from zero to blog in about five minutes — and without technical help. In Chapter 4, I go over how to make the decision between an easy, quick blog software package to a more complex, more flexible solution.

Keep in mind that a really successful blog can pull in loads of traffic. Therefore, your Web servers can take a beating, so you need quite a bit of bandwidth to meet the demand. If your company gets to a level of success where this becomes an issue — congratulations! The corresponding level of readership, interaction, and publicity that comes with this problem probably makes it all worthwhile.

Handling legal issues

The blogosphere is riddled with stories of employees who lost their jobs because of what they were posting on their personal blogs — though the actual numbers are not that high, the shocking stories were passed quickly via, what else, blog posts. In the early days of the Web, a company's employees were typically more Web-savvy than its management and felt safe in posting what was obviously inappropriate material about fellow employees, business plans, and even customers. The original personal focus of blogs, and the perception that they were written for family and friends, blinded some bloggers to the fact that a simple Web search could uncover what they posted. Heartache, loss of valuable employees, and lawsuits were often the result. Why does this concern you as you consider starting a business blog?

Be aware that starting a company blog will send a message to your staff that blogging is acceptable, even encouraged. This is no reason to be scared away from creating a blog. However, it does mean that you may want to consider establishing some blogging guidelines or at least letting employees know what kinds of business information need to stay in the office.

There's another aspect to this as well: If an employee of yours starts a personal blog, he will no doubt reveal aspects of his or her life that would normally be invisible to you and to your customers. Consider these situations:

- ✔ Do you have employees who do freelance work on the side? Would it be harmful for your company if it was known that they were freelancing for the porn industry? It may not be anyone's business — but that doesn't mean your company won't be criticized if it becomes public knowledge.

- ✔ Perhaps you employ people with strong political opinions. (Of course you employ people with strong political opinions!) Posted on the employee's personal blog, those opinions are suddenly in closer proximity to your company.

- ✔ Are you familiar with the saying "What happens in Vegas, stays in Vegas"? Well, it doesn't stay there if your employee blogs about it on his or her personal blog! Will the office gossip tomorrow be about an employee's wild weekend?

Not every company is impacted by public opinion if its employees blog, and in fact, many companies respect employees' right to free speech, and blogging isn't an issue. But if you're concerned, you can prevent a lot of attention simply by asking your employees to leave identifying business information off their personal blogs.

Chapter 2

Discovering the Buzz about Buzz Marketing

*B*uzz marketing has become a catchphrase in our culture. Generating "buzz" about a brand or product has become the cool thing to do. Whether you're trying to sell a pair of fashion jeans, iPods, or the latest movie to hit the theaters, creating buzz is a great way to generate interest and sales of your product. But what exactly is buzz marketing, and how is it done?

In this chapter, you find out more about how buzz marketing has been used successfully, and take a look at some Internet- and blog-specific examples of buzz and word-of-mouth marketing efforts.

Defining Buzz Marketing

In the strictest sense of the term, *buzz marketing* is the practice of creating talk around a product, service, company, or brand. For example, you might recruit volunteers — preferably proactive consumers who are centers of influence among their peers — to try products and then send them out to talk about their experience. One marketing agency, BzzAgent, has a network of 60,000 volunteer "agents" who go out and spread the word about products they find compelling.

Buzzmarketing (www.buzzmarketing.com) CEO Mark Hughes defines buzz marketing as "capturing the attention of consumers and the media to the point where talking about your brand becomes entertaining, fascinating, and newsworthy." Buzz is all about starting conversations.

Professional associations

A recent survey of chief marketing officers, marketing vice presidents, and brand managers showed they're spending more time seeking alternatives to traditional advertising than in previous years. The number-one alternative they were exploring? Buzz and word of mouth. So important has this tactic become that not one but two industry associations have begun as a result — Viral and Buzz Marketing Association (www.vbma.net) and Word of Mouth Marketing Association (womma.com).

The Viral and Buzz Marketing Association works to validate and promote "consumer-oriented" marketing techniques. There are members in most of the major cities of the world. Its Web site includes a very useful list of links about viral and buzz-marketing information, membership information, and a mailing list.

The Word of Mouth Marketing Association, shown in the following figure, has set out to promote word-of-mouth marketing and also to protect consumers by helping to set industry ethical standards. Members include international marketing and communications companies concerned with accountability and sound practices. The site has a blog, mailing lists, membership information, and good resources for those interested in word-of-mouth marketing.

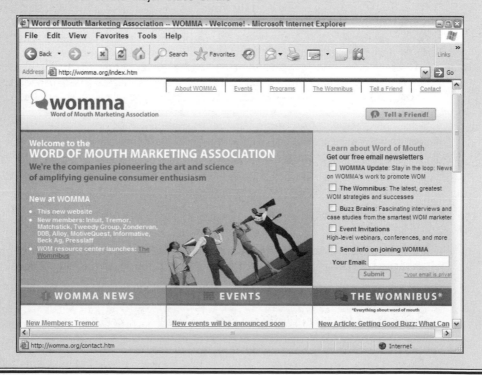

Essentially, buzz marketing is a newer spin on an older viral marketing technique: Word of mouth. Word-of-mouth marketing is a strategy that encourages individuals to pass on a marketing message to others, creating the potential for exponential growth in the message's exposure and influence.

Thanks in part to the increased fragmentation of our culture, conventional mass marketing has lost its luster — and its effectiveness. Buzz marketing has become a staple in the marketer's toolkit and is being used with greater and greater frequency. The best buzz-generating products and services, of course, are those consumers feel good talking about. Put a great product out there, and your happy customers will *want* to tell their friends, colleagues, and family about it, thus generating the buzz you're looking for.

Buzz marketing goes by a few other names: centrifugal marketing, grass-roots marketing, guerrilla marketing, referral marketing, or wildfire marketing. I've even heard the phrase "word of mouse" used to describe online-specific buzz-marketing practices.

One thing that is very difficult to do with buzz marketing is assess its success. If you can't meet demand for your product, that's a good sign that buzz marketing has worked for you, but you'll probably never be able to correlate specific efforts to specific customers, as you might once have done with a television or print advertising campaign. Though buzz is intended to boost sales, you may never be able to prove that it has done so, particularly because most buzz-marketing efforts are conducted in conjunction with more traditional marketing techniques.

Examining Buzz Marketing Examples

The advent of the Internet has given marketers new channels through which they can create buzz. Campaigns are initiated in chat rooms, e-mails, Web sites, and even instant-messaging applications.

The following sections include some specific examples of companies that used buzz-marketing campaigns to build brand awareness online.

Bacardi: Playing the "cool" card

Bacardi launched a global online viral and buzz-marketing campaign called "Planet Party" (www.planet-party.net/sucker), shown in Figure 2-1. The Planet Party theme was a "Journey from Space to Earth," where visitors traveled the galaxy and the planet looking for the best places to party. They quickly discover that Earth — not coincidentally the only planet that has Bacardi — is also the only place in the universe to truly party. An intergalactic viral film clip, "Sucker," spread around the Web, inviting partygoers to the Planet Party microsite, where they could download another clip called "Come." Visitors to the microsite could also explore a nightclub, load up Bacardi DJ, find cocktail recipes, and discover how to fit in on Earth, among other activities. The campaign was targeted to 25–30 somethings, a group considered to be entertainment-seeking, highly active online users.

Figure 2-1:
Bacardi
created
impact and
buzz with
the Planet
Party Web
site.

Burger King: Playing the "humor" card

Following Burger King's success with two other buzz campaigns — Subservient Chicken and Ugoff — the company launched one called Angus Diet. The Angus Diet was a spoof diet aimed at exploiting and countering the popularity of the ubiquitous Atkins Diet. A Web site at www.angusintervention.com featured fictional self-help guru Dr. Angus dispensing humorous interactive "Angus Interventions," designed to remind friends that life should be enjoyed. The site offered about 30 pre-made interventions, which could be tailored with a recipient's name and other personal details. The user could then e-mail a link to friends that brings them to a site where an animated Dr. Angus reads the customized script.

As with Burger King's Subservient Chicken campaign, the reasoning behind Angus Interventions was that people would spread the word about this site due to its offbeat humor and because it could be customized and personalized. The campaign targeted the elusive and highly coveted segment of 18–34-year-old men, a group that is often considered resistant to traditional ads. The campaign was designed to be a branding vehicle and worked in concert with TV and radio spots to increase the Burger King brand presence.

Hotmail: Playing the "free" card

Hotmail (`www.hotmail.com`) is probably the classic viral/buzz-marketing example. The company gives away its e-mail service for free. Hotmail, later bought by Microsoft, saw huge growth when the following clickable link was added to the foot of every message sent by its subscribers: "Sign up for your FREE Hotmail account." Every e-mail created a promotional opportunity that led to more e-mail being sent.

Using Blogs to Spread Buzz

The Internet provides tons of ways to spread and build buzz, but the topic of this book is how to create buzz using blogs. So how can blogs be used to create or facilitate buzz? I'm glad you asked.

Blogs represent a critically important Internet trend today. They are reinventing the way consumers and other influencers express themselves, as well as the way companies and consumers communicate with one another. They have the power to facilitate the spread of a message faster than any other form of Internet communication.

You can use the blogosphere in two ways to generate or spread buzz:

- Create a blog for a brand, company, product, service, event, or new initiative. By posting useful information frequently and letting your target audience know the blog is there, you can generate readership and buzz.
- Look for blogs or bloggers that might be interested in your products and services. With the right approach, you may be able to offer bloggers free trials or demo products that turn into postings and conversations in the blogosphere.

Blogs have innate qualities that make them indigenous buzz-marketing tools:

- **Blog activity is measurable and quantifiable.** Blog postings leave a digital information "trail" that exponentially extends the reach of a given message.

- **Through the use of built-in comment technology, blogs encourage conversation between blogger and reader.** Very often a conversation that begins on a blog is continued in comments, on other blogs, and via e-mail.

- **They are excellent tools for obtaining feedback.** For example, if you want to gauge consumer confidence in a particular product, you can ask your customers via a blog post. You can be sure to get honest and candid responses; no bones about it!

- **Thanks to a companion technology called RSS, blog postings can be spread more instantaneously.** *RSS* syndicates blog postings to other Web sites and newsreader software, which you find more about in Chapter 13.

- **Blogs are search engine magnets.** The leading search engine, Google, loves them. The net result is higher rankings in search returns. From an ROI (Return on Investment) perspective, they help the marketer tap into a potentially lucrative pool of traffic.

- **Blogs are a grass-roots medium that allows direct contact with the consumer.**

- **The "personal" feel of blogs tends to create trust among readers, which leads to a loyal niche following.** The blogger becomes the virtual center of influence and thought-leader. According to Intelliseek CEO Pete Blackshaw, "Blogs are tailor-made for 'influencers' and serve as pace-setting devices to other influencers."

And the list could go on . . . . The fact is, blogs are word-of-mouth marketing taken to a happy extreme.

Bloggers with marketing expertise

If you want to find more about how marketing and blogging can work together, a good place to start is with the blogs of marketing professionals who use blogs. The companion blog to this book, Buzz Marketing with Blogs (shown in the figure), is designed to do just that. Visit www.buzzmarketingwithblogs.com to keep abreast of blog-marketing happenings, blogging awards, opportunities, tips, and tools.

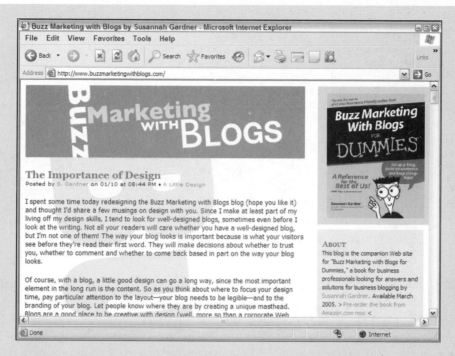

You can check out other great blogs as well, all of which are linked from Buzz Marketing with Blogs. I find these blogs and bloggers extremely helpful:

Blog Business World, by Wayne Hurlbert: Discover about blogs in business, marketing, public relations, and search engine optimization issues. blogbusinessworld.blogspot.com

The Blog Herald, edited by Duncan Riley: A portal of individual and corporate blogging news. www.blogherald.com

Business Blog Consulting, by Rick E. Bruner and others: A site devoted to demonstrating how Web logs help you communicate with customers (and prospective customers). www.businessblogconsulting.com

Common Craft, by Lee LeFever: The focus of Common Craft is innovative uses of social software in business. www.commoncraft.com

CorporateBlogging.Info, by Fredrik Wackå: This blog is designed to help you get started with corporate blogging. www.corporateblogging.info

Diva Marketing Blog, by Toby Bloomberg: Matching your brand with the opportunities of the blogosphere. bloombergmarketing.blogs.com

Easy Bake Weblogs, by Andy Wibbels: Find out about blog publishing and Internet marketing for entrepreneurs and small businesses. easybakeweblogs.com

Lip-Sticking, by Yvonne DiVita: Marketing issues with a focus on women and the Internet. windsormedia.blogs.com

Micro Persuasion, by Steve Rubel: Steve Rubel on how blogs and participatory journalism are impacting the practice of public relations. www.micropersuasion.com

Radiant Marketing Group, by Paul Chaney: Find out how to engage and interact with customers and clients via blogs, RSS, and e-mail. www.radiantmarketinggroup.com

Building conversations based on trust

Blogs serve as excellent tools to foster conversations. Of course, conversations can only happen if trust is built between the marketer and customer. Blogs are a tool well suited to serve that need. A business blogger who posts routinely, provides valuable information, and who speaks genuinely and from the heart can find himself connecting with customers in new and exciting ways.

Perhaps the most important role blogs play in generating buzz is that they put power in the hands of the consumer. According to Digital Media Communications Australia, "The most powerful selling of products and ideas is not between the marketer and consumer, but consumer to consumer. . . . The next revolution in marketing is a move from a top-down interruptive advertising approach to a more bottom-up orientated approach using network-enhanced word of mouth. So brands move from a 'command and control' consumer communication approach to a 'connect and collaborate' approach."

Looking at blogs that have built buzz

You can use blogs for specific campaigns or for long-term brand recognition; to build customer relationships; to address specific issues or problems; and even for customer service-related issues, such as technical support.

One good way to see if blogs are right for your company is to launch a blog in conjunction with a marketing campaign or new venture that has a short-term end date. Blogging for two or three months can give you a taste for the workload and the payoff. Or send your product to active bloggers to try; if they find it useful, they'll probably blog about it.

If you're looking for ideas for how you might use a blog at your company, take a look at how blogs and buzz marketing came together for these companies.

Subservient Chicken

Probably one of the best examples of how blogs were used to create buzz is the story of Subservient Chicken (www.subservientchicken.com), an online viral campaign sponsored by Burger King. This was a specialty Web site, shown in Figure 2-2, that allowed visitors to type orders to someone dressed in a chicken costume who is seen obeying, as if on a live Webcam.

Figure 2-2:
Subservient
chicken.
com
spreads
buzz
through
humor.

The site was part of a promotion for Burger King's TenderCrisp chicken sandwich line. Because of its creativity and novelty, news about the site spread rapidly through the blogosphere, making it perhaps the premiere viral campaign of 2004. Burger King deemed it such a success — projected sales over a 12-month period since starting the campaign is estimated to reach $500 million — it's launched another such campaign called the Chicken Sandwich World Championship at www.chickenfight.com.

Nokia

Nokia (www.nokia.com) got bloggers to help launch a new camera phone, the 3650. Nokia gave bloggers the phones; many thought it was a good product and blogged about it.

They looked for individual bloggers over the age of 18 who already posted photos on their sites in innovative ways, not just standard photos. Ultimately, they came up with a short list of ten bloggers, of which eight participated. After identifying bloggers, Nokia sent each a phone with two months' cell phone service.

Each blogger was asked to try taking pictures with the phone. Nokia did not ask the bloggers to post to their own sites or even mention the phone in their own blogs (though of course they hoped they would). Instead, they provided a microsite the bloggers could use to post photos if they chose.

Five of the eight included pictures taken with the phone on their blogs and wrote about the experience. Two bloggers went so far as to create their own separate "phone blogs." Most posted fairly complimentary testimonials about the phone on their own sites, and a follow-up survey showed the participants loved the product. Nokia also used an eclectic mix of online and offline marketing techniques — TV ads, banners on Web sites, ads on desktop applications such as RealPlayer, and even buzz-marketing street teams who roamed major cities.

Blogstakes

Blogstakes (www.blogstakes.com) is a sweepstakes Web site that uses blogs as marketing vehicles. Marketers make some of their products available as prizes, and bloggers promote them. The site uses a clever buzz-building twist in that there are not one but two winners for each prize. Not only does the person who entered the contest win, but so does the blogger that referred the winning entry. As people click the Blogstakes link on a given site and enter the contest, the click is automatically tracked and entered as a referring site. Some of the prizes given away include a year's worth of BrowserCam, a service that shows Web developers how their site looks in a wide range of browser platforms, and Clip-n-Seal, an easy-to-use fastener for closing and resealing opened bags.

Project Blog

Project Blog (www.projectblog.com) is an initiative of Richards Interactive, a Dallas-based interactive marketing agency. (Nokia picked this company to find bloggers for its camera phone campaign.) Richards pairs up companies with bloggers who can boast a loyal following and who would be willing to help launch products, such as Nokia's cell phone and others.

The company does not give bloggers ads to run or pay them per viewer. It simply puts products in the hands of bloggers and lets them discuss the product in any way they choose. The company emphasizes that it does not tell the blogger what to write. In other words, the product must stand on its own merits.

Marqui Blogosphere Program

Communications company Marqui (www.marqui.com/Paybloggers), shown in Figure 2-3, has begun a program that actually pays bloggers to post mentions of Marqui's services on their blogs. Each blogger is paid $800 per month to post a Marqui graphic on a Web site and blog about (and link to) Marqui once a week. Bloggers get an additional $50 per qualified sales lead they send to the company.

Figure 2-3: Marqui, a communications company, has instituted a blogosphere program designed to pay bloggers for promoting the company.

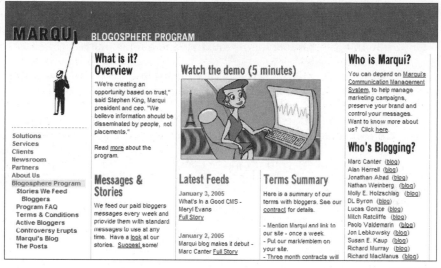

The company made it clear that the bloggers are under no obligation to be positive about companies or their products. Marqui's goal was to use the feedback, along with any comments from readers, to improve the product. You can read the agreement Marqui puts in place with each blogger at `www.marqui.com/Paybloggers/Terms.aspx`.

Nike Art of Speed

Athletic shoe manufacturer Nike contracted with leading blog publisher Gawker Media to launch the Art of Speed blog (`www.gawker.com/artof speed`), a short-term exploration of independent filmmaking. The campaign was run on a microsite and was composed of 15 short films made by up-and-coming filmmakers and artists, commissioned and selected by Nike. The blog ran for a month, and postings covered films, their creators, and the state of contemporary filmmaking and its technology.

The idea behind the campaign was that blogs allow marketers to participate in the blogosphere, rather than merely observe it as a passive sponsor.

Keeping it real

Using blogs as buzz-marketing tools can have its dark side. Blogs, in the hands of those who use the technology unscrupulously or in "stealth" mode, are a double-edged sword, as likely to generate bad publicity as they are good.

As with any other nascent marketing tool, mistakes are inevitable. Because of the viral nature and speed of cyberspace, those mistakes tend to be noticed and talked about. Face it: A lack of authenticity and transparency only buys one thing — a whole lot of trouble in the blogosphere!

Mazda made this mistake during promotion of the new Mazda M3 cars. In October 2004, a blog called HolloweenM3 appeared on Blogger.

The blog purported to be written by Kid Halloween, a 22-year-old blogger who claimed to like movies with car chases. The site's two postings both linked to videos featuring Mazda M3s that the blogger claimed to have found on Manhattan Neighborhood Network, a New York public access television station.

Though Mazda may not be responsible for the blog, many are convinced it was the brainchild of the company's marketing department, citing production values, the server the videos were hosted on, and the fact that the Manhattan Neighborhood Network doesn't sell advertising. True or not, the perception that Mazda was attempting to manipulate the blogosphere has created a negative backlash against the company. Fake is fake, folks, and consumers don't appreciate it.

The same holds true for any campaigns where marketers recruit other bloggers to spread the message on their behalf. Be up front about what you're doing, why, and what you expect from the blogger. Expect the blogger to do the same with his or her readers. And if you want to achieve authenticity, don't try to influence what the blogger has to say about the product or service.

Using ethical practices help you ensure the buzz you get is the buzz you want. People are going to talk after all, and they use blogs to do it.

Chapter 3

Building a Business Blog

*I*f you need a crash course in creating a business blog, you've come to the right chapter! I touch on nearly every aspect of creating a successful blog for you and your company, from setting up blogging editorial policies to design techniques that will give your blog flair.

It's vital to the success of your blog that you treat this new venture with respect, honoring the traditions — recent though they may be — of this medium. Your readers have certain expectations about how you will communicate with them and how they can talk back to you. You can generate amazing customer loyalty with a blog, but it's also possible to do the opposite.

In this chapter, you also discover some of the basic tools you need to run a blog, including some of the HTML tags essential to bloggers. Photos are an increasingly fun and effective format for blogs, and there is no reason you can't learn to put images to use on your blog.

One of the most important elements in any technical project is knowing your limitations. You can learn to do most of the technical details involved in running a blog on your own, but for the more complex tasks, you may find that hiring an expert just makes more sense than trying to acquire new skills yourself. You get information in this chapter on when outsourcing makes sense.

Doing the Prep Work

As you contemplate starting your business blog, you need to consider several nontechnical factors. For example, just who is going to write this blog? How often are they going to post an entry? Will the blogger be edited, and if so, how can it be done so that your blog doesn't lose immediacy and personality?

Most importantly, just what are you trying to achieve with this blog, anyway? Starting a blog just to have one is a waste of your time and your readers.

Before you begin to develop a business blog, define a purpose or goal for your blog. A good blog tells readers what they need to know and also tells you what they need to know.

As you contemplate starting a blog that can build buzz about your company, realize that what you're really doing is creating a new relationship with your customers. By opening up this new form of communication, you're agreeing to lay bare processes, motives, and knowledge that companies have traditionally kept closed off from the public. In exchange, you're going to reap the benefit of customers who feel they understand your company and who therefore trust what you tell them. Think of a blog as a way of advertising your company's attitude and values by demonstrating them. Can your company's television spots, magazine ads, or product packaging do the same thing for you? Most of those techniques reinforce a brand — they don't induce loyalty. Companies that create blogs to market their businesses accomplish the six following goals:

- **Inform or educate the public and your current customers.**

  This is the most common purpose of a business blog. Some companies are using blogs to let people know about changes in the company, new projects, and other events. Other companies have created blogs to help their readers gain knowledge — tracking news, problems, encouraging idea exchanges. These blogs serve the immediate purpose of being a useful, practical service and of demonstrating expertise to the public.

- **Provide customer service or help using a product or service.**

  Blogs can be a great way to deal with customer service issues. Dealing with customers' problems in the open is scary, but everyone benefits from the availability of the information. As well, you've just sent a message that your company cares about helping people resolve problems in a very public way. Be prepared to monitor a blog serving this purpose constantly, and respond quickly when people leave comments.

- **Convey a sense of company personality and culture.**

  The basic idea is that your blog demonstrates just how cool and fun and, well, human your company is. The blog begins to evoke emotional responses from its readers, and the final result is that your readers may actually start to *like* your company. I don't mean that they like your products. I mean that they like you like they like their friends and their pets. Think about the fanatical loyalty in many Apple users: Their feelings about the products Apple makes have often pushed them into becoming fans of the company itself. Every company can use this kind of goodwill, even if it can't be measured in revenue growth or new customer numbers.

✔ **Entertain readers and customers.**

As with the previous item, a blog devised to entertain the public pays off by building an ongoing, positive relationship with readers and customers. You don't need to find a comic to write your blog, but the addition of a joke here and there, and a generally humorous writing style, can keep readers coming back for more. A little bit of self-mockery can go a long way in this format. If the company seems to have a sense of humor about itself, its customers are more forgiving of mistakes later.

✔ **Drive users to take an action.**

Political blogs have been in the news for the past couple of years, and it's pretty clear that candidates who keep a blog are hoping to convince people to take a specific action: Voting for the blogger. Blogs can definitely be used to drive people toward taking an action, but you need to use a delicate hand.

For instance, don't expect to start a blog in order to sell more units of your latest gizmo by blogging about how great the gizmo is. The public has seen a lot of ads, and they have no reason to seek out more. Start a blog that helps current owners of the gizmo do more and better things with it, though, and you get your current customers to talk about how they're using the product and how great it is. The result is likely to be more purchases, plus your company gets credit for caring about the consumers of its product.

✔ **Encourage dialogue with current and potential customers.**

Another great use for a blog is to start an ongoing dialogue with your customers. After all, your customers are the people who know your products and services best, and they have definite opinions about how you can improve what you're doing. A blog can elicit this kind of feedback with huge efficiency and more inexpensively than user surveys and focus group testing.

Most business blogs combine several of these purposes into one blog, but don't fall into the trap of trying to do everything at once. For instance, don't combine customer service with an information exchange blog. The two approaches dilute rather than strengthen each other. A humorous customer service blog, on the other hand, might serve the joint purpose of helping customers and entertaining them during what is ordinarily not a fun process.

If you do have several purposes in mind, consider starting several blogs. Users understand that each blog is a different conversation and gravitate toward the one that serves them best. Be sure to keep your end of the conversation similarly segregated, however, or you dilute the effectiveness of what you're doing yourself. Stonyfield Farms, a Vermont dairy, (`www.stony field.com/weblog/`), has created a set of four blogs with different purposes: Strong Women Daily News, The Bovine Bugle, The Daily Scoop, and Creating Healthy Kids.

Setting the Scene

After you define a goal for your blog — or perhaps several goals — you need to set the stage for success by putting the resources in place for a good blog. Each of the following elements contributes to the overall success of your blog and should be planned carefully before you launch the blog into the world.

Finding a blogger

Because whoever writes your blog is speaking on behalf of your company, they need to be reliable, conscientious, accurate, and trustworthy. Besides that, you need to find a blogger that is thoroughly knowledgeable about the subject of the blog — and who is genuinely interested in passing that information on.

Keep in mind that a marketing professional, though trained to convey corporate messages and communicate with the public, may be a bad choice. Their very expertise can work against them; in the eyes of the public, they're "marketing shills" and not to be trusted. It's unkind but something to consider when choosing a blogger.

In Chapter 10, I talk more about what makes a good blogger.

Deciding to edit

To edit or not to edit, that is the question. In 2003, the blogosphere was rife with arguments for and against edited blogs. Today the issue has been talked to death, and the conclusion seems to be that sometimes an editor is useful, if only to check grammar and spelling. Some blogs are also edited for content.

However, maintaining the spontaneity and fresh feeling of a blog when every post has to go through an editor or committee for content approval is difficult. A better technique is to set policies for appropriate blogging practices and leave your blogger to it. If you have faith in your blogger, check his or her spelling, and let the content take care of itself.

I talk more about editing blogs before (or even after) publication in Chapter 12.

Setting policies for your business blog

For business blogs, establishing some guidelines to blog by is important. You need to create a climate where the blog can flourish that won't also turn your hair gray and keep you awake at night worrying.

The guidelines needn't be lengthy or very formal, but they should establish some working principles for the role of the blogger; an editor, if there is one; and anyone else involved in overseeing the blog. You also need to do some thinking about how to handle mistakes and corrections, preferably before they happen.

Your blog editorial policies should also include a linking policy — do you allow links to competitors or to news stories that include criticism of your products or services?

Chapter 12 contains a longer discussion of corporate blogging policies, including some real-life examples from companies using blogs today.

Becoming familiar with the blogosphere

By starting a blog, you join a whole new community — one that has no more in common with your business than random strangers off the street. Because you have chosen to use the blogging medium, the blogosphere (bloggers and those who read blogs) pay attention to what you do.

This group talks a lot, to each other and to their readers, who are often members of respected news media organizations. Because most are blogging as private individuals, they have no compunction about being critical of what you're doing or of playing watchdog for advertising in the form of blogs. Increasingly, what they say has national and international impact.

So you need to pay attention to the conventions of the blogging world and become familiar with prominent blogs and bloggers. Spend some time reading blogs, even those that don't have anything to do with your industry but are successful. Try to take note of good practices and conventions, and appropriate ways to take part in the conversations going on in the blogosphere. The payoff just may be some good buzz about your efforts from other bloggers that can send readers your way!

I talk more about reading and commenting on other blogs in Chapter 8, about avoiding common blog mistakes in Chapter 9, and about good ways to promote your blog in the blogosphere in Chapter 11.

Choosing a memorable name

This is the all-important decision: A name. You have probably already noticed that many blogs have unusual names, often one or two words that usually aren't used together or a humorous phrase. Some bloggers simply use their own name as their blog name. Some of the best-known blogs on the Web are InstaPundit (www.instapundit.com), shown in Figure 3-1, and Talking Points Memo (www.talkingpointsmemo.com). Both have unusual and memorable names that are also easy to spell or find with a search engine.

Figure 3-1:
The name
of the
InstaPundit
blog is
unusual and
memorable.

The point is to find a name that is easily remembered and one that won't be confused with other blogs and Web sites. You may find that incorporating some form of your company's name into the blog name is useful. Fast Company, for example, maintains a blog called FC Now (blog.fastcompany.com).

For a company, it's probably not a great idea to brand your blog with the name of your blogger — should he or she ever leave your company, the name of the blog won't make sense anymore. Look for inspiration in internal jokes, catch phrases, or mottoes. Does the product or service you're focusing on have a nickname you can use? If you create an informational blog, look for a name that establishes your blog as an industrywide resource. Use these tips to make your decisions as you brainstorm:

✔ **Do** choose a name that doesn't require you to use spaces or that can be collapsed (as in domain names) and still make sense.

✔ **Do** make sure your domain name won't inadvertently be a double entendre. Lumber Jack's Exchange becomes an entirely different site when the punctuation and spaces are dropped in a URL.

✔ **Do** look for a name that includes an identifying noun. For example, if you're blogging about mobile phones, using the word "phone" in the name would be a good idea.

✔ **Don't** choose a name that is hard to spell or to pronounce.

✔ **Don't** use hyphens — they are inaudible and not so useful for advertising that relies on verbal identification.

Interestingly, most bloggers avoid using the term blog, log, or Web log in the official name of a blog, much in the way you don't see the term "newspaper" in the names of *The New York Times* and *The Wall Street Journal*.

Whatever you choose to name your blog, you should consider registering the domain name for it, whether or not you plan to use the domain. You keep anyone else from registering the domain (by coincidence or design) and prevent confusion in the future.

Designing a Business Blog

You've probably seen some very slick, attractive blogs online — people who have taken the same kind of care with the visual tone of their blogs as they have with writing their entries. A particular design aesthetic has grown up around blogs that is shaped by the way a blog functions. Most blogs are arranged to display the most recent entry at the top of the page, with a column of supplementary information on the right or left.

Every blogging package comes with at least one default template, and it's often from this basic layout that a new blogger might create his or her own look. Experienced Web surfers recognize the default templates and may pass judgment on a site that hasn't taken the time to personalize its look. At the very least, they may assume this is a brand-new blog and a brand-new blogger. For personal use, many of the templates are clean and well done, but for business blogging, you want to create a design of your own. A memorable site draws more readers.

In the following sections, I describe buzz-generating elements you can use to create a distinctive business blog.

Customizing your design

Whether you modify an existing blog template or create something entirely new, design plays a big part in how your readers think about your blog. Branding is just as important here as it is on your company's business cards, stationery, and Web site. A well-designed blog typically includes:

- ✔ **A distinctive logo or banner** that clearly conveys the name of the blog.

- ✔ **A limited color palette** designed to increase the readability and attractiveness of the blog.

- ✔ **Branding** that matches your existing corporate identity, especially styles established by other Web sites.

Some bloggers have taken artful design to a technological extreme most of us can admire but not emulate. Take, for example, the interactive graphic displayed at the top of Dunstan Orchard's 1976 Design blog (`www.1976design.com/blog`). The image, which you see in Figure 3-2, is a graphic rendering of the view from the window Dunstan sat next to while designing the blog. It reflects the current time of day, phase of the moon, and weather conditions in an incredible 90 automatically updating combinations. It's over-the-top, but unforgettable, and can't be confused with any other blog.

Figure 3-2: The image at the top of Dunstan Orchard's blog reflects the current weather and time of day at his home and is updated automatically via custom programming.

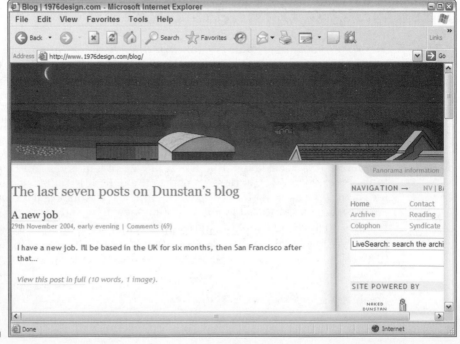

For most blogs, a nicely designed logo/header at the top of the page and some well-selected background colors or patterns that don't obscure text are more than sufficient. If you have an artist or graphic designer on staff, creating an attractive design isn't a big issue, but we aren't all blessed with big budgets or an artist's eye, and sometimes hiring a designer may be the wisest course. Even if you do have an in-house artist, be aware that designing a print brochure and designing a Web site are very different skills. The technical limitations that are part of publishing a Web site are complex enough that your print designer may be frustrated rather than challenged by the new medium.

The fact is, design strategies that work well in print may not necessarily work online. One big technical difficulty is that your potential audience may be visiting your Web site on many different kinds of computers, using many different browsers — and different browser versions, each of which has potholes into which an inexperienced designer might stumble! All those variables mean that you need a skilled designer and a skilled HTML coder to produce a Web site that looks good and works right for most of your audience.

If you're trying to decide whether to hire a contractor or use in-house expertise, turn to the "Hiring Outside Designers and Coders" section later in this chapter.

Incorporating HTML

Hosted blog solution or independent blog software aside, you'll be more comfortable and have a better blog if you have some basic HTML knowledge at your fingertips. HTML, or *Hypertext Markup Language,* is the code used to create pages for the Web. Though it can be incredibly complex when frames, dynamic database pages, or Cascading Style Sheets are used, the essentials are still quite simple to do.

As a blogger, you simply must be able to do a few things with HTML:

- ✔ Create bold or italicized text.
- ✔ Create a link to another Web page.

Adding basic formatting

HTML is a language built around the idea of enclosing, or marking up, content that you want to affect. You can also think of it as turning a tag on and then off. A *tag* is simply an individual HTML code. So in a Web page, you can make a word bold by using the following tag:

```
This <b>word</b> is bold.
```

The <b> tag starts the bolding, and the same tag preceded by a forward slash ends the bolding. If you want to bold and italicize a word, try this:

```
Use <b><i>bold and italics</i></b>.
```

Finally, you might want to indent some text, perhaps a quote. A special HTML tag is just for indenting, and you use it like this:

```
<blockquote>Four score and seven years ago our fathers
        brought forth on this continent a new nation,
        conceived in liberty and dedicated to the
        proposition that all men are created
        equal.</blockquote>
```

The entire block of text is offset from the left margin.

That wasn't so hard, was it? Just what are you paying those expensive Web developers for, anyway?! Rest assured, it does get harder, much harder. Fortunately for a blogger concentrating on writing, you don't need to get more complex once your templates are set up to your liking. You simply worry about entering the text, and the surrounding HTML is created automatically.

Creating links

You should definitely know how to make a link. Take a look at the following code example:

```
I've got to go to <a href="http://www.google.com">Google</a>
            and look up basic HTML tags!
```

In this example, the word Google is a link to the popular search engine's Web site. You create the link by using the *anchor* tag (<a>) and adding what's called an *attribute* — in this case an href (hypertext reference). The *value* of the attribute (the part in quotation marks) tells the browser what Web site to open when the link is clicked.

When creating a link using HTML, including the full URL of the Web site you are linking to is important, including the http:// at the beginning of the address. Leave that off, and the browser won't understand that it's looking for a Web server and instead tries to find a file with that name.

You can get a little fancier, still. You can create HTML links that not only take the user to a new Web site, but do so in a new browser window. This is also done with the <a> tag. To do this, use the following code:

```
<a href="http://www.google.com" target="_blank">Go to Google
            now!</a>
```

The second attribute, target, tells the browser to use a new (_blank) browser window when displaying the URL. Now you're ready to blog!

Adding photographs

In the right blog, photographs can add interest, information, candor, and color — and hopefully generate some business. Not every photo is worth 1,000 words in the blog world, but they can sometimes be the fastest, simplest way to explain something to your audience, and photos sometimes get more reaction or attention — perhaps you're launching a new logo, testing customer reaction to the playback controls of your new phone, or want to show the new artwork in the lobby of your headquarters building. Or perhaps your company's softball team just cleaned the field with the competition. Whatever the use, if you're going to use photos on your blog, you need to be able to turn images into Web-ready artwork and then display it in your blog.

Some blog solutions are built specifically for photos — if you need to present visual information more often than textual information, such as an architect or a weather site, for example — you may want to consider one of these. I talk more about photo blogs in Chapter 13.

Acquiring photos

Obtaining photos to place on your blog is pretty easy. You can use any of the following:

- **Digital camera:** These come bundled with graphics software of some kind, and they definitely come with a way to transfer images from the camera to the computer.

- **Standard film camera:** Get a digital CD of images at the time you get your film developed.

- **Scanner:** If you already have your prints back, or if you have a paper document you want to display, you've moved into the realm of scanners. Web images are rarely very high quality, so if you're going to be scanning photographs or documents and only displaying them online, you can find an inexpensive flatbed scanner quite easily. Scanners also frequently come bundled with graphic software that walks you through scanning in photographs and documents.

Formats

After you have the image on your computer, you need to save it in a Web format. There are two — GIFs and JPEGs. These dreadful-sounding acronyms are just shortened abbreviations of the compression formats used to save images for the Web, and they both handle the task of compression slightly differently. Generally speaking, JPEGs are going to work better for photographs and images that contain lots of colors and lots of variation between colors. The GIF format works well for graphics with large solid areas of few colors. This isn't always true, and the real test is always the eye: What looks better?

Most browsers can display a third format: PNG. It's not commonly used today because full support for it is simply not consistent across all browsers and browser versions. But for photos, and if you know your audience is using current browsers, PNG has its advantages.

Size

The major thing you need to worry about with Web graphics is file size. Larger images — both in terms of file size and in terms of display size — take longer to download, and your users appreciate any efforts you make to keep image sizes reasonable. This is especially true if you're going to be using a lot of images in your blog.

Now for the facts and figures — Web-ready images must be 72 ppi/dpi. This is the resolution of the image, basically the number of pixels or dots per square inch of the image. Print-quality graphics are almost always created at least at 150 ppi/dpi, but computer screens have a built-in limitation that only allows them to display 72 dpi/ppi, even if the image has a higher resolution. An 8-by-10 photograph from your digital camera that is at 150 dpi/ppi actually looks larger than 8 by 10 inches on-screen.

Choosing a graphics program

A number of other graphics programs can produce Web graphics, interface with a scanner, and import photos from a digital camera. Here's a quick selection of those programs:

- **CorelDRAW Essentials 2:** CorelDRAW Essentials has great tools for correcting and enhancing photographs, whether scanned or taken with a digital camera. The program also contains drawing and illustration tools and includes the ability to utilize a library of clip art images. CorelDRAW Essentials comes with an interactive training CD to help get you started. www.corel.com/drawessentials2/

- **JASC Paint Shop Pro 9:** You can import photos from your digital camera, scan in printed documents, and turn them all into Web graphics. JASC Paint Shop Pro deals especially well with photo touch-up problems — graininess, white balance, color adjustments. The program allows you to create graphics using standard tools such as the pencil, pen, paintbrush, and text tool. www.jasc.com/products/paintshoppro/

- **Macromedia Fireworks MX 2004:** This program from the leader in Web design software was created specifically with the Internet in mind. Fully featured, it doesn't include functions and features that don't apply to Web graphic creation. Fireworks includes photo retouching, cropping, and the usual tools, and also has some powerful built-in tools to allow you to create animated graphics. If you're using Macromedia Dreamweaver MX 2004, you'll enjoy the integration between these two programs that allows you to work a little faster. www.macromedia.com/fireworks/

- **Adobe Photoshop Elements:** Adobe Photoshop Elements is a lighter edition of the industry-standard graphics program Adobe Photoshop, and you can size, crop, rotate, and retouch photos with it. You can also use it to create original graphics and illustrations. Elements is very affordable and one of the best graphics packages available. Best of all, it has a 30-day free trial version. `www.adobe.com/products/photoshopelwin`

- **Adobe Photoshop CS:** If you want the industry leader in graphics design and creation, Adobe Photoshop CS is the program for you. Used by designers working in all kinds of mediums, this powerful program offers drawing, font, photo retouching, cropping, and other tools, in addition to an array of filters and other high-end production goodies. If you're working on print brochures or other graphics programs as well as producing Web graphics, Adobe Photoshop more than meets both your needs. `www.adobe.com/photoshop/`

Finding stock photo and clip art resources

You can use or adapt a number of good resources for stock photography and clip art for your blog design.

- **Creative Commons:** This nonprofit organization allows you to find, use, and publish works under a range of copyright protections. You can find blogging tools such as audio, images, video for free. Check out `www.creativecommons.org`

- **Comstock:** Comstock offers a wide selection of royalty-free, flat-rate, and rights-managed stock imagery. Its special Ask Angela feature can suggest suitable images based on your search. Be sure that you buy the right license for the image you want to use. `www.comstock.com`

- **GettyImages:** If you're looking for something very specific, try the Getty-Images vast database of royalty-free and rights-managed photographs. It has a great news and film archive. Be sure that you buy the right license for the image you want to use. `www.gettyimages.com`

- **Hemera:** Hemera sells clip art and stock photography compilations. Buy a CD or search the online database of images in Hemera Images Express for what you need. You can buy unlimited access for one month or one year, or purchase single images. `www.hemera.com`

- **Photos.com:** For a lower-cost alternative and unlimited access, consider a subscription to photos.com. You can subscribe for one month or one year, and you receive unlimited access to the 100,000 images in the service's library, with the ability to use most images for business purposes. `www.photos.com`

- **Clipart.com:** Clipart.com is a very low-cost image resource, in part because you can subscribe for just a week and still have unlimited access to their collection of clip art, photos, Web animations, fonts, and sounds. You can also choose a three-, six-, or twelve-month subscription. `www.clipart.com`

Hiring Outside Designers and Coders

For many years there was a great hue and cry about the Internet making it possible for "anyone to publish!" While this notion is true, you'll note that the phrase is not "anyone can publish *well*." Registering a domain name and buying Web hosting are often quite easy to do, and you can learn basic Web coding in an afternoon. This doesn't necessarily mean that your site looks as professional and credible as it really could. Just because you own a printer, for example, doesn't mean that you can create a *New York Times*-quality newsletter right out of the starting gate.

Nonetheless, you can effectively learn much of what goes into a blog, and you should spend the time to do it — developing a readable writing style, establishing and editing policy, even setting up a blog in the first place. For some things, however, you may want to hire a professional, and setting up the HTML templates or creating the site design are the usual candidates for outsourcing.

If you're wondering whether buying the help of an expert is really necessary, take a look through these issues, and apply them to your situation.

- ✔ **Do you have technical expertise in-house? What kind?** If you have an artist without Web experience or a Webmaster who wears stripes with plaid, it will show on the Web site.

- ✔ **If you have in-house expertise of the kind you need, do you have access to it?** We're all overworked in this busy world, and it may be difficult to turn the focus to this new project. This is especially true when another department loans you resources, and managerial relationships and firm deadlines may be difficult to establish.

- ✔ **Have you ever created a Web site before or managed a Web project?** Your own preparedness and expertise play a huge role in getting what you need out of in-house staff, especially when you are trying something for the first time.

- ✔ **Do you have the time and budget to bring outsiders into the picture?** Estimating what your costs will be like if you choose to outsource can be difficult — everyone's blog scope differs, after all! Sticking to your budget is probably the greatest factor in whether you choose to learn how to create complicated Cascading Style Sheet pages, install software on a server, or become an artist.

  A blog project doesn't have to be a huge budgetary item, however. The design needs of a blog are minimal. For instance, most blogs use a standard layout that remains much the same from page to page. Even the graphic header at the top of the page usually doesn't change. So when you approach a Web designer, be aware that what you're looking for is help creating one standard page design and the templates for the home page, archive pages, and individual entry pages. Because many elements remain the same from page to page and probably won't change much over time, you may be able to buy more designer time than you think.

✔ **How good are your technical skills?** How much time do you have to devote to learning new skills that you may use now and then not come back to for a couple of years? Web sites are usually redesigned every couple of years, so it can be difficult to keep your technical skills sharp if you aren't practicing them daily. You can also get easily excited about learning something new and forget that you don't really have time to become an expert in something completely outside your expertise.

Figuring out whether you need outside help to set up your blog has no easy formula, but as you go into the process, you can find some ways to make the process work more smoothly and save yourself money.

Part II
Setting Up a Business Blog

The 5th Wave   By Rich Tennant

FREELANCER NED WILLIS CONSULTS WITH A MEMBER OF HIS TECHNICAL STAFF

"I can help you with that, Mr. Dotter. Let's look at this blog about underpaid kids who went on to make big money dispensing technical advice in their spare time."

In this part . . .

Now that you have a taste of what goes into a successful blog, it's time to get started blogging. Part II helps get a blog up and running quickly. Use the information in Chapter 4 to decide what blogging software solution can work best for you. I make it easy for you to get through making that decision so you can get to the fun part: Chapter 5. Newbies and experienced bloggers alike can find the detailed instructions in Chapter 5 helpful in setting up a hosted blog in just 10 minutes. In Chapter 6, find out how independent blog software can help you customize your blog in powerful ways. You won't leave this section of the book without a thorough grounding in the technological intricacies of business blogs.

Chapter 4

Picking a Blog Solution

*I*f you're taking the plunge and starting a blog, you've got some immediate decisions to make. What solution you use depends on who you are: Are you a technophobe who wants a quick solution to get you started blogging today or a computer guru who wants the ability to fine-tune every aspect of the design and functionality of your blog?

Either way, your first big task is to pick a blogging platform. You can use an outside company that handles everything for you, or install an independent solution and set up everything yourself. In this chapter, I help you figure out your blogging needs. At the end, you'll have a much better idea of just which blogging solution fits your situation.

Deciding Which Blog Solution to Use

There are many ways to start a blog, and more are made available every day. You must decide between two blogging scenarios:

- ✔ **A *hosted* blog solution:** You blog, and the publishing interface that creates it resides on the server of a blog company.

- ✔ **An *independent* blog solution:** You install a blogging package on your own Web server.

A hosted blog solution is one where all the technical headaches are taken care of for you. If you're a technophobe, or even just very pressed for time, using a hosted blog solution gets you started blogging quickly, and you don't have to invest much time in set up or learning new skills. The financial investment required to use these services is usually quite reasonable; some are even free.

If you want control over all aspects of your blog, an *independent* blog solution may be a better choice for you. If you go this route, be prepared to buy, install, and customize blog software on your own server. You'll have a very powerful, flexible blog solution that you can tweak to your heart's content, way beyond simply getting the company logo placed at the top of the page and customizing the link color. All that flexibility comes with a price tag, however.

Discovering hosted blog solutions

When you sign up with a hosted blog company, such as Blogger or TypePad, you purchase space on their servers and use of a blogging tool to make entries. With most of these solutions, you can make changes to the design and code if you have the skills to do so, but they're designed to be used by people who are new to blogging.

Pros and cons of a hosted blog

The best part of a hosted blog — the fact that someone else takes care of the technical issues — can also be the worst part. You get the benefit of all the technical development the blog maker put into the product, but you're also subject to any technical problems the blog may have, such as server downtime. There are nontechnical risks as well, because companies (especially Internet companies) come and go — and your data could be gone with them.

Nonetheless, for many companies, a hosted blog is a great alternative to learning a bunch of new technical skills or hiring a techie to install software on your server.

In Chapter 5, I give you some specific recommendations for companies with robust hosted blog solutions, and if you're ready to start blogging today, you can set up a hosted blog right away.

Knowing when to use a hosted solution

Though blog software (both hosted and independent) is designed to be easy to use, hosted blog software is simply more accessible to users with little to no technical experience. Using a hosted blog means you have access to some tools other people built and a customer support e-mail address or phone number for when you get stuck. Consider the following points:

✔ **Time limits:** Your previous Web experience means you might be able to puzzle through installing independent blog software yourself, and you may even be excited about learning some new skills. But setting up an independent blog can take time.

Time, unfortunately, is a commodity many businesspeople simply don't have, and you're probably no exception. As you decide which route to take, think hard about whether you really have time to spend learning how to install and configure blog software — a task that may take you hours and become a skill you may not need to use again in a hurry.

Don't let your own enthusiasm to have the most customized blog ever blind you to the fact that an expert, or a hosted blog company, may be able to do the job better and faster, allowing you to focus on the real business at hand — blogging.

✔ **Financial constraints:** You did the hard part when you persuaded the CEO that blogging wasn't something he needed a plumber for. You did the impossible when you got him to agree that it might be worth trying.

  • **No budget whatsoever:** You need a free hosted blog solution. Never fear; they exist. Don't despair that you will lose access to the powerful features common to more expensive solutions; even the free blogging solutions come with a nice package of technical tools.

  • **A budget, albeit a very small one:** While a hosted blog solution is probably the right one for you, you can choose from several, at various pricing levels. Think not only about what you want to do now, but what you need to do in the future, and assess the possible traffic and storage needs you have.

    Choosing a blog solution based on a small budget is limiting, but not something that needs to affect whether you have a successful blog or not. Spend those dollars in ways that will make success more likely, and plan to go looking for a larger budget when you have demonstrated that success.

It might be wiser, for example, to spend the money for a unique domain name and a custom logo than on the fancier technical bells and whistles. Bells and whistles are easy to add later, but branding needs to be present from the beginning.

✔ **Trial run:** A hosted blog solution gives you an inexpensive, even free, way to try blogging on for size without committing to a large project you don't have the time or resources to maintain.

A surprisingly large number of blogs are created and then abandoned — some in the same day. The fact is, blogging isn't for everyone,or for every company. A blog is a lot of work, and you may want to simply try doing it for a week before you jump wholeheartedly into buying a domain, choosing blog software, and finding Web hosting.

✔ **Blogging anonymously:** Setting up a blog anonymously on a hosted service is easier than setting up one on your own server. If you'd prefer to blend in with the rest of the blogging hordes, and you don't want your blog traced to a particular source, think hosted blog.

You have no guarantees of staying anonymous. If your identity is the source of speculation, the tenacious, clever community of bloggers can piece together the clues, hunt down the asides, and figure out who you are. I talk more about blog safety in Chapter 12.

See Chapter 5 for more information about hosted blog software solutions, including how to set up a blog and start posting right away.

Discovering independent blog solutions

When you purchase an independent blog solution, for example, from Movable Type or pMachine software vendors, you purchase a permanent license to install and use its software on your own Web server. The software gives you an interface with which to customize the look, feel, and behavior of your blog and also allows you to make and edit entries to the blog.

You almost always need to install and configure independent blog software before using it, a process that takes time and several different technical skills to accomplish. Even the easiest installation can go awry, and you may not have the supporting software necessary to install the blog software. After it is installed, the software is powerful but not for the technically faint of heart. In addition, the HTML coding on which most blogs are built is among the most complex Web page coding being done today.

Of course, if you buy software that needs to be installed on a Web server, you may also need to find a Web hosting company and, probably, register a domain name for your blog. I talk more about registering a domain name and choosing Web hosting at the end of this chapter.

Having a firm grasp on HTML and Cascading Style Sheets is key to really making this software work hard for you. The resulting blog is personalized entirely to you, though most of the available software comes with a selection of generic and recognizable templates from which to start.

Turn to Chapter 6 to find out more about choosing and setting up an independent blog solution.

Assessing your technical skills

Although you spend some dollars for an independent blog solution, the real cost is counted in terms of learning and setup time. You must have strong technical skills to take full advantage of your blog software or work with someone who can handle the configuration for you. And after you start tweaking, you may find keeping your blog up to date is a never-ending process. There's always a new plug-in to try or a new Web tool to add.

Lots of blogs are created by and for technical folks, and if you're part of that community, you may already know that an independent blog software solution is what you want to do. As you set up and configure your blog, these skills are helpful:

- ✔ **A background in creating Web sites, writing HTML, designing Web graphics, and programming:** Even if you don't have all those skills at your fingertips, being familiar with how the Internet and Web publishing work and being willing to experiment are good indicators that you can make independent blog software work for you.

- ✔ **Experience with other blog software, even a hosted blog solution:** This isn't to say, however, that everyone with a strong technical background needs to go with an independent blog software solution, but it is more likely that you'll succeed in using one effectively if you do have good technical skills.

Knowing when to use independent software

As you think about whether an independent blog software package is right for you, consider these points:

- ✔ **Customization:** Maybe your company has a certain graphic design style that you need to emulate as you create a blog. Many hosted blog solutions let you customize templates or change color palettes, but if you want to have final control over every aspect of how your blog looks, feels, and acts, an independent blog solution is the best method. Figure 4-1 shows an example of one of the default Blogger templates.

  Look for a system of templates and style sheets that allows you to change the following items:

  - Colors, graphics, layout, and wording

  - How to create URLs and make custom error and search result pages

  You should also look for an independent blog that allows you to install plug-ins so you can expand you blog's capabilities in the future.

- ✔ **Finances:** If money isn't an issue, you're free to choose the best software solution for the job. Since independent blog software is typically more expensive that hosted solutions, having a generous budget puts you in a better position to consider using one. A generous budget for starting a blog might be in the $500 to $1000 range to cover software and hosting costs.

  Your budget may also allow you to pay for a top Web designer and/or developer to install and customize that software for you.

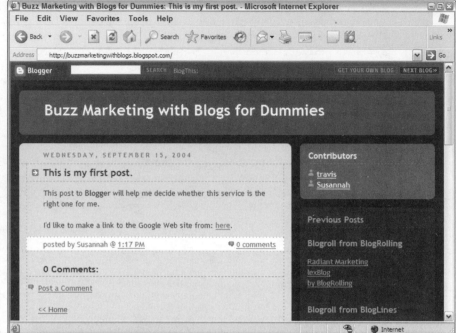

Figure 4-1:
Is this
hosted blog
from
Blogger.com
a little bland
for you? If
you want to
tweak, you
need an
independent
blog
software
solution.

Rates for contract Web designers vary regionally, but be sure to get quotes from at least three different designers. Go with the one that's the best fit for your needs, and don't equate a high price tag with high quality.

✔ **Bells and whistles:** Blogs are a hot technology area on the Web right now, and that means a lot of innovation is in the field. Audio, video, mobile, and photo blogs are only some of the interesting ways people are choosing to blog. If you want to use all the latest tools on your blog, and perhaps increase your traffic while doing so, independent blog software often keeps pace with developments better than a hosted solution.

Independent blog software developers are catering to a technically savvy, cutting-edge audience that knows and demands current technology. And even if they don't extend their software regularly, many independent blog software companies encourage third-party developers to create plug-ins that can be used with their software. You can take advantage of newer technology or even contribute your own code to handle your specific need. A hosted blog solution simply can't match the nimbleness of independent blog software — at least as long as innovation continues in blogging.

At the same time, all this additional functionality can come at the sacrifice of stability or compatibility. Nothing's certain, but hosted solutions tend to be less buggy in regular use.

✔ **Reputation:** The blogosphere is a relatively small world and a tightly knit community to boot. Chances are that visitors who are also bloggers will take note of the software you create your blog with, and you'll get just a little bit more blog credibility if you're using independent blog software rather than a hosted solution. While this isn't completely fair to the many excellent bloggers on hosted blog solutions, it is nonetheless a blogosphere reality.

If you want to test this theory, start looking at the blogs you read regularly. Many blogs indicate which software they're using, even when they don't need to. This is a bit of technical showmanship, or perhaps one-upmanship — one blogger saying to another that he's got the smarts and skills to go with the difficult solution. Waxy (www.waxy.org) is one popular blog that displays a "Powered by Movable Type" graphic; it is shown in Figure 4-2.

Because one of the best ways you can build buzz around your blog is to attract other bloggers, you may want to play this game yourself — if you go with an independent blog, add the logo to the final design of your blog.

✔ **Existing Web sites:** Perhaps you're creating a blog that will actually live on your company's Web site, as part of a larger package of information your company is providing to the public. You need a blog solution that permits you to publish your blog on your company server. Some hosted blog solutions permit you do to this, but an independent blog solution is likely the way you need to go.

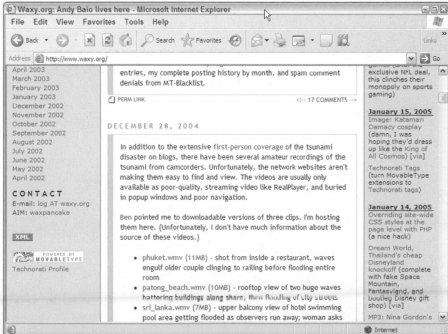

Figure 4-2: Tech-savvy blogger Andrew Baio uses Movable Type to run his blog.

Before you get too carried away: The server software in use with your current site may dictate what blog software you can use. Several different kinds of server platforms are in common use, and most independent blog software is only available for one or two of those platforms. When in doubt, look up the technical requirements of the blog software you want to use, and consult with your IT staff about whether the technologies are compatible.

Never underestimate the value of having someone close at hand who can help you figure out a new technology. Having someone who can help you who already knows and uses a blog technology is better than the best customer support out there. If the technology your friend or colleague uses suits your needs, stop agonizing over choosing the right solution — you've already found it. Buy him or her lunch, and bring your notebook.

Getting Ready to Blog

If you're going to blog, you simply must get your own domain. Having your own domain gives you credibility and a permanent address that stays constant even if you decide to switch underlying services later.

If you don't register a name, you're in danger of someone else coming along and registering the name — you don't want that.

If you choose to go with an independent blog software solution, and you don't have a company Web server to install that software on, you definitely need to find some Web hosting as well.

For more information on choosing a name for your blog, look to Chapter 3. This decision is important even when you're using a hosted blog solution, if only for marketing purposes. After all, `buzzmarketingwithblogs.com` is easier for your audience to remember than `buzzmarketingwithblogs.blogspot.com`.

If you need information on how domain names are structured, see Appendix D.

Finding out if your domain name is available

To find out whether the domain you want to use is available, don't just type your preferred name into a Web browser. Even if no Web site appears, the domain name may already be taken. Follow these tips to ensure you get the domain name you want:

- ✔ **Check out a domain registration company:** Many, many domain registration companies are out there, such as Network Solutions, GoDaddy, 1&1, and Dotster. They offer a range of different services at varying prices, so be sure to check around before you make your purchase.

- ✔ **Look up availability for free and then register a domain for as long as ten years, in one-year increments.**

- ✔ **Look for extra services offered for free.** When choosing a domain registrar, you might want to see whether the domain registrar offers *domain forwarding* or *domain masking* as free services or requires an extra fee.

Domain forwarding is a little like that message you get when you call a number that's been disconnected that tells you the new number. A user types in `www.buzzmarketingwithblogsfordummies.com`, and after the forwarding kicks in, the browser displays the hosted blog at `buzzmarketingwithblogs.blogspot.com`, where the blog actually lives. Anyone who bookmarks the site bookmarks the final address.

Domain masking is sometimes a little more expensive and works like calling a big hotel chain — you call the local number, and your call ends up in a call center across the country. Masking ensures that the Web address always shows in the browser address bar as `www.buzzmarketingwithblogsfordummies.com`, even if the underlying Web site is on a hosted blog software company's site. This feature can be a little more technically complicated to implement, but if someone bookmarks or forwards the page, they get the permanent URL you prefer they use.

Masking is sometimes also called *domain mapping*. If your name of choice isn't available, put on your thinking cap. It's time to come up with some alternatives.

As you think of good names, avoid domain names that are only slightly different from one already in use, as visitors will undoubtedly end up visiting the other Web site when they mean to come to yours. For example, if `buzzmarketing withblogs.com` is already registered, `buzz-marketing-with-blogs.com` (with a hyphen) isn't a good choice alternative, especially if the owner of `buzz marketingwithblogs.com` is a competitor!

If you have your heart set on a domain name that isn't available, consider contacting the owner and offering to pay for the domain. If the Web site is inactive, the owner might consider letting it go. Expect to make an offer for the domain at quite a bit more than if buying an unregistered domain. Nevertheless, the days when a domain like `business.com` sold for $7.5 million — as happened in 1999 — are over, and you might consider opening with an offer of $150.

In any case, if you have a name in mind to use and find it's available, register it right away! Nothing is more frustrating than discovering that a domain name that was available yesterday was snapped up this morning.

I talk more about choosing a name for your blog in Chapter 3.

I use 1&1 Internet in my examples because its registration process is straight-forward and its prices are very competitive. Follow these steps to use 1&1 Internet to find out whether the domain name you're interested is available:

1. **Go to** www.1and1.com.

2. **Type the domain name you're interested in into the Get Your Domain box, and click Go.**

3. **Select the suffix you prefer to use.**

    Figure 4-3 shows how to conduct a search. The registrar checks the Internet domain registry and lets you know whether the domain is available for purchase or not.

If your domain name is available, congratulations! You're one step closer to making your business blog a reality.

Figure 4-3:
You can use the domain registrar 1&1 Internet to find out if a domain name is available to purchase and use.

Registering a domain name

After you find an available domain name to use, you need to register it. (See the previous section, "Finding out if your domain name is available," to find a domain name.) You can use a similar process to the one below to register a domain name with any domain registrar. Follow these steps to register your domain with 1&1 Internet:

1. **Select the domain name you wish to purchase, and click Continue.**

   It may already be selected for you.

2. **Click Continue if you're ready to purchase and don't want to add additional domain names to your order, and then select the 1&1 Instant Domain package.**

   1&1 may give you an opportunity to add more domain names to your order. You can do so if you wish, or simply click Continue until you have the option to select the 1&1 Instant Domain package.

3. **Click Continue until you reach the Address entry page.**

   If you are already a 1&1 customer, you can bypass the Address entry by entering your username and password. If you are not already a 1&1 customer, fill out the required address information and then click Continue.

4. **Choose a six- to eight-character password to use with the 1&1 Web site, and click Continue.**

5. **Tell 1&1 how you heard about them, and click Continue.**

6. **Enter your credit card information, and click Continue.**

7. **Review the information on the check-out screen for errors, read through the Terms and Conditions policy, and click Order Now to complete your purchase.**

   Your order is complete. 1&1 sends you a confirmation e-mail verifying your purchase. You may also want to print a copy of your order for your records.

Finding a Web host

Having a domain name is only half the equation in creating the Web site. If you aren't using a hosted blog solution, you also need to arrange Web hosting. A Web hosting company maintains computers (usually quite a few) on which the pages of your Web site live. When you register your domain, you tell the registrar which Web host you are using. Then, when someone wants to visit your Web site, the registrar tells that visitor's browser which computer the pages live on.

If you think about the domain name as an address, a Web host is the actual house that sits at that address — that is, the actual pages of your Web site.

The variations between Web hosts and their technical options and pricing are endless. Don't make the mistake of simply buying the cheapest solution, however! Blog software packages often have some specific technical requirements in order to run, and you need to make sure that your Web host can handle them before you buy. And if you need technical assistance, the cheapest solution may not have the best customer service.

Choose a blog software package and *then* contact the Web hosting companies you want to use. Ask them specifically if they support that package. Even better, ask them to refer you to a customer of theirs that is currently using the software. You can't get better evidence of software and Web hosting compatibility than seeing it in action!

Don't confuse a hosted blog solution with Web hosting — they are not the same. A hosted blog is a blog that lives on another company's server. Your postings, photographs, comments, and pages are all created by their software and stay on their server.

Web hosting is necessary for every Web site. A hosted blog solution includes Web hosting as part of the whole package, but Web hosting almost never includes blogging software. A hosted blog provider doesn't also include things you get from Web hosting — such as e-mail forwarding, an FTP site, or traffic logs. If you choose an independent blog software package, you don't get Web hosting, only the software, so you still need a host where you can install that software.

There are some blog companies that have also begun to offer Web hosting, and these can be a good option for an all-in-one package that guarantees server and software will be a match. Wordpress and Movable Type are two examples of blogging companies that also offer hosting.

Chapter 5

Setting Up a Hosted Blog

A hosted blog is one that lives on the server of a blog company and is also maintained through that company's production interface. Hosted blogs are quick to set up and easy to use, and you usually don't need to download and install software. And some of these services are even free!

Using a hosted blog solution means that you can begin blogging very quickly and also that you don't need to have all the technical skills required to install and configure software on your own Web server. A hosted blogging solution will let you get right to blogging rather than distracting you with complicated technical issues.

Although using a hosted blog can simplify the process a great deal, you still have some decisions to make. Quite a few really excellent hosted Web solutions are out there to choose from. You can find a company whose package suits you, but you may have to shop around a bit to do it.

Focusing on Important Blog Features

The right hosted blog solution for you depends on a number of factors:

▸ **Budget:** Hosted blog solutions come in several price ranges. Some are free; some require a monthly fee that varies depending on the use you are making of the blog.

✔ **Flexibility:** Depending on which hosted blog solution you choose, you will have different built-in functionalities. Look for one that will give you the ability to add tools and make changes, even if you don't plan to do so right away.

✔ **Future plans:** Be sure to consider your long-term plans for the blog when you choose your blog solution; if you choose a stripped-down service now, you may limit yourself in the future.

Moving a blog of any significant size to a new host is a task to be avoided if you can possibly help it!

Use Chapter 4 to determine whether hosted or independent blog software better meets your needs.

Choosing Functionalities

Good blogs have some important features in common that you should look for while shopping for a hosted blog solution.

Even if you're not sure what kind of use you'll be making of your blog at this point, the following functionalities are found on most good blogs, and having them can make yours more usable and flexible in the future.

✔ **Categories:** As you blog, you may find that you are doing things differently than when you started — you might even develop a new goal for it. A blog created to talk about technical trends, for example, might start to have a significant number of posts about one trend in particular. So you can use this trend as a category. It can be challenging to make sure people get the information they are looking for, and categorizing your entries can help you deal with this. Most blogs archive entries by date (for example, you can look at all entries for September 2004), but that only tells part of the story if you're looking for a specific piece of information. Using categories for your entries lets you subdivide things logically and gives your users a better chance of finding information that was posted last month or last year.

Some categories will get more use than others, and you'll undoubtedly add some over time (and even stop using others), but not having this functionality makes your life harder. For an example of a categorized blog, check out Stonyfield Farm's Bovine Bugle (www.stonyfield.com/weblog/BovineBugle), shown in Figure 5-1. This blog is devoted to the cows that contribute the raw materials for Stonyfield's products. Each entry is assigned a category, like Christmas Trees or Cows. Archived entries can then be sorted and read by category instead of chronologically.

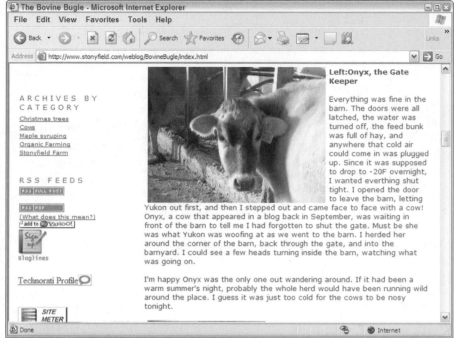

The Bovine Bugle - Microsoft Internet Explorer

File   Edit   View   Favorites   Tools   Help

Back   Search   Favorites   Links

Address   http://www.stonyfield.com/weblog/BovineBugle/index.html   Go

ARCHIVES BY CATEGORY

Christmas trees
Cows
Maple syruping
Organic Farming
Stonyfield Farm

RSS FEEDS

RSS FULL POST

RSS PDF
(What does this mean?)
add to YAHOO!

Bloglines

Technorati Profile

SITE METER

Done   Internet

Left:Onyx, the Gate Keeper

Everything was fine in the barn. The doors were all latched, the water was turned off, the feed bunk was full of hay, and anywhere that cold air could come in was plugged up. Since it was supposed to drop to -20F overnight, I wanted everthing shut tight. I opened the door to leave the barn, letting Yukon out first, and then I stepped out and came face to face with a cow! Onyx, a cow that appeared in a blog back in September, was waiting in front of the barn to tell me I had forgotten to shut the gate. Must be she was what Yukon was woofing at as we went to the barn. I herded her around the corner of the barn, back through the gate, and into the barnyard. I could see a few heads turning inside the barn, watching what was going on.

I'm happy Onyx was the only one out wandering around. If it had been a warm summer's night, probably the whole herd would have been running wild around the place. I guess it was just too cold for the cows to be nosy tonight.

Figure 5-1:
The Bovine Bugle blog sorts entries into categories to help readers focus or find things later.

✔ **RSS:** What the acronym *RSS* stands for is a little unclear — it could be Really Simple Syndication or Rich Site Summary, depending on who you ask. In any case, an RSS feed is an XML-based technology that creates short summaries of every entry posted on your blog. These summaries can then be:

- Picked up by blog syndication Web sites

- Displayed on other Web logs or sites

- Accessed through newsreader software

To see how RSS works, visit Bloglines at `www.bloglines.com`. Bloglines is a Web site that aggregates RSS feeds from all over the Web and allows you to subscribe to and read those that interest you. Incidentally, this site is a great way to get familiar with the blogosphere. Figure 5-2 shows Bloglines at work.

✔ **Blogrolls:** Nearly every blog you visit includes a list of blogs read by the blogger. Typically, this list is compiled to recommend blogs or to give readers an idea about his or her blog-reading habits. This list is usually called a *blogroll.*

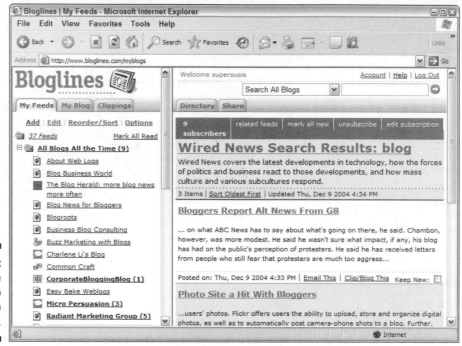

Figure 5-2:
Use
BlogLines to
subscribe to
RSS feeds.

Creating a list is good blog etiquette, so you want to find a hosted blog solution that lets you do this.

If you fall in love with a hosted blog solution that doesn't offer this service, look to see whether you can edit the templates. With some HTML know-how, you can make a list and put it on the page yourself, but this solution is only viable if you have some good HTML skills.

✔ **Comments:** Reader feedback is what make blogs blogs. Without comments, your blog is just another Web site, a platform for your views and nothing more. If you're serious about fostering dialogue on your blog, you simply must have the ability to handle comments.

There are exceptions to the general rule that a blog has comments, but most do. Even if you don't think you want this technology now, you'll get requests for it in the future, so you should look for a hosted blog solution that provides it. If you're concerned about comments, look for a hosted solution that allows you to turn off comments for a single entry.

✔ **Design:** The ability to create a unique look and feel for your blog may seem secondary to the idea of getting started today, but over time you will find you want to make your blog different from all the rest. Many of the hosted blog solutions offer a series of designs you can choose from, but the selection isn't huge. There are so many blogs out there that choosing a design template in this way guarantees that hundreds of other blogs will have the same look.

Look for a blog solution that offers you either the ability to further customize these templates or that lets you access the template code yourself. Better yet, look for one that does both! This gives you the flexibility down the line to pep things up or even to redesign.

In Chapter 3, I discuss design tools and resources.

Getting Familiar with Hosted Solutions

This list is by no means comprehensive, but the following companies each provide a great package of services and an easy-to-use interface.

Blogger

`www.blogger.com`

Blogger, shown in Figure 5-3, is one of the oldest of the hosted blog solutions. The company opened in 1999 during the economic frenzy of the dot-com boom. It survived the crash and is still going strong, thanks to a solid set of services. In 2002, Blogger was bought by Google, which provides solid financial backing and some assurance that this company will be around for some time to come. Best of all, Blogger continues to innovate and add functionality. Here are some advantages to using Blogger:

- ✔ It's free and includes a blog that lives on the Blogger server.
- ✔ You receive a unique Web site address.
- ✔ You can choose from a variety of features to personalize your blog, including a selection of designs and user comments.
- ✔ Multiple authors can use Blogger, and you can post e-mail, photos, and audio files.
- ✔ You can add a button on your browser toolbar for easy access to your blog.

If you know some HTML, Blogger gives you access to the guts of your blog so you can customize your design. You can also choose to display a Blogger blog on your own Web site, if you have one.

Blogger claims that setting up a blog takes only five minutes, and that seems to be true. Go to the "Opening a Blogger account" section later in this chapter to find out how easily you can set up a new account with Blogger.

Figure 5-3:
Start a free
hosted blog
with
Blogger.

TypePad

`www.typepad.com`

TypePad's functionality, while more powerful than you find with Blogger, is also a little more complex to use. The system is designed to permit the maximum in customization, from design personalization to photo albums. TypePad is a great choice for someone who wants to give their blog a unique look and feel without spending months learning HTML.

TypePad, shown in Figure 5-4, lets you do the following things:

- ✔ **Host your blog:** A unique Web site address.
- ✔ **A photo album:** Upload photos to share with your readers.
- ✔ **Add links:** A feature called TypeLists allows you to easily add lists of links — or other blogs, books, Webrings, news stories, or other groups as well — to your blog.
- ✔ **Personalize your design and your layout:** Your blog can have photos, comments, categories, multiple authors, search, and statistical information about the use your blog gets.

- ✔ **Protect your blog with a password:** Limit your audience to those you send the password to.

- ✔ **Mobile blogging:** *Moblogging* is when you send text or pictures to your blog from your digital camera, PDA, or phone.

Unlike Blogger, TypePad charges for its services. There are three service levels, and depending on the amount of customization and the number of features you want, using TypePad costs between $4.95 and $14.95 a month. You can start your TypePad blog with a 30-day free trial. If you choose to use the prepay option for a year, you receive two months free.

Radio UserLand

radio.userland.com

Radio UserLand works a little differently from Blogger or TypePad. With this solution, you actually download and install a piece of software that lets you create and edit your blog on your own computer. This software is available for both Macs and PCs. You can even get it in English, French, German, or Italian.

Figure 5-4:
TypePad offers a strong blogging tool for a monthly fee.

Radio UserLand features include:

- ✔ **RSS:** A file containing summaries of your posts that can be viewed via newsreader software or displayed on Web sites that track new blog posts. Having an RSS feed will give your readers faster access to your posts.

- ✔ **News aggregation:** This technology allows you to tell Radio UserLand about your news interests. The company searches news sites and other blogs for articles that match your interests. You can view these headlines through the Radio UserLand software or receive them by e-mail and then create an entry with a link to a news story you're blogging about instantly.

- ✔ **Multiple authoring:** Some blogs are the efforts of several bloggers, all contributing expertise and content. They are a good way to include several viewpoints and decrease the workload of blogging.

Radio UserLand, shown in Figure 5-5, also has e-mail updating, content categories, a unique Web site address, comments, a hit counter, and statistical information about how your blog is used. Advanced users can access the blog code, and you can also use Radio UserLand to post a blog to your own Web site instead of the Radio servers.

Radio UserLand offers a 30-day free trial. Afterwards, Radio UserLand costs $39.95 a month.

Figure 5-5:
Install Radio UserLand and blog from your computer.

Using other hosted solutions

You can find quite a few other hosted blog solutions. Xanga and LiveJournal have good blogging tools, and both offer free service levels but are also focused on serving the needs of online diarists rather than businesses. Even AOL has gotten into the blog space with its AOL Journals service. The online e-zine *Salon* offers a *Salon*-branded version of Radio UserLand.

See Appendix C for more hosted blog solutions.

Setting Up a Hosted Blog

If you're trying to decide which hosted blog service to use, try setting up an account with each and then using them for a couple of weeks. Most of the pay solutions offer a free trial period you can use to do this. This strategy really pays off in the long run, because you can make the most informed decision possible. Each of the hosted solutions works a little differently, and some are targeted at slightly different levels of technical experience, so it takes some experimentation to know which is best for you.

Opening a Blogger account

Setting up a Blogger account is a great way to get started. Its sign-up process is simple, and you don't need to have anything but a name for your blog in mind. Follow these steps:

1. **Open a browser, and go to** `www.blogger.com`.

2. **Click the Create Your Blog Now arrow on the home page.**

3. **Fill out the information it requests, read the terms of service, and click Continue.**

   You may need to experiment to find an available username. Be creative!

4. **Name your blog, choose a blog address (see Figure 5-6), and click Continue.**

   Again, you may have try a few different names to find one that is available.

5. **Choose a template design (see Figure 5-7), and click Continue.**

   If you don't like those that are available, remember that with some HTML skills you can alter the code to make a design that suits you better.

6. **Click the Start Posting button to begin using your new blog.**

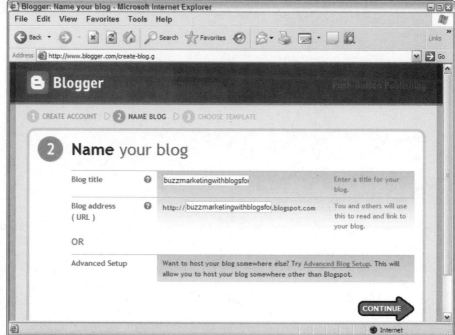

Figure 5-6:
This is the second step in setting up a Blogger account.

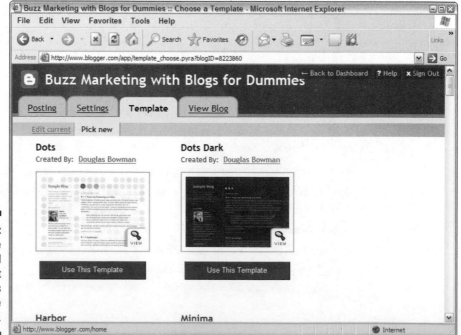

Figure 5-7:
There are several different blog designs to choose from.

Posting to your blog

Blogger provides an interface from which to post your entries. If you need to, go to the Blogger Web site and sign in.

You can choose to click the Remember Me box so that you don't have to sign in every time you go to `blogger.com`.

You can have multiple blogs under the same user account with Blogger, so when you sign in you have to select which blog you want to post to, even if you only have one blog. Follow these steps to create a new post:

1. **Select your blog.**
2. **Click the Create a New Post button.**
3. **Type a title.**
4. **Type the text of your entry.**

   If you want to bold some text, click and drag to highlight it. Click the B button and the HTML code that creates bolded text is inserted. You can also italicize text and indent it.

5. **Decide what you want to do with your post:**

   • To save this post and come back to it later, click the Save as Draft button.

   • To post the entry to your blog, click the Publish Post button.

   Figure 5-8 shows a sample post page. The entry appears on your blog.

Adding links

Blogger has a built-in tool that allows you to create links in your posts. Follow these steps to add a link:

1. **Select the text you want to be clickable.**
2. **Click the Insert Link icon (it looks like a small globe with a chain link on top of it).**

   An Enter URL dialog box opens.

3. **Enter the URL of the site you want to link to, as shown in Figure 5-9.**

   Be sure to include the `http://` before the address.

4. **Click OK.**

   The HTML that creates a link is added to your entry.

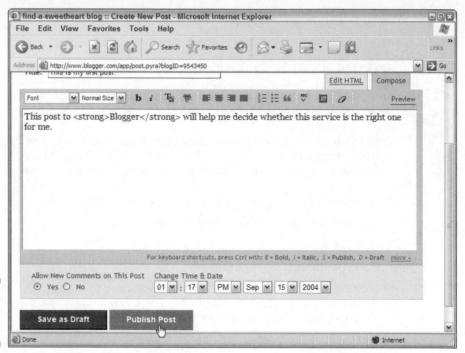

Figure 5-8:
Post your
entry.

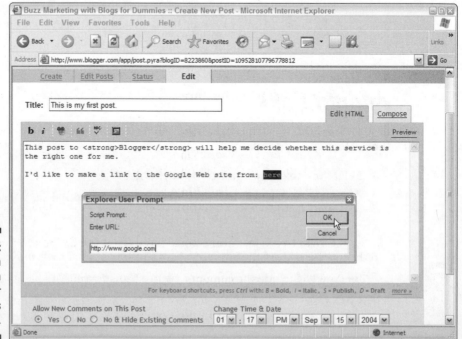

Figure 5-9:
Adding a
link to a
Blogger
entry is
simple.

Adding images

Blogger does not allow you to post images on its server, so you need to place your images online in another location. For example, you can put your image on your own Web site or use a photo service such as Flickr (www.flickr.com) or BloggerBot (www.hello.com) to post your images online. Some of these services, like Flickr, resize your images for you.

Take note of the URL where you post your images so you can provide a link to them on your blog.

Windows users can download the BloggerBot Hello software to their computers and use their Blogger usernames to upload images for free.

Turning on comments

Blogger permits you to allow comments on your blog, but you may want to change some of the settings. Follow these steps after logging into your account to update your comments settings:

1. **Select the blog you want to work on.**

2. **Click the Settings tab and then click the Comments link.**

   The settings page for comments appears (see Figure 5-10).

3. **Choose to show or hide comments.**

   If you choose to hide comments on your site, they don't display, but they aren't deleted. To show all comments, choose Show.

4. **Choose from the following three options in the Who Can Comment? drop-down list:**

   • **Anyone:** Any visitor to the blog can comment.

   • **Only Registered Users:** Only members of the Blogger service can comment. (Readers can register for free.)

   • **Only Members of This Blog:** If you add members to your blog (see the "Adding another author" section later in this chapter), only they will be permitted to post comments.

5. **Select what behavior future posts have from the Default for Post drop-down list.**

   The New Posts Have Comments option turns comments on in the future.

6. **If you want to know when someone posts a comment on your blog, enter your e-mail address in the Comment Notification Address box.**

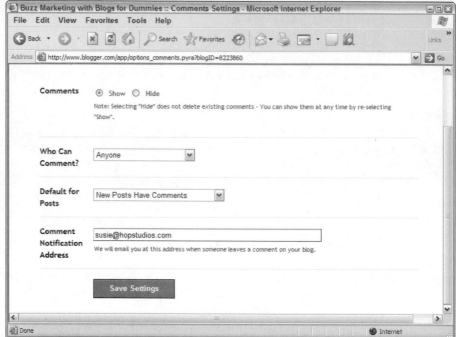

Figure 5-10:
Use these
settings in
Blogger to
turn on
comments
for everyone
who visits
your blog.

7. Click the Save Settings button.

Blogger reloads the page with the Republish button visible.

8. Click the Republish button to make these settings changes active.

Your next post has comments turned on.

Adding another author

Blogger allows you to have more than one contributor to a blog. You can use this feature to create collaborative blogs or to allow a guest blogger to run your blog for a week. Follow these steps to add another contributor (Blogger calls them team members) to your Blogger blog:

1. Log in, and select the blog you want to add a new contributor to.

2. Click the Settings tab and then click the Members link.

3. Click Add Team Member(s).

You can add up to three new members at a time. To add them, enter one new member per box next to New User (see Figure 5-11).

4. If you want to include a message with that e-mail, type your message in the Message box.

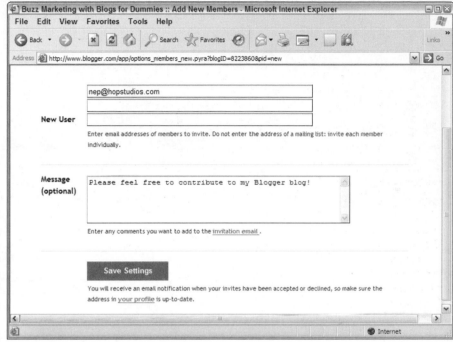

Figure 5-11:
Add up to
three new
contributors
to your
blog with
Blogger.

5. **Click the Save Settings button.**

   Blogger sends invitations to the new team members with a link that
   allows them to set up a Blogger account or connect an existing Blogger
   account to your blog.

Chapter 6

Taking Control with Independent Blog Software

In This Chapter

▶ Selecting an independent blog software solution

▶ Important technical features to look for

▶ Installing and using pMachine's ExpressionEngine

*I*n this chapter, I focus on installing and using independent blog software — that is, blog software that you put on your own server and configure yourself. Although the technical hurdles are much greater than with most hosted blog solutions, using an independent solution provides greater flexibility.

Bloggers who choose to use independent blog software are usually those with very strong technical skills in Web site creation, programming, or graphic design, or those with access to people with those skills. Because of the degree of complexity of such software packages, many bloggers consider using them a mark of prestige — sort of a digital calling card that demonstrates skill and know-how. This is especially true of blogs that have been further customized with additional programming and functionality.

Using independent blog software is hard to do, but the really savvy bloggers choose this solution, so you know you're on to something good when you go this route.

Go to Chapter 4 to find out how to determine whether hosted or independent blog software better meets your needs.

Independent Blog Software Solutions

As with hosted blog solutions, you can choose from many options. Most of these software packages include the following:

- Instructions on acquiring and installing the software on your Web server
- Guidance on server technical requirements
- A user guide

Be sure to review all these documents as you assess the different software packages. If you're constrained by a certain set of server capabilities or can't make heads or tails of the installation instructions, the software package may not be for you!

Many independent blog software solutions are available; the list could go on for pages. To get you blogging quickly, the companies I discuss in the following sections are those with very strong software packages, competitive pricing, and a robust set of functionalities.

Choosing functionalities

Good blogs have some important features in common that you need to look for in any independent blogging software solution you consider (and in hosted solutions, too). Whatever solution you decide to use, make sure you have access to the following technologies, even if you don't plan to use them right away. If your blog is a success, you will undoubtedly want to add some of these features down the line.

- **Categories:** One of the best ways to help your readers get the information they're most interested in is to categorize your content. If you post frequently, allow multiple authors, or cover a number of topics, you'll find categories essential.

  For an example of a categorized blog, check out Steve Rubel's Micro Persuasion blog (www.micropersuasion.com), shown in Figure 6-1. Steve writes about the impact of blogs and journalism on public relations, and assigns each post a category like Citizen Journalism, Marketing, and Free Advice. Archived entries can then be sorted and read by category, instead of chronologically.

- **RSS:** Most blogs — and, increasingly, many Web sites with regularly updated content — provide an RSS feed for readers. An RSS feed is an XML-based file that creates short summaries of every entry posted on your blog. The RSS feed pushes your content to blog aggregation sites and permits it to be:

  - Picked up by Web sites that syndicate blog content

- Pulled in by other Web logs or other Web sites
- Displayed by newsreader software

Figure 6-2 shows Bloglines (`www.bloglines.com`), a free RSS reader, at work.

✔ **Blogrolls/links:** Creating a list of links to blogs you read regularly, or a *blogroll,* is considered good form and a way of being a participating member of the blogosphere.

Some independent blog software solutions provide a tool for you to build the blogroll; others let you edit the templates and code yourself. If you pick a blog software package that requires you to write some HTML to create a list of links, see Chapter 4 for an HTML brush-up.

✔ **Comments:** Look for an independent blog software solution that not only permits comments, but allows you to track them to keep up with what people are saying.

You set apart your blog from a run-of-the-mill Web site with comments. They are the dialogue, the interaction, that makes blogs exciting and unique — and they're important avenues for your readers to give you information and criticism.

Readers can comment on Stonyfield Farm's Bovine Bugle (`www.stonyfield.com/weblog/BovineBugle`), shown in Figure 6-3.

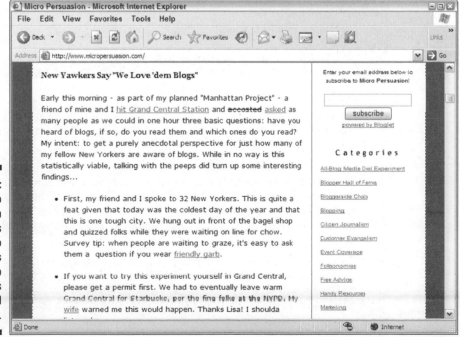

Figure 6-1:
The Micro Persuasion blog sorts entries into categories to help readers focus or find things later.

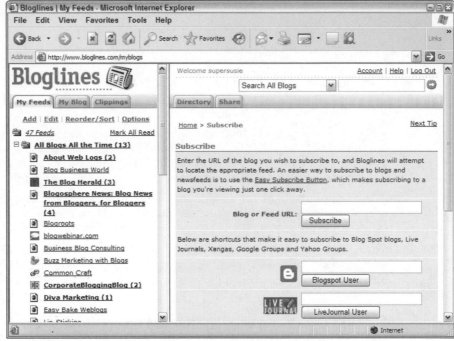

Figure 6-2:
Bloglines is a Web site that gives you access to the RSS feeds of many blogs.

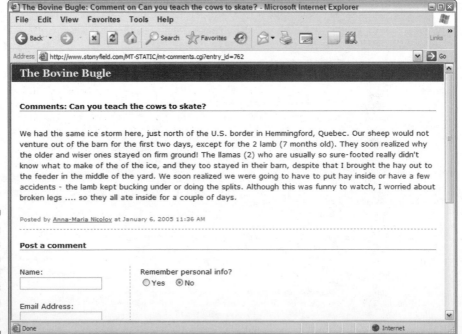

Figure 6-3:
Comments from Stonyfield Farm's Bovine Bugle blog.

pMachine's ExpressionEngine

ExpressionEngine (www.pmachine.com/expressionengine/) is the higher-end of pMachine's two blogging solutions and contains an impressive array of functionalities, including the following:

- ✔ Multiple blogs.
- ✔ Categories, comments, and templates.
- ✔ Multiple authors. Each author can have different levels of access to the system. Some folks can write but not publish; others can edit or delete content.
- ✔ A search engine.
- ✔ A versioning system. Tracks changes to the code and allows you to revert if things go haywire.
- ✔ A built-in mailing list. Send e-mails to your members.
- ✔ Photo capability. Upload and resize images, and create thumbnails.

What's most exciting about ExpressionEngine is that it's completely customizable — you can create fields in your blog for every type of content you create and use the templates to control the way that content appears on the page. ExpressionEngine runs your blog out of a database, so changes you make to the design in the future ripple back through your archives.

I used ExpressionEngine to create the companion blog to this book, Buzz Marketing with Blogs (www.buzzmarketingwithblogs.com), which is shown in Figure 6-4.

ExpressionEngine 1.2 is written in PHP and uses a MySQL database. To use it, you must have a server with XML support, PHP version 4.1 or better, and MySQL version 3.23.32 or better.

A commercial license for ExpressionEngine is $199; nonprofits can buy a non-commercial license for $149. You can download, install, and test a free 14-day trial version of ExpressionEngine. If ExpressionEngine is more than you really need, take a look at pMachine's other blog offering, pMachine Pro (www.pmachine.com/pmachinepro/).

pMachine can also install ExpressionEngine for you for $50.

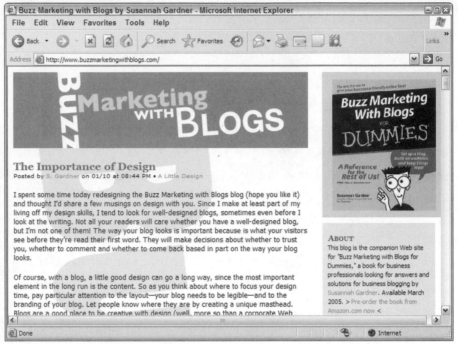

Figure 6-4: Buzz Marketing with Blogs, the companion blog for this book, was created using Expression-Engine.

Six Apart's Movable Type

Movable Type (www.movabletype.org) is perhaps the most well-known independent blogging solution available today. Its creators, husband and wife Benjamin and Mena Trott, wrote the first version of the software in 2001. It was one of the first available independent blog software solutions and does a great job of addressing the functionality needs of bloggers.

Movable Type features includes:

- ✔ Comments and categories.
- ✔ A search engine.
- ✔ Multiple authors, templates, and multiple blogs. You can assign different permission levels to the blog authors and control which authors can edit or publish to the blog.
- ✔ Thumbnail images from uploaded images.
- ✔ Publish your blog *dynamically* (when a visitor requests a page) or *statically* (when the blog entry is written).
- ✔ Plug-in capability. Because Movable Type has been used by so many technically inclined bloggers, you can add quite a few plug-ins to your Movable Type installation to increase functionality. The MT Blacklist

plug-in, for example, gives you the ability to ban use of certain URLs or certain IP addresses in comments on your blog, thus cutting down on comment spam. Another popular plug-in, NowPlaying, lets you display the names of songs you are currently listening to in iTunes. Learn more about available plug-ins at www.mt-plugins.org.

In Figure 6-5, you can see an example of a blog run using Movable Type. Joi Ito, chairman of Six Apart Japan (Six Apart is the company behind Movable Type), runs his own blog using MT at joi.ito.com.

Movable Type 3.1 can be run on several operating systems but does require that your Web server allow you to run CGI scripts and have Perl 5.004_04 or better installed.

Movable Type has several pricing options, but for commercial purposes the costs range from $199.95 to $1,299.95 depending on the number of users. The $199.95 package includes an unlimited number of Web logs and five users. Not-for-profit organizations can get a similar software package for $49.95. No matter which package you ultimately need, you can begin by using a limited version of the software for free.

Six Apart can also install Movable Type on your Web server for you for a fee.

Figure 6-5:
Joi Ito's
Blog is run
using the
independent
blogging
software
Movable
Type.

Other independent blog software solutions

You can find several other good independent blogging software solutions. Many are targeted toward a very technical user and aren't good solutions unless you're a fairly competent programmer, or can work with someone who is. At this level, some of these systems are also great content management tools, and you can use them for entire Web sites and not just blogs.

Whichever solution you choose, you need to be aware that committing to independent blog software gives your blog added flexibility now and in the future, even if you don't know what your blog needs to be accomplishing two years from now. Keep in mind also that although you can switch platforms — and most software solutions offer a porting option from other major blog software solutions — it's usually a huge headache to do so.

Make a list of all the features you know you need, you think you might need, and those that you think might be great but don't seem realistic right now. Choosing the right platform now saves you time and money later.

Setting Up an Independent Blog

Are you ready for a challenge? Installing and customizing an independent blog solution isn't a task for the faint of heart.

I use pMachine's ExpressionEngine as my example, but if you choose another independent blog solution you may still find the information here useful, because many of these software packages work similarly.

If you have not already done so, acquire Web hosting and a domain name to use with your blog. Make sure the Web hosting you choose is compatible with the blog software you want to use! For more on Web hosting and registering a domain name, see Chapter 4.

Purchasing ExpressionEngine

Your first step in this process is to purchase the appropriate software license for ExpressionEngine from pMachine.

1. **Visit** www.pmachine.com, **and go to the pMachine store. Select ExpressionEngine from the list of available products.**

2. **pMachine asks you to enter the quantity of licenses you want to purchase.**

These licenses are for separate *installations* of the software, not the number of users or blogs you plan to run with a single copy of the software, so chances are you only need one license.

3. **Follow the Web site's process for registering and purchasing the license(s).**

The ExpressionEngine license is a lifetime license to use the software. When you make your purchase, you're given access to technical support forums and to future software updates. This differs dramatically from the way in which most software manufacturers make their money and means that there won't be additional software costs down the line.

Installing ExpressionEngine

After you purchase your ExpressionEngine license, you need to download the software itself and then install it on your Web server. The best part of installing an independent blog software package is that it only has to be done once. If you've never used FTP, or file transfer protocol, to move files to and from your Web server, this process will be confusing to you.

Downloading

To get started, download the software from pMachine's Web site. During the purchase process, pMachine should have sent you a URL or otherwise given you access to a location where you can download your software. You will also need the username and password you created when you bought the license. Clicking on the Download Area found in the navigation bar should require you to login and then give you access to your software.

When you click to download the software, the browser should ask you what you want to do with the file you are downloading. If you have the option, save the file to your desktop so that you can find it easily once it has finished downloading.

Unzipping

The ExpressionEngine is zipped, or compressed, for downloading purposes. This means you don't have to download lots of files individually and helps to keep the file size down as well. In order to use the files, you must unzip, or uncompress, the file you downloaded.

On most Windows computers you can unzip compressed files simply by double-clicking on them. If you don't have that capability on your computer, visit www.stuffit.com. The StuffIt program will let you compress and uncompressed files and is available for Macintosh, PC and Linux computers. You can choose to purchase the Standard or Deluxe edition, but the free trial of StuffIt Expander will be sufficient to unzip the ExpressionEngine file.

Once you install StuffIt Expander, double-click the zipped ExpressionEngine file and extract the contents to your desktop. The result will be a folder that contains all the software and installation instructions necessary to install ExpressionEngine on your Web server.

Getting the installation instructions

Once you have the folder of ExpressionEngine content on your computer, open it and look for the readme.txt file. This file explains where you can find the documentation and installation instructions in the folder and online. You can see all the latest ExpressionEngine documentation and installation instructions online at www.pmachine.com/expressionengine/docs/.

Installing

Use the instructions provided to actually install the software on your Web server. You may need to check with your Web server technical support person or documents to gather all the information you need.

You will definitely need an FTP program to upload the files to your computer. The ExpressionEngine instructions mention several, and you can download all of them by visiting download.com and doing a search.

For Windows, consider using WS_FTP, which allows you to set file permissions easily. For the Macintosh, consider Transmit. Read more about WS_FTP at www.ws-ftp.com and Transmit at www.panic.com/transmit.

Navigating ExpressionEngine

With power and flexibility comes complexity; all independent blog software solutions have a distinct learning curve, and ExpressionEngine is no exception. As you get started, review these important concepts to make the system a little more understandable.

Cascading Style Sheets

CSS, or *Cascading Style Sheets,* is at the heart of a truly flexible blog environment. If you're not familiar with this very powerful tool for design, layout, and customization of Web pages, consider buying some of the excellent CSS books on the market today. *Any* time you invest in learning this technology truly makes your blog better.

Looking for a good CSS book? Try *CSS Web Design For Dummies* by Richard Mansfield.

Cascading Style Sheets are used to set up custom styles that you can then apply across an entire Web site. They work something like this:

1. You create a style that makes all headlines 30-point Courier.

2. You apply that style to every headline, creating a consistent design experience. Even better, you add that style to a single document called a *style sheet*.

3. When you decide that headlines really need to be 20-point Arial instead, you update the style sheet instead of editing every single page of the Web site to change the code.

Blogs lend themselves to the use of style sheets so well because the format is so regulated — every post contains a headline, some body text, maybe a link or quote, and some comments. This regularity of content means that using CSS pays off when you need to redesign your blog — change the style sheet and you're sitting pretty.

Like most blogging software, ExpressionEngine uses style sheets to build your blog, and you can simply edit that style sheet to customize the design. To take a look at the style sheet that's created when you installed ExpressionEngine, log in and follow these steps:

1. **Click the Templates tab.**

2. **Click the weblog group of templates.**

   The list of templates opens (see Figure 6-6).

3. **Click the Edit link next to the** `weblog-css` **file.**

   The template editing page opens. You can edit the style sheet here, or copy and paste the style sheet code into any text editor (such as Notepad) to make changes.

Control Panel Home › Templates				Create a New Template Group	
Template Management		Global Variables | Edit Group Order | Template Preferences			
weblog	Preferences				
	New Template	**Template Name:**	**Hits**	**Edit**	**Access**	**Delete**
	Edit Group	archives	0	Edit	Access	Delete
	Delete Group	categories	0	Edit	Access	Delete
	Export Templates	comments	0	Edit	Access	Delete
		* index	0	Edit	Access	--
		preview	0	Edit	Access	Delete
		referrers	0	Edit	Access	Delete
		rss_1.0	0	Edit	Access	Delete
		rss_2.0	0	Edit	Access	Delete
		rss_atom	0	Edit	Access	Delete
		smiliesg	0	Edit	Access	Delete
		trackbacks	0	Edit	Access	Delete
		weblog_css	0	Edit	Access	Delete

Figure 6-6: You can customize these templates in Expression-Engine.

Templates

Templates aren't a new concept. You've probably used them yourself at some point. Templates are useful when you have a document that you reuse many times, changing only some items each time you use it. Most company letterhead includes a logo or some kind of identifying mark and preprinted address at the top. When you use it, you add the address of the person you're sending the letter to, a greeting, and the text of the actual letter. This is a template — some elements are always the same and never change, and some elements change every time the stationery is used.

Most Web sites are actually designed using templates, and using them is considered good form to provide a consistent user experience. As with CSS, blogs lend themselves very well to templates because the content is so consistent. ExpressionEngine includes templates for the following types of pages, organized into groups.

Weblog Templates

- A monthly archive page: Lists all the postings for a given month
- A category archive page: Lists all the postings for a given category
- A comments template: Formats the layout of comments readers leave on your site
- Several RSS feed templates: Sets up the content you want to include in your RSS feeds.
- A Trackback page: Formats the Trackback information for each blog entry
- A style sheet: Controls the layout and look of every element of your blog
- A home page: Lays out the page visitors see when they arrive

Member Templates

- A member profile page

Search Templates

- A search page: Controls the layout of simple and advanced search forms
- A search results page: Formats the results returned from a search
- A search page style sheet: Controls the layout and look of the search page elements

You don't have to use every template and you can add more, but these are good starting places for customizing ExpressionEngine to your blog. The best place to start is by editing the weblog_css template itself; most of the layout and design styles are controlled by this template. The next most important template to customize is the index template, or the home page of your blog. Both of these are part of the weblog group of templates.

You can edit any of the existing template pages by logging into EE and following these steps:

1. **Click the Templates tab.**

2. **Click the template group containing the template you want to edit. When the list of templates opens, click the Edit link next to the template name.**

    The template editing page opens, as shown in Figure 6-7. You can edit it here or copy and paste the HTML code into any text editor to make changes. I opened the index template in this example, but you can use the same steps to open any template.

ExpressionEngine 1.2 permits you to save your templates as files on your Web server and then download them via an FTP program so that you can edit them using any text or Web design editor (such as Macromedia Dreamweaver). For more information on how to do this, read the documentation at www. pmachine.com/expressionengine/docs/templates/flat_file_ templates.html.

Databases

All the style sheets and templates in the world would be useless without the database that ExpressionEngine uses to build your blog. The database is the skeleton that pulls together the style sheet, the templates, and the blog content into a coherent Web site — and that provides the production system that lets you edit the templates, style sheet, and content.

Figure 6-7:
You can edit templates directly in Expression-Engine.

When you installed Expression Engine, you created the database that controls your blog. If you ever need to change any of the general configuration settings, log into ExpressionEngine and click the Admin tab. The System Preferences section allows you to control macro-level database settings.

Working with your EE blog

When you install ExpressionEngine, it creates a blog for you. Before you jump into customizing templates and style sheets, you can use this default blog to understand the capabilities of ExpressionEngine. The best place to start? Create a few new posts to your blog and then view the resulting pages EE creates.

Adding an entry

Are you ready to post to your blog? Log into ExpressionEngine and click the Publish tab. What you see is the default blog entry page.

You can customize or even add more fields if you need to by visiting the tools located in the Admin tab and following the instructions in the User Guide.

To post to your blog, follow these steps:

1. **Title your blog entry.**

   This is the only required field in the blog posting.

   You can leave the URL Title field blank. ExpressionEngine generates the URL title, which is used in the full address of the blog entry, based on the information in the Title field.

2. **Write a short summary of the entry.**

   Use the summary to pique your readers' interest and get them to read more. Many bloggers don't bother with a summary. Other bloggers display the summary only on the first page of their blog and make readers click to get the full post.

3. **Fill in the following fields:**

   • **Body:** Contains the bulk of your blog posting. In most cases you won't go on and fill in the Extended field, but put all of your entry in the Body field.

   Your blog posting reflects the spacing you use in the Body field. Want to skip a line and start a new paragraph? Use the Enter key as you do in a word processor; there's no need to insert spacing using HTML tags.

- **Extended:** This field is for occasions when you have an extra-long blog entry and don't want the entire posting to display on the home page of your blog. Text that you place in the Extended field is only visible to users who click the permalink. The best way to get a feel for this field is to go ahead and try it!

- **Trackbacks:** Use this field to include a Trackback URL from someone else's blog you're citing in your posting. When you publish your entry, ExpressionEngine uses the Trackback information to notify that blog publisher that you've referred to their blog. I cover Trackbacks in more detail in Chapter 11. You don't have to use Trackbacks, but they are an easy way to create links from other blogs without lots of work on your part.

- **Entry Status:** Determines whether content is visible on your blog or only entered into the production system. Set your entry status to Open, and your entry is published to your blog when you submit it. Choose Closed, and ExpressionEngine saves the entry so that you can come back to it later.

- **Author:** Normally this field reflects the name of the person who is currently logged into the system. It is most useful for blogs with multiple authors.

- **Date:** Determines what date and time you use to publish this entry. Set the date and time to a point in the future, and ExpressionEngine holds your entry off the blog until then.

   The date and time are generated the moment you begin your posting, so if you want it to go live right away, you don't need to make any changes at all.

- **Expiration Date:** Tells ExpressionEngine when to remove a posting from the blog. Most bloggers only do this in rare instances, and there is no need to set a date if you don't want your post to ever expire.

- **Comment Expiration Date:** Set the date to remove comments from the blog at some point in the future. Again, this is rarely done. Comments are usually allowed to live on the blog forever, and you don't need to set any expiration date at all.

4. **Under Options, make some choices about the behavior of this blog entry.**

   Sticky entries always stay at the top of a group of blog postings and are useful for announcements you want to make sure everyone sees. ***Note:*** You can turn off comments for individual blog entries here. In Figure 6-8, I choose to allow comments in this blog posting.

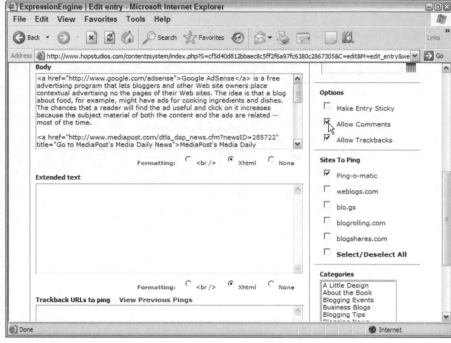

Figure 6-8:
You can choose whether to permit comments in each of your blog posts.

When you publish your blog entry, ExpressionEngine gives you the choice to *ping,* or notify, blog aggregation sites that you've posted something new to your blog. You can select which sites to ping in the Sites to Ping section before you publish your post. See Chapter 11 for more information about pinging sites.

5. Select a category for this posting.

ExpressionEngine's default installation provides three categories to choose from: Blogging, News, and Personal. When you customize EE, you can change or delete these categories, or add more. Select any of these to place this posting into a category.

6. Jump back up to the top of the page, and click the Submit button.

You've just published your first blog entry! Don't forget to see how it looks on the blog by clicking the My Weblog link at the top of your ExpressionEngine window. In Figure 6-9, you can see the entry I just created on the Buzz Marketing with Blogs blog.

Editing an entry

Now that you know how to publish a new entry, you may be wondering about going back to add content or make corrections to it. You can edit old entries at any time, but do consider indicating when you're making a correction so that your readers understand why you've made an edit.

To edit an existing entry, log into ExpressionEngine and follow these steps:

1. **Click the Edit tab.**

   The most recent entries display in descending date order. If your entry was posted recently, you can probably find it near the top of the list.

2. **After you find the entry you want to edit, click the Edit link next to the title.**

   ExpressionEngine opens the entry for editing.

3. **Make your changes or corrections and then click the Update button to make your changes visible on your blog.**

Adding images

In Chapter 3, I tell you how to format images for use on the Web. After you have some Web-ready images, you can use ExpressionEngine to upload those images to your blog posting. Log into ExpressionEngine and open an existing blog entry or begin a new one and then follow these steps to upload an image:

1. **Click the File Upload link from the Formatting Buttons box.**

   The File Upload window opens.

2. **Click the Browse button to find the image on your computer.**

   The Open dialog box opens, as shown in Figure 6-10.

3. **Select your image and click Open.**

   The File Upload window reappears.

Using the formatting buttons

If you want to include HTML in your blog entries, you can do so by simply pasting it into Expression-Engine from another application or typing it in. Alternatively, you can use the formatting buttons ExpressionEngine provides to accomplish common formatting tasks and add links. The following figure shows the formatting buttons.

Highlight the text you want to affect and then click the appropriate button. For example, highlight a word in the Body field and click the <b> button. ExpressionEngine inserts the HTML code for bold text around the word you highlighted.

Button Mode:	Guided ○	Normal ⊙		File Upload		Emoticons	

<b>	<i>	<u>	<bq>	<strike>	Link	Email	Image	Close All

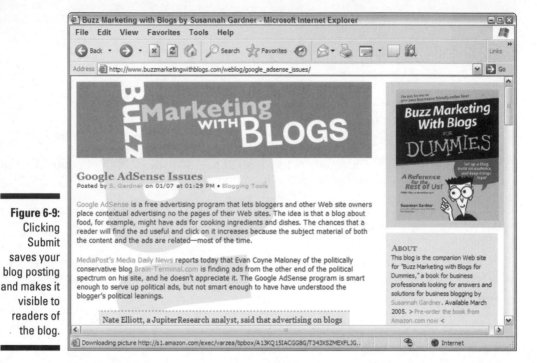

Figure 6-9:
Clicking
Submit
saves your
blog posting
and makes it
visible to
readers of
the blog.

Figure 6-10:
Select an
image on
your
computer to
upload.

4. **Click the Upload button.**

   ExpressionEngine uploads the file you've selected to your Web server.

5. **Select the file type and location.**

   If you want the image to display in your blog posting, select Embedded in Entry as your file type and then choose which field to contain the image.

6. **Choose whether to resize the image or click the Close Window link.**

   You can resize the image to create a thumbnail of the image you just uploaded, but doing so is not necessary.

   ExpressionEngine creates the HTML code to display the image and inserts that code in the field you selected in Step 5. If you see something like this, ExpressionEngine has successfully added the HTML to your entry:

```
<img src="{filedir_1}logo.gif" border="0" alt="image"
          name="image" width="197" height="83" border="0" />
```

   If you want to move the image around, be sure to select the entire chunk of code so that you don't break the image.

7. **Click Submit or Update to publish your blog entry.**

   When you view the blog posting, you will see the image.

You can use the File Upload functionality to upload all kinds of documents, not just images. For example, you can upload a PDF, Microsoft Word document, or any other digital file. ExpressionEngine recognizes that the file is not an image and inserts it as a link instead of using the HTML tag for displaying images.

Adding a category

Earlier in this chapter, I mentioned that you can add categories to your blog in ExpressionEngine. You can also add subcategories. For example, if you created a blog with a Books category, you can further divide that category by creating Fiction and Non-Fiction subcategories. To create a new category or edit the name of an existing category, log into ExpressionEngine and then follow these steps:

1. **Click the Admin tab and then the Category Management link in the Weblog Administration column.**

   Because ExpressionEngine allows you to have multiple blogs, the categories for each are divided into groups. The default Web log uses the Default Category Group.

2. **Click the Add/Edit Categories link to see a list of the current categories in the group.**

3. **To add a new category, click the Create a New Category link on the top right of the page.**

   ExpressionEngine opens the new category page.

4. **Give your category a name.**

   You can choose to provide a description and an image, but these aren't necessary for your blog to function.

5. **If you want this category to be a subcategory of one that already exists, choose the parent category from the drop-down menu.**

6. **Click the Submit button, as shown in Figure 6-11.**

   ExpressionEngine returns you to the list of current categories for the group. You can use the up and down arrows to change the display order of the categories — this affects the order of the list in the entry publishing pages.

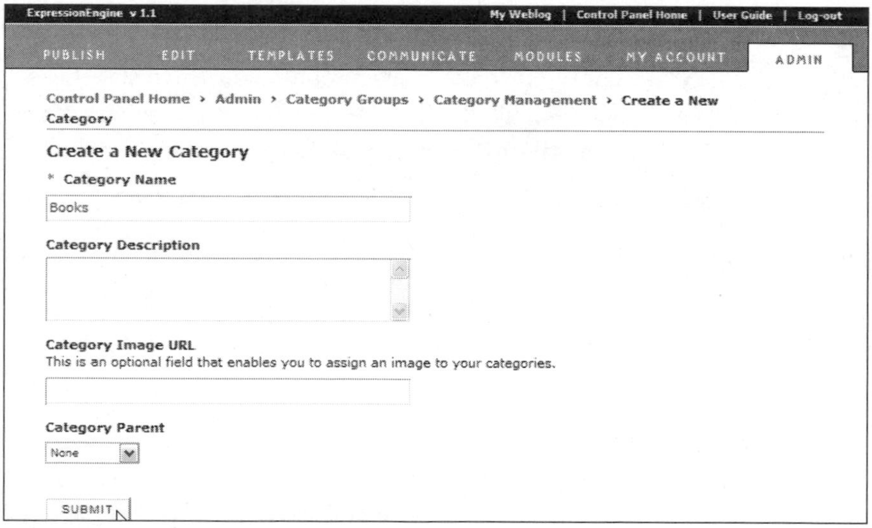

Figure 6-11:
You must give your new category a name, but it isn't required that you write a description or create an image link.

```
ExpressionEngine v 1.1                        My Weblog  |  Control Panel Home  |  User Guide  |  Log-out

  PUBLISH        EDIT       TEMPLATES     COMMUNICATE     MODULES     MY ACCOUNT      ADMIN

  Control Panel Home  >  Admin  >  Category Groups  >  Category Management  >  Create a New
  Category

  Create a New Category
  * Category Name

  [Books                                    ]

  Category Description

  [                                      ]
  [                                      ]

  Category Image URL
  This is an optional field that enables you to assign an image to your categories.

  [                                      ]

  Category Parent

  [None    v]

  [ SUBMIT ]
```

Adding a member

If your blog includes contributions from multiple authors, or if you want to allow an editor access to the ExpressionEngine production system, you need to add a new member to the system. To do so, log into ExpressionEngine and follow these steps:

1. **Click the Admin tab, and look for the New Member Registration link in the Members and Groups column.**

2. **Fill in the username, password, password confirmation, screen name, and e-mail address fields.**

These fields are all required.

Make a note of the username and password fields for your own records.

3. **Choose a Member Group Assignment.**

   ExpressionEngine permits you to set up different levels of access to the blog production system and provides some default levels for you to choose from. Members can create new blog postings but can't edit templates or change the administration settings. Super Admins have access to everything.

4. **Click the Submit button.**

   Don't forget to notify your new member of their username and password, and the URL of the production system to contribute to the blog!

Part III
Minding Blog Etiquette and Culture

The 5th Wave   By Rich Tennant

"I think it started as a result of a discussion about proper blog etiquette."

In this part . . .

Being technologically savvy is no excuse for breaking common etiquette rules. Use Part III to make sure other bloggers welcome you to the blogosphere, and even lend you support! Find out who your audience is and how to attract them to your blog in Chapter 7. Meet your fellow bloggers in Chapter 8. Treat them well and they'll be your friends. They are a vocal group! Find out how to get them talking about you in a good way. Your readers are your most important resource, so I spend some time in Part III identifying ways in which you can do them wrong and chase them away. Use Chapter 9 to avoid common missteps and mistakes, and to deal with the mistakes you do make.

Chapter 7

Understanding Your Audience

As you prepare your blog for launch, you discuss design, content, and who's going to be writing it. The day after it launches, though, you are focused on a different question: Who's looking at it? You should have a traffic reporting system in place from the very first day — especially if you plan to launch with some fanfare or simultaneous advertising of the blog.

The tools available to you are many and varied — you may not use every solution with your particular blog. And depending on your traffic volume, different tools may be more or less helpful.

This chapter introduces you to the concepts involved in Web traffic analysis. You discover the various software or Web-based traffic tools. Finally, you get some advice on what to do with all this information — turning numbers into actions.

Understanding Web Site Traffic Numbers

Figure 7-1 shows the results of a typical statistic-gathering tool. These statistics are taken from Gawker (www.gawker.com), a popular New York gossip blog. They include a handy chart summarizing a month of traffic and separate sub-reports for things such as operating systems, browser versions, and search keywords. You can find Gawker's traffic stats at www.gawker.com/stats/awstats.pl.

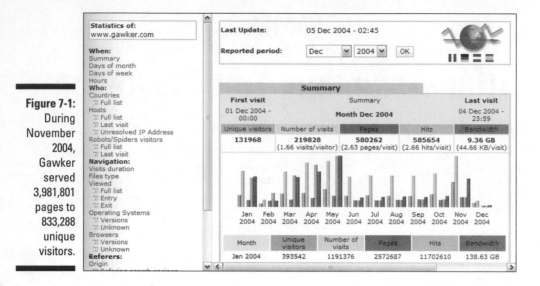

Figure 7-1:
During
November
2004,
Gawker
served
3,981,801
pages to
833,288
unique
visitors.

As you look at the output of any Web traffic tool, you need to fully understand the terms being used to slice and dice the statistics. Three measurements are commonly associated with Web site traffic: hits, pages, and visits. Each has its own hidden pitfalls and uses, and none is a sure-fire way to compare your site with another. Most, but not all, statistic-measuring tools give you all three figures.

Bringing on the hits

The number of *hits* a Web site gets is always a big number, but it's essentially a meaningless one and can even be misleading to those who don't really understand what's being measured. Here's why: When someone views a single page on your Web site, their browser actually makes several requests for the Web server. The browser asks for every element it must have in order to display the page: the HTML, external style sheets, external JavaScript files, and each unique image.

For a basic blog, elements can add up quickly. Most blogs have a logo, a background image, an image used for spacing content, and sometimes a graphical navigation bar or graphic advertising banner. The server also counts Flash files, audio and video files, and even incomplete or erroneous Web requests (for example missing files).

Hits are sometimes misleadingly called "page hits," but they're not pages. Every Web page results in a different number of hits; there is no average. Even Google's simple, clean, crisp home page registers two hits (and sometimes three) when viewed.

If you craft your Web pages to cause fewer hits, they, on average, load more quickly. Browsers make fewer separate requests of the Web server, and your server spends less time answering new requests.

Hits were an early unit of measure on the Web because they were easy to count. They fell out of favor because they're also very easy to manipulate. For instance, if you want to increase the number of hits your site gets, simply add more images to your pages. Or make the images you do serve into multiple files — the user won't notice the difference, but the computer counts each file separately as it's served. Making your hits skyrocket is quite easy without actually getting more readers or even serving more pages. You also have higher bandwidth costs and a slower site, but saying you had a million hits last month is fun.

Ultimately, hits are easy to count, but they don't tell you much about your readers.

Web cookies: Yummy or scary?

A *cookie* is simply a small bit of information handed by the server to the browser and later by the browser back to the server. A cookie is a unique identifier used by the site to keep track of who the user is so that it can keep tabs on how many pages that user visits, what services they sign up for, and what ads they have seen. The information in a cookie is only ever handed back to the server that created it. Cookies themselves are inert bits of data; they can't contain malicious code, and they make it possible for you to be "remembered" by a Web site when you return — Amazon.com can show you books you like, and Google can remember your preferred search settings.

However, with cookies, information can be aggregated and tracked across multiple sites. When you first go to a site, you get a generic cookie, and later if you register, your previous visits are merged with the e-mail address you registered with. Later, if you give your address for a contest promotion or a catalog, that's merged with your e-mail address. Or if a giant ad company serves a banner ad to you on a beer site, and later you visit a sports site with banners served by the same company, you're tracked and served a beer banner ad. For this reason, some people block or erase cookies, which causes difficulty in tracking visits and visitors.

Turning pages

Pages, also called page views, are a little harder to quantify but are more meaningful indicators of actual site value and success than hits. A page is a single HTML Web document as perceived by the end user, excluding non-HTML file formats such as PDF or Microsoft Word documents. When you call up the home page of Google, Yahoo!, or *The Washington Post,* what's displayed in the browser is a page, or page view.

Page views are useful information. You probably don't care how many times your logo was viewed, but you do care how many times the About Us page was. For most Web sites, a high page view number is indicative of some measure of popularity with readers.

However, as with all Web traffic measurements, page views can be misleading. For example, use of HTML frames inflate the page count number by showing visitors three Web pages at once in different sections of a single browser window. For an example of a page that uses frames, visit the Gawker traffic stats (refer to Figure 7-1).

Knowing who is visiting

The most current and valid traffic numbers are *visits* and *unique visitors.* Both are tied to the ability to distinguish between different folks using your Web site at the same time, and because of this, the measurements are somewhat, shall I say, fuzzy.

A *visit* is what it sounds like — one person coming to your site and looking at some pages. A *unique visitor* means you can tell whether the one person looking at your site right now is different from the one who came by this morning.

A visit is usually considered one or more page views from a unique user separated by an hour from any other page views. If your biggest fan checks your blog every 30 minutes from work, that shows up as a single, 8-hour visit. If someone else starts reading your blog, wanders off to have dinner, and then comes back to finish, that's two visits from one unique user.

A visit is usually measured by the Web server setting a cookie when your site is first accessed and then by tracking that cookie as the reader browses to different pages on your site. It's not completely foolproof: Some people disable cookies.

Cookies are pieces of information storied on your computer that let Web sites remember something about you, such as a username. For more information on cookies, see the sidebar "Web cookies: Yummy or scary?" in this chapter.

With cookies turned off, the same visitor looking at five different pages looks like five visits rather than one.

Visit and unique visitor counts can also be skewed by networks, such as those in schools and libraries, that use the same identifying information for each computer. A classroom of students all looking at your blog at the same time, for instance, might all appear to come from the same Internet connection, and that's reported as a single visit (a strange one that consisted of 30 visits to your home page at the same time. . .).

So will your unique visitor count be underreported or overreported? Yes, probably. Different blogs, with different users (education, corporate, press, privacy fanatics), have different traffic tracking problems to resolve. Every site suffers from this inexactness.

You can take steps to reduce this uncertainty by requesting that visitors register or require that visitors allow cookies, but high-handed demands tend to drive away readers.

Ultimately, it's a little like the Heisenberg uncertainty principle: You can know exactly how many hits your site is getting, but not how many people are viewing your site. And if you take steps to force a more exact count, you'll probably end up losing some visitors.

Reading Your Log Files

If you have your own Web hosting solution, you have access to your log files. A *log file* is simply a recording of every hit registered by the Web server. They are the raw, unfiltered base that most site traffic tools use to serve up traffic reports.

I'll be honest here: Few bloggers look through their raw log files. However, knowing what information they contain is helpful, so you know what you can get out of your traffic tools.

The following is a sample of Apache Combined Log Format (`httpd.apache.org/docs/logs.html#combined`). Not every log file is structured exactly as this one is, but it can give you a good idea of a typical file.

```
213.245.147.28 - - [28/Nov/2004:17:39:42 -0500] "GET
        /whatwedo.html HTTP/1.1" 200 2487
        "http://www.hopstudios.com/" "Mozilla/4.0
        (compatible; MSIE 6.0; Windows 98)"
83.67.20.193 - - [28/Nov/2004:17:58:23 -0500] "GET
        /nep/column/surfersISOthis.html HTTP/1.1" 200
        83088
        "http://www.mamma.com/Mamma?&query=jib+jab+lyrics"
        "Mozilla/4.0 (compatible; MSIE 6.0; Windows NT
        5.1)"
66.196.91.116 - - [28/Nov/2004:18:02:42 -0500] "GET
        /gallery/22.html HTTP/1.0" 304 - "-" "Mozilla/5.0
        (compatible; Yahoo! Slurp)"
68.100.211.202 - - [28/Nov/2004:18:32:01 -0500] "GET
        /brokenlink HTTP/1.1" 404 1641 "-" "Mozilla/4.0
        (compatible; MSIE 6.0; Windows NT 5.0)"
38.144.36.16 - - [28/Nov/2004:18:04:53 -0500] "GET
        /nep/five/index.rdf HTTP/1.1" 304 - "-"
        "Mozilla/4.0 (compatible; MSIE 6.0; Windows NT
        5.1; SV1
```

In the following list, I break down the elements of a file:

- **IP address:** The beginning set of four numbers separated by periods is the visitor's IP address — the unique number associated with the computer connecting to the Internet. Traffic tools can look up that number to find out if computer using it is based in `.com`, `.edu`, or an internationally based network.

- **Date:** Inside the [] brackets is the date. You can see what day of the week, or what hour of the day, your traffic spikes happen. You can use this information to make strategic decisions about posting entries when your blog is busiest — and running site modifications when things are slowest.

- **Page URL:** Between the first set of quotation marks you find the URL of the page being requested contained between the terms `GET` and `HTTP`. The traffic tool determines if the request is for a page or just a hit and what content to serve back.

- **Server response code:** Next comes a number indicating the computer's response to the request. A 200 means, "I gave back the data properly." A 404 means, "I couldn't find the data to give back," which is a serious error. Any 404 responses mean someone tried to follow a link or request a page that wasn't there. Getting rid of all 404s is impossible, but you can minimize them by fixing broken links and getting other sites to update or fix incorrect links to you, and if you see a page that's frequently requested but doesn't exist — consider making one there!

✔ **File size:** The next number is the size of the file that was returned. Smaller files download more quickly.

✔ **Referrer URL:** In the second set of quotation marks you find what is, frankly, the most interesting bit of data in your log files: The page from which the request originated, is called the *referrer.*

The referrer might be another page on your site, another site that linked to you, or a search engine that returned your page in its results. By analyzing what Web heads call your refers, you can tell who is sending you traffic and what search terms are resulting in the most clicks to your site. You can't tell, though, what sites have links to you or what search terms make your site appear — you only find that out when someone clicks a link.

✔ **User Agent:** After the refer comes the *User Agent,* which is the name of the program requesting the page. This information is handy because it tells you which browsers people are using to view your blog. You can focus your testing and features to these browsers. But watch that this statistic doesn't become a self-fulfilling prophecy. If you don't see many Mac users with Safari on your blog, it could be that it doesn't work for them — and if you fix your site, you might see an increase in use.

Spend too much time looking at your log files and you'll go blind, but checking in every so often may be an eye-opener. There may be some surprises: uncommon browsers used by more people than you expected, page requests for old content, high traffic numbers from a country where your products aren't sold. It is a wide and diverse Internet out there, and you should design and write your blog accordingly.

Implementing Traffic Tools

Even a moderately well-read blog can produce 10,000 new lines in a log file every day. To keep yourself sane, consider using a site traffic tool to interpret your log files for you.

You can use three possible sources of traffic tools: built-in tools that are part of the blogging software you're already using, software that's installed on your Web server, and JavaScript-implemented code that tracks your stats on a Web-hosted tool.

Built-in tools

A few blogging software applications have implemented traffic tracking tools as part of their administrative interfaces. Most of these services are limited and will probably whet your appetite for more detailed information.

TypePad

The popular hosted blogging software TypePad does track some site statistics: basic data about how many hits (or is it pages? It's unclear.) you've ever served and how many per day; and a clunky way to see the last 20 or 40 refers, but no way to find out which sites are your best traffic generators.

ExpressionEngine

If you use the independent blog software ExpressionEngine, some built-in site statistics are available, including limited data about the templates that have been visited, the refers to your site, and the total number of visitors, as shown in Figure 7-2.

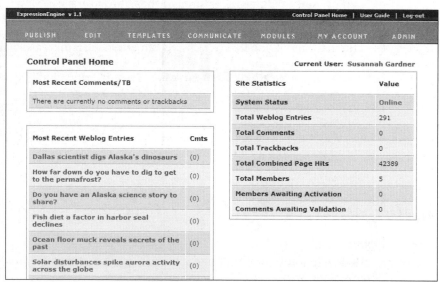

Figure 7-2: Expression Engine provides some site statistics, as shown here for Alaska Science Outreach (www. alaska science outreach. com).

Locally installed tools

If you have set up your blog on your own Web server or bought Web hosting to use, think about installing a traffic tracking tool. These packages are the most robust of the tracking software available and let you maintain control of who has access to log and statistics files.

Many Web hosting companies build a tracking program into their hosting package, so check to see if you already have one available to you.

The Webalizer

Unix-based hosts often have The Webalizer preinstalled, and it is a very functional program — and free. The Webalizer generates reports on a monthly basis, breaks the numbers down further to show you daily and hourly usage, top URLs accessed, top entry pages, top exit pages, top refers, top search strings, and country numbers. The last significant update to The Webalizer was in 2000; there have been some bug fixes since then.

Visit `www.mrunix.net/webalizer/` to find out more and download the program. You can see a sample of the data The Webalizer produces in Figure 7-3.

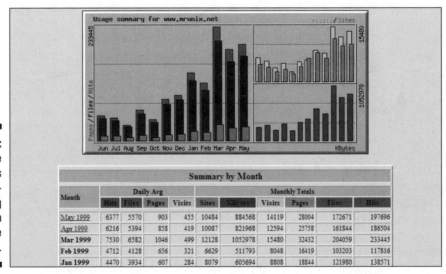

Figure 7-3: The Webalizer is a good traffic tracking program and is free to use.

Month	Daily Avg				Monthly Totals					
	Hits	Files	Pages	Visits	Sites	KBytes	Visits	Pages	Files	Hits
May 1999	6377	5570	903	455	10484	884568	14119	28004	172671	197696
Apr 1999	6216	5394	858	419	10087	821968	12594	25758	161844	186504
Mar 1999	7530	6582	1046	499	12128	1052978	15480	32432	204059	233445
Feb 1999	4712	4128	656	321	6629	511793	8048	16419	103203	117816
Jan 1999	4470	3934	607	284	8079	605694	8808	18844	121980	138571

Urchin

Another frequently used traffic tool is Urchin, available for Windows and Unix Web servers or as a Web service. There are both free and paid versions. The free version of Urchin is very hobbled. The pay version is gratifyingly robust. Neither the hosted nor the installable package comes cheap. Urchin On Demand, the Web-based service, is $495 a month. Urchin Software is $895.

The most recent version of the Urchin software features visitor tracking, support for tracking Flash, banner ads, and e-mail campaigns. Urchin's Web site is at `www.urchin.com`.

AWStats

AWStats is a Perl-based stats tool, available for free. It runs on any platform but is slower than The Webalizer. On the plus side, it's still in active development and offers numerous features not available elsewhere, including tracking of hits by robots and spiders, site visit lengths, and monitor screen sizes. Assuming your site doesn't need to handle zillions of lines of log files, this tool is a decent choice. It also analysis FTP and mail logs.

AWStats is used by Gawker.com (refer to Figure 7-1). You can download the software at awstats.sourceforge.net.

WebTrends

On Windows Web servers, WebTrends is a common software solution. It does an excellent job of mapping the path visitors take through your site and the results of Web visits. WebTrends is ideal if you want to measure the financial impact and actions of a site visitor, rather than simply collecting the overall numbers describing your Web traffic. There's no free version available, but the pricing, if you have less than 1million page views a year, is $495. WebTrends has also started offering a Web-based On Demand solution. Costs vary depending on the amount of traffic your site gets.

The WebTrends site offers a guided interactive tour that shows off its heavily graphical interface and is at www.webtrends.com.

Web-based tools

Regardless of your blogging setup, you can always use a Web-based traffic tracker. You place a small piece of JavaScript code on every page on your site, which then reports activity back to the service you're using.

Because these tools require JavaScript to run, they aren't as comprehensive about recording every visit, and they have no way of tracking non-HTML files, such as PDFs and images.

On the other hand, you can track information with JavaScript that just isn't available with log files, including monitor size, DHTML compliance, plug-in status, and more.

Site Meter

Gawker also uses a Web counter from Site Meter (www.sitemeter.com). By using more than one piece of tracking software, Gawker staff can more easily pinpoint discrepancies in site statistics. The free Site Meter services provide basic information about visits and visitors, types of browsers, and referring URLs. It's updated constantly as people come to the site. In exchange, Gawker must display a relatively unobtrusive Site Meter graphic on every page of the site. Figure 7-4 shows Gawker's Site Meter stats. Site Meter's oddly colored tools and cluttered site interface aren't all that appealing to use, unfortunately.

Figure 7-4:
Gawker also uses Site Meter to tracks traffic data.

	Home	Help	Search	Login		
General		**Gawker**		Ads by Google
Summary		**Site Summary**		
Who's On?				**Free Visitor Counters**
Traffic Prediction				Track your site's visitors.
Recent Visitors	**VISITS**			Tons of styles and no registration needed!
By Details				www.CounterData.com
By Referrals	Total		5,748,197	
By Search Words	Average Per Day		87,091	
By Entry Pages	Average Visit Length		0:20	**Free Counters & Stats**
By Exit Pages	Last Hour		2,862	Get your web counter for free, with full stats. In just
Visits	Today		34,790	1 minute.
Day Week Month Year	This Week		609,635	www.RankingStats.com
Visits and Page Views				
Day Week Month Year	**PAGE VIEWS**			
Moving Average				**Hit Counter & Site Stats**
Visits 7 / 30				Multiple site tracking,
Page Views 7 / 30	Total		7,579,268	traffic, referrer, search engine stats more.
Referral Ranking	Average Per Day		122,125	www.tdstats.com
Web pages ranked by	Average Per Visit		1.4	
Visits	Last Hour		3,898	
Page Views	Today		51,052	**Hit Counter & Statistics**
Visit Length	This Week		854,872	Real-time analysis with
Web sites ranked by				
Visits				
Page Views				

As a Site Meter user, you have the option of making your stats public or private. Many blogs have taken to making their stats public; if you're trying to attract advertising and have good traffic, you should consider making these statistics public. For most blogs, there is little point in making this information public.

Bravenet

Counters are only one of the Web tools offered by Bravenet — it also offers hosting, classifieds, chat, site search, and more (but not blog software, unfortunately). It's all free, at least for the basic level of service.

Bravenet offers one stat that isn't always available elsewhere: first-time versus returning visitors. Though it's a suspect number that hits the same limits as other visitor-counting tools, it's still a nice metric to watch change over time.

For an example of this in action, visit `counter2.bravenet.com/index.php?id=370586&usernum=137405393`. Sign up for Bravenet services at `www.bravenet.com`.

StatCounter

The nicest thing about StatCounter, better than its clear interface and simple signup, is that you don't need to display a link back to StatCounter, even for the free package. As well, it's a very robust service at a price that can't be beat. StatCounter breaks down your current unique, returning, and repeat visitors, as well as tracks statistics on browser, resolution, operating system, country, search engine, keyword, referring link, and more.

The only limitation on this service is that you must have fewer than 250,000 page views a month to escape paying. More traffic than that, and you need to get out your wallet.

Sign up for StatCounter at www.statcounter.com. There is a good demo of the service available on the site, which you can check out in Figure 7-5.

Figure 7-5:
StatCounter is free for sites with fewer than 250,000 page views a month.

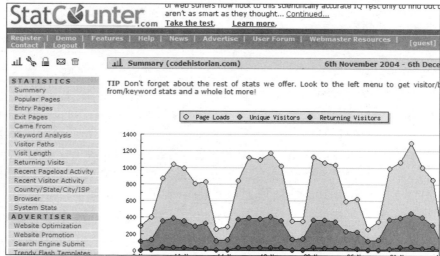

FastCounterPro

Microsoft's Web site traffic tool costs $19.95 a month (as long as you're below 50,000 page views a month) and gives you stats on everything from keywords to conversions to general page view data. Downloadable reports are in CVS format (easy to import into Excel). FastCounterPro is at www.microsoft.com/smallbusiness/products/online/fs/detail.mspx.

HBX

One of the more advanced Web tools, HBX (once known as HitBox) offers an amazing cross-section of tools but is better suited for sites that have large, complex traffic analysis needs. Cost isn't mentioned anywhere on the Web site. HBX is at www.hbxondemand.com.

For more site tracking tools, take a look at the Google Directory listing for Counters and Trackers at `directory.google.com/Top/Computers/Internet/Web_Design_and_Development/Hosted_Components_and_Services/Counters_and_Trackers/`.

Use Table 7-1 to help you choose between local tools and Web-based ones. There are always exceptions, but as a general rule, these differences hold true for most site traffic tools.

Table 7-1	Web-Based Tools versus Local Tools
Web-Based	**Local**
Works regardless of your hosting limitations	Need to find a package that works with your host
Your information is stored on another company's servers; often aggregate information is shared	Keeps your traffic information completely private
Has limits on traffic volume unless you pay extra	Costs the same regardless of traffic volume (usually)
Pay each month	Pay once
Pay per site	Pay once
Doesn't track hits for certain file types such as PDFs and Flash	Records every Web server hit, regardless of file type or visitor's browser
Can slow down your page slightly	No extra download required
Some visitors object because of the ability to track them from site to site	Is completely transparent to the visitor
May require a visible counter or link to the counter service	Is completely transparent to the visitor
You get upgrades and fixes as necessary	May not be actively updated; updates may not be free
Live stats usually available	Usually run once a day or less frequently
Requires code on every page	No extra page code required (usually)
Installation is extremely simple, if you can edit an HTML page	Installation difficulty varies widely
Same tool can be used if you switch hosting providers	Changing hosts usually results in a change in tracking; comparing stats becomes difficult
Doesn't include page size data	Includes page size data — helps you track your bandwidth usage

What they won't tell you

None of these traffic systems tells you specifics about the people who visit your site. Specifically, you won't know:

- ✔ Ages
- ✔ Gender
- ✔ Income
- ✔ Title
- ✔ Employment status
- ✔ Whether they own or use one of your products or services
- ✔ Contact information

Demographic information is generally available only when it's requested through a survey or registration mechanism. A blog rarely requires registration, and most blogs even allow readers to leave anonymous comments. Even a survey doesn't give you really reliable results, because not all your readers take it, and you have no guarantee they tell the truth if they do.

Swimming in Data

The goal of collecting data is that by having information about your audience, you can make some decisions about how to change, update, or improve your blog — and you may also find out that change isn't necessarily needed. Analysis of all that log data can be tricky, and not all of it is useful, especially as you just start out. However, this list gives you some idea of the kinds of questions you can use stats to find answers for:

- ✔ **What pages are getting the most traffic?** This is probably the most important question, and sometimes the answers are surprising! Keep track of highly trafficked pages over time to get some idea of the kinds of content your readers find most appealing.

- ✔ **What pages do people leave from?** These are usually called *exit pages,* and while you can't stop people from leaving (and you irritate them if you try), you may notice problems or patterns that you can address. This is an inexact science, at best, so don't forget that you may want to ask your readers just why they're leaving rather than hazard guesses. Of course, every reader eventually leaves, so don't view these numbers too negatively.

Some exits are desired outcomes! Your readers may be clicking interesting links that you provided. By including some extra HTML code in your links, you can make sure external links open in a new browser window, but not many blogs do this. Find out how to create links in Chapter 3.

✔ **Am I blogging on the days, and at the times, that most people are visiting my site?** It may be easiest to blog first thing in the morning, but if your traffic peak is in the afternoon, you ought to have something fresh at that time. Many blogging software tools allow you to create posts that go live at a time you specify, so you can easily adjust your publication schedule with significantly changing your production schedule.

✔ **Is my site being visited by all browsers and operating systems?** Unless you're writing for a specific technical audience (The Linux Lover's Hockey Blog, for instance), you should expect to see a broad cross-section of browsers in your Web stats. If you don't, your site may not be displaying properly in the missing browsers. Be sure to test the site on different kinds of computers, different browsers, and different browser versions. If everyone in your office has the same computer, try using computers at the library, at a Kinko's, in your kid's room or school, or at a neighbor's house to access the blog.

✔ **What sites are sending me the most traffic?** And how can you thank them and encourage them to continue?

✔ **What search words are people using to find my site?** Search terms people use to get to your site can be a great indicator of hot subjects to blog about. On the other hand, you can get a pretty dismal vision of the human race — you can receive a disproportionate amount of traffic just by quoting Alexander Pope saying "Hope springs eternal in the human breast."

Of course, search term data isn't a complete picture — you can't tell what words people are using that *don't* result in a visit to your site. So while you may focus on topics that seem to draw visitors from search engines, you can also figure out what logical, appropriate search words should be getting your visitors but aren't.

✔ **Are there gaps in my traffic?** This can point to server outages or problems with your site's infrastructure.

✔ **Is my blog's traffic growing?** You want to see regular, reasonable growth in your reader numbers. If your stats are stagnant, that's a sign that something is going wrong. If you are experiencing a slump, see if you detect what might be causing. The biggest culprit is posting infrequently — you need to be providing enough content to keep the site from seeming stale and to reward the repeat visitor with something new.

Chapter 8

Joining the Blogosphere

As a blogger, you're in good company. Bloggers are a smart, dedicated group, many of whom are staunch defenders of the format and medium. If you want to make friends and not enemies, spend a few minutes in this chapter learning about the history of blogs. You want to make friends, not enemies, in the blogosphere so understanding the buzz around blogs is important.

Influential bloggers know the significant events that have shaped the blogosphere as it exists today. You can more easily find your own spot in the blogosphere if you fill in the background.

In this chapter, I give you specific advice on reading and participating in blog conversations. I also discuss several blogs from which you can find out a lot about the ins and outs of the blogosphere and a lot of historical material that has shaped that dialogue. Understanding what happened in the past can help you participate without being criticized for making rookie mistakes.

Lurking and Learning

So far, blogging has been a very American activity. Good bloggers exist all over the world, but tons of them are in the United States, from political commentators right down to middle schoolers communicating with friends.

Blogs to lurk on

Your first task as a blogger is to pay attention to what other bloggers are doing, regardless of content or intention. Though not the kind of blog you might be planning to create, these five blogs are well-regarded, well-trafficked, and are a great place to learn more about how a good blog functions:

FC Now (`blog.fastcompany.com`): This blog from the publishers of Fast Company is devoted to talking about business practices that rise to the top between regular publication dates. Though a unique combination of multiple bloggers, guest bloggers, and active comments, the site stays current and fresh, without losing focus.

BoingBoing (`www.boingboing.net`): This "directory of wonderful things" is a group blog that brings together the weird, wonderful, and remarkable sites on the Web today. Not every entry appeals to all readers, who nonetheless stick around because there is no other Boing Boing.

InstaPundit (`www.instapundit.com`): This mostly political blog by University of Tennessee professor Glenn Reynolds is widely read. Reynolds' posts are usually short, often include quotes, and nearly always link to another Web site. The following figure shows the InstaPundit blog.

Romenesko (`www.poynter.org/romenesko`): Jim Romenesko tracks and comments on all media-related happenings in his blog on Poynter Institute's Web site. This blog is a must read for media professionals trying to stay on top of hirings, firings, media scandals, and more.

Dooce (`www.dooce.com`): Dooce is the personal blog of Heather Armstrong. Heather has readers all over the world that visit for a daily fix of news about her family, health, friends, thoughts, and photos. This is a quality production: The writing is funny, irreverent, and smart, and the site is beautifully designed.

Gizmodo (`www.gizmodo.com`): A blog about all kinds of tech gadgets, Gizmodo is a popular resource for daily readers and those looking for specific information on a product they are thinking of purchasing.

Begin your experience with the blogosphere by *lurking* and *learning*. Lurking is an old Internet term (as far as the Internet has *old* anything) that describes people who read Internet content but don't participate in discussion or make themselves known. The first lurkers were those that merely read mailing lists, newsgroups, and forums without ever posting. Plenty of lurkers are on major blogs. Lurking sounds kind of sinister, but the activity is anything but. In fact, you can learn the ropes without making any mistakes by lurking.

I recommend that you begin your campaign to become part of the blogosphere by being a silent lurker in order to learn how the format works. Start by picking a few prominent blogs, and establish a regular schedule of visiting and reading every post and commenting on them. The content may be interesting, but don't forget that you are there to:

- ✔ See how, when, and why bloggers choose to post on a subject

- ✔ Discover what kind of posts engender comment and discussion, and which simply sink into the background

- ✔ When and how links are used to add information or extended the discussion

- ✔ Note common design and layout practices that you can use on your blog

- ✔ Get ideas for writing styles, technical tools, and topics you can apply to your own blog

While you're in this learning phase, click every link you can. Make note of when readers are willing to include an e-mail or URL address in comments. Watch how experienced bloggers deal with inappropriate, off-topic comments. You can learn a lot from noting how often a good blogger posts and the length of those posts, too. Realize that you may have to lurk on blogs that aren't necessarily business or marketing efforts in order to learn the ropes.

Make notes about practices you think are useful and those that you don't think work at all. Think about how you can apply those practices to your own blog. Will you link to other Web sites? How thoroughly will you screen those sites before blogging about them? Will you allow readers to comment on every post? When might you turn comments off? What's the best way to handle corrections?

Remember that blogging is a very young medium. By observing how the concepts are practiced, you are learning the how a format that hasn't been around very long works, even though it is made up of individuals in a loose network that don't necessarily agree with each other. Not everything you read applies to you and your blog, but by watching you can find out how this format works — and that is invaluable.

Knowing When to Comment

After you spend some time lurking, you can add your own voice to the mix. The contribution you make by creating your own blog is important, but the interaction with other bloggers is equally so. When you add a comment to a post, you become part of the dialogue. You can distinguish yourself with smart comments that bring up new points or add new information. Or you can brand yourself a flack by blatantly trying to drive traffic to your own blog or Web site. You definitely *want* to bring readers to your site, but you need to do it by creating genuine interest rather than using a straight-out advertising message. You must create buzz by demonstrating your expertise and knowledge, and by simply getting people interested in what you have to say.

When you comment on another person's blog, you're usually asked to include an e-mail and/or URL address that is then linked to your name. You can see how to insert an address along with a comment on Steve Rubel's Micro Persuasion blog in Figure 8-1.

Let that link be your calling card — don't include links and sales language in your comment. Unless you're commenting on your own product, and maybe not even then, other people's blogs aren't a place to make blatant sales pitches. If you want to be accepted in the blogosphere, concentrate on creating valuable content. The links to your blog that push traffic, generate buzz, and maybe bring you sales will follow, but only after you've proved yourself.

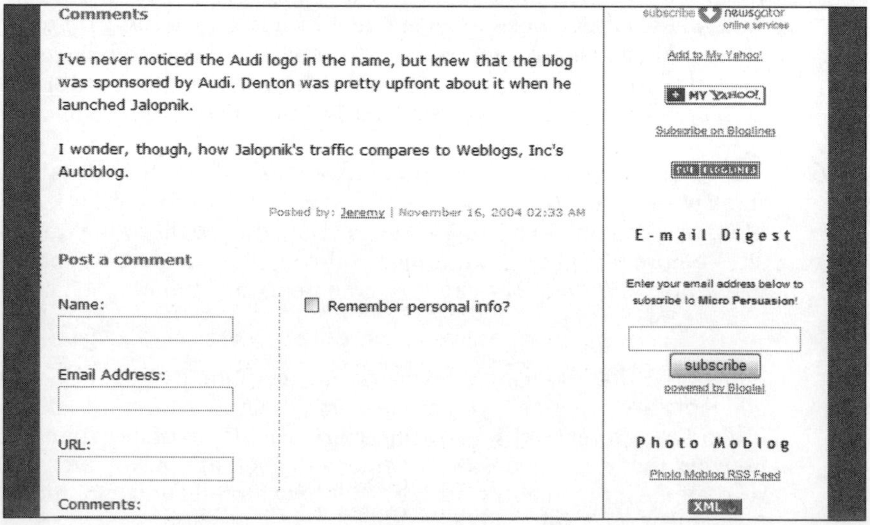

Figure 8-1:
This comment on the Micro Persuasion automatically includes a link to the commenter's Web site.

Comments

I've never noticed the Audi logo in the name, but knew that the blog was sponsored by Audi. Denton was pretty upfront about it when he launched Jalopnik.

I wonder, though, how Jalopnik's traffic compares to Weblogs, Inc's Autoblog.

Posted by: Jeremy | November 16, 2004 02:33 AM

Post a comment

Name:

Email Address:

URL:

Comments:

☐ Remember personal info?

subscribe ❤ newsgator
online services

Add to My Yahoo!

MY YAHOO!

Subscribe on Bloglines

THE BLOGLINES

E-mail Digest

Enter your email address below to
subscribe to Micro Persuasion!

subscribe
powered by Bloglist

Photo Moblog

Photo Moblog RSS Feed

XML

Don't fool yourself by being complimentary in order to get your name and link on a prominent blogger's site, either. Saying "I agree!" or "Nice site" doesn't further the conversation and won't pique the interest of others.

Joining Online Communities

The Internet is a great resource of information, and I could talk for a long time about how it has revolutionized access to information. The more exciting innovation, however, is in the realm of community.

The Internet has allowed large groups of people who are geographically distant to come together as (more or less) functioning community groups, with social habits, rules, and customs. Whatever your personal interests or issues, the Internet likely gives you resources for finding others like you and mechanisms for sharing and supporting each other.

You need to be aware of two important online communities if you plan to have an active blog. MetaFilter and Slashdot are huge, ever-changing online discussions of every topic possible.

Slashdot

Slashdot's tongue-in-cheek tagline is "News for Nerds. Stuff that matters." The Slashdot community, shown in Figure 8-2, is smart, highly technical, and interested in the world. Users create all the content. Slashdot users talk about everything, all the time, so the site (at www.slashdot.org) is an amazing measure of what's current on the Web.

Here's how Slashdot works:

1. Anyone can submit stories to the editors of Slashdot. You can even submit a story anonymously.

2. Slashdot Authors review stories for timeliness, relevancy, and appeal to the Slashdot audience. Some are selected for use on Slashdot; many are rejected, quite a few because the subject has already appeared on Slashdot.

3. A Slashdot Author posts the story.

4. Readers post comments, questions, and follow-up information to the story. A story usually generates many comments. I've seen stories with 50 comments, and I've seen others with more than 1,000.

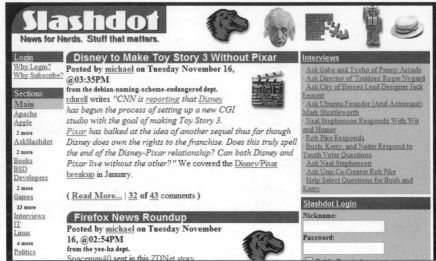

Figure 8-2:
Slashdot
is home to
the most
talkative
technical
group
online.

5. Comments are moderated. The moderation system is one of the really novel things about Slashdot. Moderators are chosen randomly from among the registered users and are given a certain number of points. While they read comments, the moderator chooses an adjective to describe the comment: Informative, Redundant, Funny, and so on. Each time they do, they lose a point. After using up the points, they're no longer moderators, though they can be selected again. The comments are scored and displayed with higher-ranking comments on top.

The system is a little more complex, but this should give you the general idea: Conversation on Slashdot is filtered through the submission of stories from users, selection by editors, and then self-moderation of comments by the community. You can see the breadth and frequency of comment posting in Figure 8-3.

The result of this process is an ongoing conversation in which users are sometimes moderators, sometimes consumers, but are always aware of the level of dialogue around a topic. The site retains its original Slashdot "flavor" because stories are chosen by editors, who maintain a certain level of discourse and direction. Slashdot doesn't appeal to everyone, but the site has an enormous following. While you don't need to submit stories or comments to Slashdot, checking in occasionally and watching for mentions of your company is important.

Slashdot was created by Rob Malda and a group of other Slashdot Authors in 1997. Though ownership of the site has changed hands several times, Malda is still the main developer for the site, as well as its Editor. Slashdot's name is a play on the general awkwardness of URLs — trying saying `http://www.slashdot.org` out loud to see what Malda was getting at.

Today Slashdot serves an average 80 million pages a month, with somewhat higher traffic on weekdays than weekends. Anyone can read Slashdot and post to Slashdot, but only registered users are permitted to participate in the various administrative functions that influence the site's editorial content. Basic registration is free, and users that want to surf ad-free can pay a subscription. Interestingly, the amount you pay for your subscription is determined by the number of pages you visit and is not a flat-rate time period.

One interesting feature of Slashdot is the Hall of Fame page. It tracks the most active and most visited stories (not necessarily the same), among other things. You can keep constant tabs on conversations, giving you instant feedback about tech buzz. In mid-November 2004, the most active stories were mainly concerned with politics: Kerry's concession, Hussein's arrest, *Fahrenheit 9/11*.

Why should you care about Slashdot? Well, get mentioned in an interesting Slashdot story, and your site will be deluged with visitors. Think of Slashdot as an enormous spotlight that can be swung in your direction at any time, and remember that Slashdot users are charged with verifying facts for themselves, so they don't hold back in what they say.

Getting linked from a Slashdot story and the resulting number of visitors sounds like a good thing, but servers that aren't prepared to handle the load often choke and fail — in other words, *Slashdotted*.

Figure 8-3:
Slashdot's community is interested in every-thing — they post comments constantly on a huge variety of subjects.

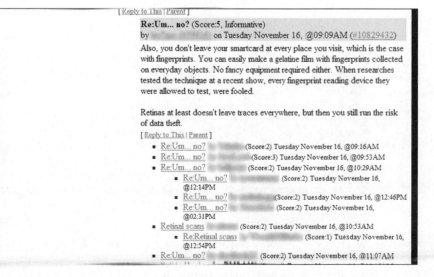

MetaFilter

MetaFilter (www.metafilter.com) is an enormous Web log — the Web log of anyone in the world. It is open to *anyone* who wants to post to it, on any topic. The site exists to remove communication barriers and to encourage interaction. The whole idea is that participants create a collaborative discussion, shaped by shared information and mutual respect.

Postings are sorted into discussions: You can start with the original post and read responses, or you can jump into the middle of the discussion. In order to post, you must register (free). Be a member long enough, and you can actually post links directly to the home page.

MetaFilter has somewhere in the neighborhood of 17,000 members, 32,000 discussion threads, and more than 750,000 comments. In mid-November 2004, the home page showed discussions on the decline of the U.S. dollar, the anniversary of a famous murder case, Apple iPod tools for the PC, and the psychology of reunions. Though not edited, the site is moderated by community members, and users can lose membership for inflammatory comments.

Matt Haughey, a software engineer, started MetaFilter in 1999. The site, which is shown in Figure 8-4, has experienced some growing pains because of its popularity and has sometimes had to limit new registrations while the site is altered to handle the mass of content and activity it experiences.

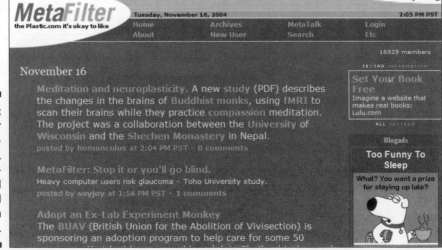

Figure 8-4: MetaFilter is a free-wheeling, community-driven, and moderated discussion blog.

Social networking tools

Partly because blogging is a form of networking and partly because a lot of blogging is being done by Web innovators, many bloggers are heavily involved with social networks, such as LinkedIn, Audioscrobbler, and Friendster.

What these sites aim to do is better connect you with your current group of friends or colleagues and to build relationships between those with similar interests. Sound a little like the network of relationships inherent to blogs and blogging? It should! Being a member of these communities has intangible benefits but definitely demonstrates an understanding of Internet trends and technologies that only speaks well of you. Additionally, your accessibility through these mediums encourages curious bloggers and readers to get in touch directly. And, of course, getting hooked into the conversations going on within these networks can generate buzz and readership for your blog.

Not all of these networks are useful to you, but think creatively about how you can leverage these networks to add value and functionality to your business blog.

Audioscrobbler

Audioscrobbler (www.audioscrobbler.com) collects information about the music you listen to and then matches your musical tastes with that of other users. The result is a list of recommended music and contacts with whom you can talk in forums and form into groups (see Figure 8-5).

Figure 8-5:
Share your musical tastes on Audioscrobbler and find others with similar interests.

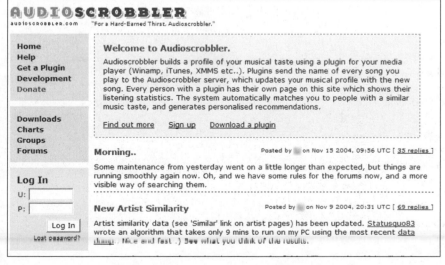

Friendster

Friendster is a purely social networking tool designed to connect groups of friends and allows you to build relationships with your friends' friends. The basic premise is that this is a friend-making tool where the people you come in contact with are already known to your friends or friends' friends. This is a great tool for making contacts with young, single people!

LinkedIn

LinkedIn (www.linkedin.com) is a purely professional network of 1.4 million people. Register and provide some basic information about yourself and then feed your Rolodex into the system. If you have colleagues that aren't registered, you can invite them. Use the system to search for people and organizations you want to make contact with. For example, if you want to make contact with the CEO of a company to establish a business relationship, do a search for that person's name. If the CEO is in the system, LinkedIn tells you how many contacts you have in common, or trace a route from your contacts, your contacts' contacts, and hence to the CEO.

The entire system is based on referrals, so the chances are high that you can make a connection to a potential business partner. I used LinkedIn, which is shown in Figure 8-6, frequently while writing this book to find and request contact with bloggers and technology companies.

Figure 8-6:
The LinkedIn professional network allows you to leverage the contacts of your contacts to make new business relation-ships.

Blogging History and Events

Being a member of a group means understanding its shared history so that you can participate appropriately. Blogging, though young, has its share of format-shaping events that have hugely impacted the evolution and form of the blogosphere.

The following events are generally thought to be significant moments in the history of blogging or events of which most bloggers are aware. Some reflect the nature of blogs, and others have shaped the medium itself. This information is useful to you because of the connected nature of the blogosphere — being savvy about significant events in the history of blogging means you can avoid common mistakes and understand references that crop up in conversation. At this stage, even business bloggers need to know about these events, if only to keep from looking uninformed!

The first use of the term *blog* in regard to an online journal seems to have happened in 1999, but not everyone agrees on the exact date and who should get the credit for the word. *Web log* was used somewhat earlier, but not before 1997. Pitas developed the first real software intended specifically for blogging in 1999, and Blogger followed close on its heels.

Most early blogs were directories that catalogued links that the blogger found entertaining or informative. They were sifting information for their readers, a truly valuable service in the early days of the Internet when search engines weren't as robust as they are today. Rebecca Blood, blogger and author, has written a good essay on these early days that is at `www.rebeccablood.net/essays/weblog_history.html`.

2001: September 11

After the attacks on September 11, people all over the United States and the world reached out for comfort and knowledge. Like all of us, Web loggers wanted and needed to talk, and they did so in their blogs. Several blogs were even started in response to September 11, as their authors sought to understand why the attacks had happened.

The country was united in many ways, and bloggers were able to put those feelings into words. September 11 has connected Americans in many different ways; blogging is one of them.

For more about what was blogged about after September 11, visit NYC Bloggers at www.nycbloggers.com/911.asp. You have to sift through some broken links from blogs that are no longer active, but some real gems of emotion and sharing are included.

2001: Kaycee Nicole Hoax

Kaycee Nicole played basketball and attended high school in a small Kansas town. On her blog, she also wrote about her ongoing fight with leukemia, a cancer of the blood and bone marrow. Kaycee was an outgoing girl who made a lot of online friends, with whom she shared her poetry and bravery in the face of awful medical procedures, and her hope about the future.

People exchanged e-mails with Kaycee, talked to her in chat rooms, and even spoke with her on the phone. Kaycee's mom, Debbie, also kept a blog where she talked about having a seriously ill child. Kaycee and Debbie weren't celebrities, but they were strongly supported by the online community that invested emotionally in Kaycee's struggle.

When she died of an aneurysm on May 15, 2004, her online friends were devastated — and then puzzled. Debbie, Kaycee's mom, wouldn't provide information about the funeral or an address to send cards and flowers. It was strange, but many assumed the family just wanted to grieve privately. A posting on MetaFilter, however, suggested that it would be possible to fake the life of someone like Kaycee, and with that suspicion planted, people began to ask questions. The biggest question was why no one had ever met or seen Kaycee in person.

Enterprising MetaFilter members started to check out the facts and learned that there was no obituary or record of her death. In fact, there wasn't any official record of her life! Confronted, Debbie Swenson admitted the girl's life and death had been a hoax. The girl shown in photographs of Kaycee was a family friend who was unaware of the hoax. Debbie Swenson claimed the story was based on the lives of three people she had known with cancer, though this may not be true either.

Just what Debbie Swenson thought she was doing is unclear. What is clear is that people invest themselves emotionally on the Internet and that communities can build up around issues, causes, and people. These new communities have the strength to achieve real results, too — as they did in uncovering the Kaycee Nicole hoax.

For more information on the Kaycee Nicole hoax, visit the Kaycee Nicole (Swenson) FAQ at rootnode.org/article.php?sid=26.

2002: War blogs and Trent Lott

In 2002, the war blogs entered the scene. War bloggers tapped a vein of outrage and political skepticism to keep the White House in the hot seat about the war in Afghanistan. Others expressed support and arguments for what was happening.

Joshua Micah Marshall, journalist and blogger, started his Talking Points Memo blog (at `www.talkingpointsmemo.com`) in late 2000. Marshall also writes for the *Washington Monthly* and several other traditional media publications.

During a speech at Strom Thurmond's 100th birthday celebration on December 5, 2002, Senate Majority Leader Trent Lott remarked: "I want to say this about my state. When Strom Thurmond ran for president, we voted for him. We're proud of it. And if the rest of the country had followed our lead, we wouldn't have had all these problems over the years either." As Marshall pointed out, Thurmond ran on a presidential platform of racial segregation of schools and public facilities. Lott was, in fact, lamenting the loss of those good old days of legislated racism.

For whatever reason, most reporters gave Lott a pass on his statement, either because they didn't know the history or, perhaps, out of political ennui. Marshall, however, reported what had happened on his blog. And then reported some more. Other bloggers also picked it up and posted about it. Together, they brought Lott's statement back into the public eye, and into newspaper stories, and radio and television newscasts. By December 20, Lott had submitted his resignation.

Blogs can do a better job than traditional media of focusing on details and of keeping the conversation current and emotions fresh. Lott's resignation was evidence the bloggers had power in the real world and not just the virtual one — and that they could use it by drawing on the strengths of the medium: links, comments, and interaction.

Here are some additional resources for this event:

- Marshall's original post on Lott's remarks: `www.talkingpointsmemo.com/archives/week_2002_12_01.php#000451`
- Andrew Sullivan, another political blogger, jumps into the fray: `www.andrewsullivan.com/index.php?dish_inc=archives/2002_12_08_dish_archive.html#90029180`
- *The Washington Post* reports on Lott's resignation: `www.washingtonpost.com/ac2/wp-dyn?pagename=article&contentId=A17080-2002Dec20`

2003: Google buys Blogger

In February of 2003, Google — one of the most popular and successful Internet search engines — bought Blogger, a Pyra Labs company that hosted thousands of Web logs.

Why would Google be interested in Blogger? Many bloggers theorized that the purchase meant big things for blogging: Self-publishing was now mainstream. If a profitable company such as Google saw fit to invest in blogging, it certainly wasn't *only* the realm of self-obsessed gadget geeks! The marketplace had endorsed the medium.

2003: Blogging from Baghdad

During the war in Iraq, soldiers, journalists, and Iraqis blogged from Iraq, offering a novel mix of viewpoints and opinions on what was happening there. The appetite for these blogs was high, especially in light of the coming 2004 presidential election, and several achieved notoriety.

Stuart Hughes was one such war blogger. A journalist working for the BBC, Hughes spent several months in Northern Iraq. Hughes started his blog to keep in touch with friends, family, and colleagues. Early entries read like an unusually adventurous travelogue, complete with snapshots. But on April 2, 2003, Hughes stepped on an anti-personnel landmine. He lost his right leg below the knee; a colleague lost his life. The travelogue became something of a medical journal. Hughes quickly became active in anti-landmine campaigns. He continues to blog at stuarthughes.blogspot.com.

Not all of these blogs are still being updated, but each qualifies as a war blog:

- Baghdad Burning: Girl Blog from Iraq — Riverbendblog.blogspot.com
- Back to Iraq: www.back-to-iraq.com
- Soldier's Paradise: www.soldiersparadise.blogspot.com and www.soldiersparadiseii.blogspot.com

2003-2004: Howard Dean

During the run-up to the 2004 presidential election, Howard Dean started a grass-roots campaign that positioned him as an outsider willing to listen to the people and to effect real change for the country. The Dean for America campaign strategy utilized the Internet as presidential candidates never had before. The immediacy and interaction of blogging suited Dean's style perfectly.

Dean for America did some very unusual things: got younger voters to meet and listen to Dean in person while he was on the campaign trail; raised millions of dollars through small, individual donations; and involved voters directly in the campaign. Many Americans responded well to the openness and accessibility of the blog, and Dean was highly praised for having activated traditionally apathetic voter blocks.

The process had significant plusses for Dean as well — it made supporters feel like part of the campaign team, which in turn made them more likely to invest time, money, and eventually their vote in the candidate. The blog, in combination with his other efforts, raised millions for Dean's campaign. (He also got major geek points from the technical community using blogging technologies such as Trackbacks and comments.) You can see the archived blog at archive.deanforamerica.com and in Figure 8-7.

When he failed to win the primary, Dean turned the power of the Dean for America team into Democracy for America, a political action committee that continued to endorse, raise funds, and support democratic nominees through the election in November 2004.

Figure 8-7:
Howard Dean blogged for America and for the presidency during his bid for the White House.

Tying Up Loose Ends

In this section I bring together some small tidbits of information that aren't easy to categorize, but are nonetheless interesting facets of blog culture. You will definitely run across blog memes, or viral ideas, as you read blogs. In fact, participating in a blog meme can be a good way to become a member of the blogosphere.

No blogger worth his salt should miss the amazing service provided by Technorati — use it to track phrases and URLs around the blogosphere.

Blog memes

Blog *memes* are trends that bloggers choose consciously to participate in. Some are running jokes, some are obscure, some are simply for fun.

Defined by Webster, a meme is "an idea, behavior, style, or usage that spreads from person to person within a culture." Chain letters, joke, slogans, and catch phrases are all memes. The McDonald's "I'm lovin' it" tagline is a meme, as is Arnold Schwarzenegger's accented "I'll be back."

Any blogger can participate in a meme, and it can bring a lighthearted note to the most serious blog. Blog memes occur when a group of bloggers all post on the same subject, deliberately creating a group of cross-blog answers to the same question or opinions on the same topic. Some examples:

- **Page 23, sentence 5:** Bloggers open the closest book, turn to page 23, and blog the fifth sentence on the page.

- **Catblogging:** Bloggers interrupt their regularly schedule commentary on Fridays with a photograph of their cats. Begun by Kevin Drum, the meme is a reminder that life doesn't have to be entirely serious.

The Long Bet

Blogs are seen as an amazing tool for personal journalism — citizens turned reporter. The Long Bet goes something like this: There's only one *New York Times*. By 2007, there will be so many popular bloggers that they will rank higher in Google Web searches for the five top news stories of the day than the *Times*. Because Google uses clicks and links (in part) to build its search result rankings, this indicates that blogs are a more popular source of news than the most respected newspaper in the country.

Don't Control the Message

The number-one way to guarantee that your blog won't succeed is to over-sanitize, overedit, and overspin your blog postings.

Blogs are about sharing information — whatever that information is — not controlling it. If your company can't share without keeping your CEO up at night in a cold sweat, think again about starting a blog.

Ideally, a blog is an outreach, a service, and a way to give more to the people who buy and use your products and services. Do that, and in exchange, you get their good will, loyalty, and help in improving your company.

Don't lose sight of what sharing information means in practice. You don't have to spill your trade secrets or put your lawyers on the chopping block! You just need to be real.

For example, in Figure 9-1, take a look at the Halloween entry of the official Google Blog. Google may not sell more advertising accounts by posting pictures of staff dressed up for Halloween, but doing so proves that Google is made up of *real* people, that it isn't a faceless behemoth sitting on a pile of gold, scheming to get more.

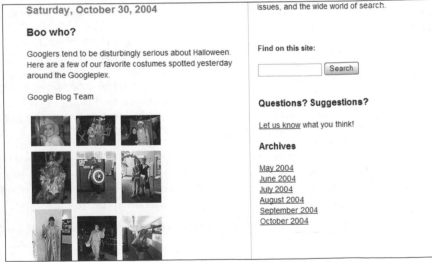

Figure 9-1:
The Google blog entry for October 30 shows staff and their families and pets enjoying the Halloween holiday.

The bet was placed in 2002, with a $1,000 stake from Dave Winer and Martin Nisenholtz. Winer made the prediction; Nisenholtz disagrees. Whoever wins will donate the money to a charity. Winer is CEO of Userland.com, a blogging technology company, and a blogger himself. Nisenholtz is CEO of *New York Times* Digital.

Read more about The Long Bet and vote on whether you think Winder is right at www.longbets.org/2.

Technorati

Technorati (www.technorati.com) is a Web site that tracks the connections between blogs. Type a URL or keywords into Technorati, and the system tells you how many links there are to that URL, from how many blogs. It also shows you a list of those links. You can track conversations and buzz on topics and to see how well your own blog is faring in the blogosphere.

In late 2004, Technorati was tracking 4.6 million blogs and paying particular attention to politics, news, books, and the most popular blogs (as determined by incoming links).

Chapter 9

Avoiding Business Blog No-Nos

• •

In This Chapter

▶ Following your own blog policies

▶ Handling criticism gracefully

▶ Asking readers for help

• •

*W*eb logs have traditionally been one of two things:

✔ The personal journal — interesting to the general public or not — with the feeling and flavor of an individual putting his or her heart on the line honestly.

✔ The outlet of a pundit, critic, or social commentator who cries wolf when warranted and keeps chosen opponents on their toes.

You may have noticed that I didn't mention business blogs in that list. The truth is, business blogging is a new phenomenon, and by creating one you're breaking new ground. However, just because earlier blogs had a different focus doesn't mean you can't learn a thing or two about blogging well from them. All kinds of bloggers have learned that blogs, when they're used correctly, can revolutionize the relationship between the public and the blogger. They do by being faithful to the medium: being open, honest, and transparent.

In this chapter, I discuss what not to do when using blogs to build buzz for your business. If you use blogs the wrong way and get on the wrong side of the blogosphere, you risk failing to connect with customers. Finding out about how you can go wrong can help you blog correctly.

Lesson learned: Overcontrolling the content of your blog leaves it dull and lifeless. No one tells their friends to take a look at dull, lifeless blogs.

Don't Put Your Integrity at Risk

Though you should think creatively about your blog and keep it interesting and fresh, don't push your creativity too far. Bloggers that don't exist in real life, or that don't have the experiences they claim to, aren't appreciated in the blogosphere, which is exceptionally sensitive to deception. If you can't use a real blogger, and let him or her blog about real information and events, rethink the whole blog idea.

I talk more about developing a good blogging style in Chapter 10.

In March 2003, Dr Pepper/Seven Up learned this lesson the hard way when it tried to use the blogosphere to generate buzz for a new milk-based drink called Raging Cow. Dr Pepper located six young bloggers, gave them samples of the drink and some Amazon gift certificates, as well as a trip to Dallas. In return, Dr Pepper hoped the youths would talk about Raging Cow on their blogs, hopefully building buzz and enthusiasm for the product. The bloggers weren't asked, much less paid, to talk about Raging Cow or endorse it.

Some of the six posted; some didn't. Those that did appear to have tried and actually liked the drink; nor did they include innocuous links to the product Web site. Unfortunately, none of the bloggers disclosed the fact that Dr Pepper had provided them with gifts or the drink itself on their blogs. When the nature of the relationship — despite the fact that Dr Pepper hadn't paid the bloggers to post — between Dr Pepper and the bloggers was discovered, readers felt conned — by the bloggers and by Dr Pepper.

At least one boycott of Raging Cow was proposed, and in news stories Dr Pepper admitted that it would do things differently next time. Nonetheless, the drink was talked about — and talked about and talked about — all over the Web on Web sites and blogs that would never have mentioned milk-based drinks targeted to teens under normal circumstances. The big lesson here, however, is that even the appearance of impropriety can get you into trouble in the blog world, although it can also get you talked about. If the goal was to get people talking about Raging Cow, Dr Pepper achieved it, but a better effort might have resulted in positive, rather than negative, buzz.

Fake blogs are fictional blogs that you can use to get creative. You can create a story, as long all concerned realized that it's fiction. As well as involving real bloggers with Raging Cow, Dr Pepper created a completely fake Web site that was the blog of a "cow with attitude." The site chronicled the cow's travels while promoting the beverage. Clearly, the site wasn't the blog of a real person, and if it had launched sans the controversy with the real bloggers, it might have earned Dr Pepper points for innovation.

In Chapter 13, I discuss more creative ways to add pizzazz to your blogs.

Lesson learned: Disclose all marketing relationships and sponsorships with bloggers you give products or services to in exchange for posts. Ask those bloggers to do so when they post, so that you don't risk looking like you're trying to pull a fast one.

Don't Be Defensive

Your company already has critics. Maybe you deal with these folks already, maybe you have a customer service department that handles problems as they arise. But if you start a blog, you will be criticized, and in a very public medium. Your strategy in dealing with criticism, warranted or not, is pretty simple: be informative, not defensive. Do the following:

- **Apologize for mistakes.** You've probably noticed that staying mad at someone who makes a sincere apology is difficult. Acknowledging the problem instead of ignoring it — especially if you can also do something about it — gets noticed and respected.

  I experienced this myself when I was responsible for getting the *Los Angeles Times* crossword puzzle onto the Web. Because I was inputting the answers and clues by hand, I sometimes made a mistake — and puzzlers definitely let me know! Some were polite, but many wrote scathing attacks via the Web site's customer service page. When I wrote back and simply apologized for the typo, usually also thanking them for using the site, I very often got a response like this: "Gee, I never realized a real person would read this. I guess I kind of flew off the handle there. I think you guys are doing a great job." Users started off angry and ended up pleased that they'd received a personal response. Not a bad outcome! All that was needed to turn the situation around was a simple "I'm sorry."

- **Explain, but don't make excuses, when mistakes do happen.** This one is a fine line to walk, but your readers will probably respond well to factual explanations of why something happened. Your explanations have a greater impact if you can talk about what you did to fix the issue or what you're doing to make sure it doesn't happen again.

Readers do not appreciate excuses or blame-passing, especially if they think you're trying to avoid taking responsibility for whatever the problem is. You can almost always defuse irritation with graciousness and an explanation of what happened, even in situations where you can't actually fix the problem.

✔ **Acknowledge valid criticism.** You'll deserve some criticism, and you can do yourself and your readers a great service if you respond forthrightly to it. Let readers know you're paying attention and responding. It is the best possible outcome they can expect from making criticism. Besides, your readers know your products and services well — they may very well give you criticism that helps you improve what you're doing and just maybe sell more of that better product or service as a result.

✔ **Don't give scathing, vicious attackers the satisfaction.** *Trolls* (commenters who post offensive feedback) and folks who just plain don't like your company will find your blog. If they post abusive criticism that is more invective than informative, feel free to delete the comment and ban the user. No one benefits from remarks clearly intended to stir up trouble, but make sure the criticism isn't valid before you get rid of the comment. In his blog, www.bbrown.info, Bill Brown makes clear he doesn't accept dialogue of this nature in his blogging policy, as shown in Figure 9-2. You can go directly to his blogging policy at www.bbrown.info/blogs/policy.cfm.

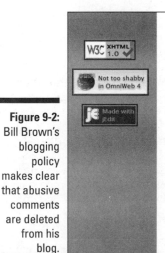

Figure 9-2:
Bill Brown's blogging policy makes clear that abusive comments are deleted from his blog.

Ideas, on the other hand, are freely credited. You can assume that any uncredited content is my own handiwork, though it is a stretch to say that it is uninfluenced by others. I have well integrated Ayn Rand's philosophy of Objectivism into my life and her ideas inform virtually all of my content.

If you want to see where I visit, your best bet is to stand over my shoulder as I peruse the Web throughout the day. The bookmarks area of my site is but a general guide and doesn't reflect my actual travels, though I would certainly love it if it could.

5. If I find out I am mistaken on an issue, I will add an "[UPDATE" to the entry no matter how far past the entry is. I am fallible and often jump to conclusions too quickly. I'm big enough to admit my mistakes and missteps no matter how embarassing they might be.

6. I will only delete comments when they are offtopic, spam, or abusive. Someone posted a comment recently that read "You are such a fag." Not that there's anything wrong with that, but I didn't see how that furthered discussion one iota so I deleted it.

7. The views expressed within this site do represent the views of the management, the BBIC, and all of its subsidiaries.

Updated: 8/10/2003

Lesson learned: You can't escape criticism, but you can turn it into a positive interaction and good buzz by handling it well.

Don't Break Your Own Rules

You can adapt a number of good blogging resolutions to ensure that your blog is useful to your readers. If you do adapt a set of standards or guidelines, be sure to stick to them, especially if you have made them public!

In Chapter 12, I discuss establishing some guidelines for the kinds of blogging and dialogue you should encourage and discourage on your blog.

Many bloggers resolve to:

- ✔ Be truthful and accurate.
- ✔ Delete comments only when they are spam or don't contribute to the conversation.
- ✔ Make corrections and updates without materially changing the substance of the original blog posting.
- ✔ Respond promptly to comments and e-mails.

These are admirable resolutions and do make your stance and standards obvious to your readers. They are especially helpful when you plan to have multiple bloggers or a blog editor. Once set, however, don't start to make exceptions if the policies become inconvenient. Thanks to caching, syndication, and printers, your readers can easily make comparisons and realize that you aren't being consistent with your own standards.

Many bloggers choose to post these resolutions on their blogs so that their readers also know how the blog is being run. You can post them or not, as long as you actually follow them.

Breaking your own rules is a fast way to lose the respect of your audience.

You can change your policies if you have a genuine need to do so. For example, perhaps in your original blogging policy you promised that you would never delete user comments. This rule worked for a while until your blog became popular and was discovered by spammers. They began posting about pharmaceutical products and online gaming Web sites, but you violate your own policy if you delete those comments!

In the case of spammers, make an amendment to your policy, announce it to your blog readers, and carry on.

Lesson learned: Setting a blogging policy is a good idea, but only if you actually stick to it.

Don't Be Greedy

You can pitch, and even sell, your own products and services via your blog. You can also add a number of other revenue-generating functionalities to your blog, including advertising, affiliate program links, and donation requests. (I talk more about these tools in Chapter 14.) Carry all this too far, however, and your blog becomes a sales tool rather than a communication tool. You lose readers and you certainly won't sell anything when you get carried away by the desire to make money with your blog.

Many commercial bloggers don't take any risks in this area at all, often for very good reasons. In the Community MX blog, `www.communitymx.com/blog`, postings often cover fixes, tricks, and tips for various Macromedia software products. It would be pretty obnoxious if every mention of a software application also involved a link to the purchase page — especially because readers of this highly technical blog are likely to already own and use the software being discussed. Take a look at this blog in Figure 9-3.

Figure 9-3:
The Community MX blog rarely links readers to software purchase pages.

Don't let the possibilities of the marketplace overwhelm your sense of serving the readers. If your readers can benefit from links to purchase books from Amazon.com, don't hesitate to include them. But rely mostly on your company's traditional revenue streams to bring in money.

With any luck, an informative, helpful blog that allows your customers to really communicate with your company results in new and repeat customers, which is more valuable to your business than any possible gain you might make from an affiliate program or advertisement.

What do you think? Do you find the appeals for donations and the advertising on Little Green Footballs (shown in Figure 9-4) distracting or just the price you have to pay for great political commentary?

Lesson learned: Business bloggers should be careful of soliciting donations or overt commercial efforts, for fear of appearing greedy.

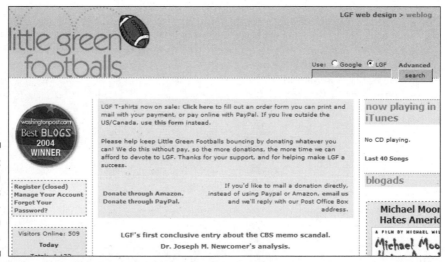

Figure 9-4:
Little Green
Footballs
has a dona-
tion link on
every page.

Don't Be Scared to Link

Links are a huge part of what makes your blog valuable to your readers — links to other blogs, news stories, resources on your company Web site, and even to your competition!

The blogosphere is based on a network of linking and referrals. Some of the oldest blogs were nothing more than a collection of links that readers might find of use. In fact, many blogs are still a collection of links around a particular topic — a news aggregation service is perfect for readers interested in that topic.

LAObserved, the blog of journalist Kevin Roderick, collects information about Los Angeles news and journalism. At www.laobserved.com, the blog is a collection of pointers to other Web sites accompanied by a quick summary and comment as to why the link is significant.

He includes at least one, and usually more, links to news stories, newspaper Web sites, e-mail addresses, and often to the institution where Roderick obtained the information in each post, as you can see in Figure 9-5.

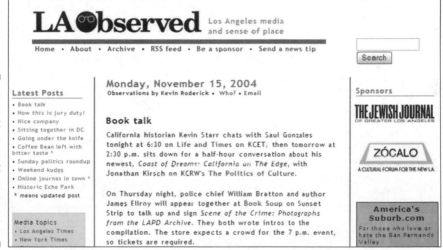

Figure 9-5: LAObserved is a blog that aggregates all the news of interest to the Los Angeles journalism industry.

Don't be afraid to send your readers to other Web sites — including your competitor; if you're doing your job right, they will come back to you. If something your competitor posts on its Web site helps inform your reader, include the link. Ignoring the competition doesn't make them go away!

Lesson learned: Links add value and earn you points for being helpful to your readers. Plus they encourage other sites to link back to you and send you potential readers.

Don't Be Afraid to Try New Things

If your traffic could be higher and your readers don't seem enthusiastic about your blog, try something new! You generate conversation and attention when you do, even if the attempt doesn't succeed (or doesn't accomplish quite what you thought it might).

Here are a few things you can try:

- **Redesign your blog.** Better yet, get your readers to help you redesign by contributing a new logo, a new name, vote on the color palette, and so on.

- **Do a survey or quiz.** People love to test their knowledge or compare their experiences with those of others. Ask them to weigh in, and don't forget to show the results!

  In his blog (www.tompeters.com), management expert Tom Peters puts a weekly poll on his blog and also displays the results from previous polls, as shown in Figure 9-6.

- **Add a new technical tool you aren't already using.** If you haven't already implemented a search tool, RSS feeds (which I discuss in Chapter 13), or comments, these are logical places to start.

- **Get a prominent member of your company or industry to be a guest blogger for a week.** Don't forget to promote the guest blogger before he or she begins posting so that your readers know to come to the site.

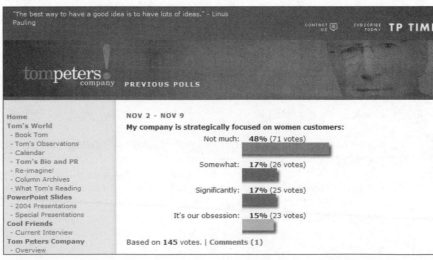

Figure 9-6: Polls can be a way to generate interest and repeat visits from your blog's readers.

Photo credit: Allison Sherriffs

In Chapter 11, I discuss how to promote your blog, drive traffic, and generate user interest and participation.

Lesson learned: Generate buzz about your blog by trying something new, especially if things are getting a little stale.

Don't Show Off

Make sure that your blog displays expertise and intelligence, especially about your industry and business. But don't let that become the purpose of the blog. Avoid showing off. Never post something just to make yourself look smart, unique, well-read, or well-educated.

Let your knowledge and expertise show by choosing your words, topics, and links carefully. Never choose a topic solely because it makes you or your company look good. A successful blogger puts the readers' interests and needs first.

Lesson learned: Be smart, but don't alienate your readers by showing off.

Don't Forget to Ask for Help

Blogs are a give and take, an ongoing conversation between blogger(s) and readers. If you're wondering something, ask your readers! Here are a few things your readers can help you do:

- ✔ Evaluate your products and services
- ✔ Decide whether to expand your business
- ✔ Decide where to focus your development dollars
- ✔ Change your Web site
- ✔ Rewrite your user manuals

Through your blog, you may find out about problems faster than you might ordinarily and even what your customers are doing to fix problems.

I came across a blog posting recently that mentioned the blogger's problem with a recently purchased bed frame that broke after only two months of use. Response to the posting was strong — the entry had nearly 30 comments.

Some commenters reported the same problem, some talked about their experiences with the furniture manufacturer's customer service, others talked about how they fixed the bed frame, and still others recommended where to purchase sturdier frames. Imagine if the furniture manufacturer had a blog — it could see the trend, learn how it's being fixed from those that would never bother to contact customer service, and adjust its manufacturing process. As it is, the company is probably completely unaware of the ongoing discussion happening on another blog — one that's apparently influenced at least two people to change their minds about purchasing the bed frame.

Blogs are a fast, inexpensive, and easy way to get feedback from people who know your company, products, and services very well. Don't let these people slip away. The service you provide them can be a two-way street that benefits you and your customers.

I should also mention that soliciting help from your customers makes them feel more involved in your company, invested in your products, and more likely to give you the benefit of the doubt if they ever experience a problem with a product or service.

Lesson learned: Your blog's readers may have valuable information for you that can help you improve your business.

Don't Take Your Blog Too Seriously

It's a blog, not a mission statement! Have a little fun, and keep your sense of humor about you. Be funny. Everyone loves funny. Funny and informative is even better.

You don't have to be a comedian, but sharp, humorous writing has been a recipe for success in the blogosphere and results in repeat visits from readers and attention from the press.

Visit "the dullest blog in the world" at www.wibsite.com/wiblog/dull for a laugh and a constructive look at what not to do with your blog, shown in Figure 9-7.

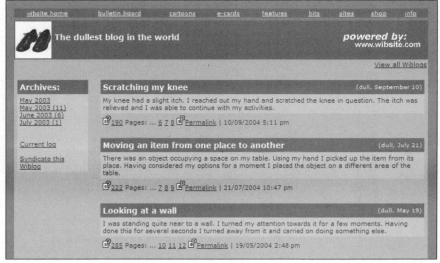

Dave Walker/Wibsite.com

Figure 9-7:
Check out "the dullest blog in the world" for more inspiration on what *not* to do with your blog.

Part IV
Positioning Your Blog

The 5th Wave   By Rich Tennant

"The bad news is our Web hosts' servers crashed last night, the good news is it was our blog that caused it."

In this part . . .

Blogging can look easy, but not everyone is really suited to being a blogger. In Chapter 10, you discover just how to identify the best person for the job of speaking on behalf of your company, and you may be surprised by my advice. I also have some focused advice for how to develop a strong blog writing style. Chapter 11 helps you become a member of the blogosphere by using comments and posts to communicate with other bloggers and your readers. Finally, blogs come with a new set of rules, standards and yes, ethical and legal problems. Steer clear of new liabilities by refreshing your understanding of copyright and libel in Chapter 12.

Chapter 10

Finding a Voice

*B*efore a blog can serve as an effective buzz-marketing tool, it must establish dialogue. For dialogue to be successful, you need a blogger whose style, personality, and knowledge meet the needs of the audience. In this chapter, you discover how to select an appropriate person to write the blog — and get some help understanding just what kinds of communication are best for blogs.

Establishing a friendly, open, and credible tone with your blog is fundamental — whatever its purpose. In the early days of the World Wide Web, a culture of openness and information sharing sprang up. Blogs are an extension of that tradition, a form of communication in which much is exposed. Even the process is transparent! Use this chapter to determine what kind of voice your blogger should use to create dialogue. As well, I give you some blog-specific writing tips to help you get started.

In this chapter, I discuss the basics of good blog writing. If you're faced with the task of finding the right person to be the voice of your company's blog, you'll find this chapter helpful.

Developing a Writing Style and Voice

If you are like most business professionals, you've spent a long time cultivating a professional writing style suited to memos and reports. Sadly, the blog writing style is vastly different — shorter, tighter, and more informal. As you get started blogging, watch how other bloggers approach the writing issue, and read this section to get some specific pointers on being more bloggy in your writing.

A great site design and technical gimmicks are no replacement for developing an interesting, readable writing style. Writing is never easy, and informal writing is almost always harder than a professional paper or memo. You may freeze up in front of the computer screen, or your writing may become stilted and unnecessarily verbose. Even the conversational style of the *For Dummies* series can be tough to maintain!

Finding your writing style

You can apply these consistent writing techniques to make your style more "bloglike":

- **Keep posts short, informative, and to the point — like an e-mail:** In fact, blog posts share many similarities with writing effective e-mails, more so than with writing memos, reports, or academic papers. On a blog, as with an e-mail, you're addressing a specific person or a group of people, and you usually know something about the person you're writing to. Most important — in both formats — you're writing something short and to the point, containing information the reader actually needs or wants. As with e-mail, a blogger can expect to get some response to what is written. (Unless, of course, you're writing one of those "help me get money out of my country by giving me access to your bank account" e-mails.)

- **Write in the first person, and include links to other Web sites, blogs, and resources:** You don't always have to use these techniques, but they make your blog entries more well-rounded. The shortest entry I've seen was a single word; most blog entries aren't more than a few hundred words at a time.

- **Inform your readers through humor and commentary:** Think of your blog as a conversation that you get to start. Think about who your readers are (you should already have a good idea about who your customers are) and what they are interested in.

- ✔ **Keep your posts conversational:** Try to write the way you speak. Avoid jargon, and don't use a thesaurus. You may find speaking your entry out loud helpful before trying to type it in — or read it aloud to yourself after you've written it. If you find yourself struggling or speaking unnaturally as you read aloud, think about what you might say if you were talking to a colleague or friend instead of writing.

- ✔ **Write with a friend in mind:** This tip relates closely to the conversational tone — write your blog with a specific friend or customer in mind. Thinking of someone you know well and who might want to read your blog while you write allows you to relax your writing style. As a result, your writing sounds more like you. Write your blog entries casually, as you would a personal letter or e-mail.

- ✔ **Learn from other bloggers:** Before you start blogging, spend some time visiting other blogs that are like the one you're thinking of starting. Read one or two for a couple of weeks, and pay attention to things such as posting lengths, frequency, writing style, and subject material. You don't need to copy them, but you may get some good ideas for your own blog by noting what you find interesting and compelling reading in others.

Blog writing isn't . . .

Don't confuse short and informal with inconsequential — your blog entries need to be focused and on topic. Avoid doing the following:

- ✔ Don't use your blog to post press releases, corporate communications, technical reports, or other lengthy official documents. You may choose to blog about some things in those documents — and link to them — but the blog format isn't designed to handle long, impersonal communication.

- ✔ As you post, make sure you're not giving in to personal interest as you select your topics. Although your tone and delivery are personal, your topics should always be focused on the reader and the reader's interests. You don't need to pander to them, but you should always have them in mind as you write.

- ✔ Avoid showing off with your blog. Let your erudition, knowledge, and general *savoir-faire* shine through in the words you choose and the topics you discuss. Never choose a topic solely because it will make you or your company look good.

Checking spelling, grammar, and punctuation

You undoubtedly come across blogs, mostly personal journals, in which the blogger has decided to dispense with the niceties of spell checking, grammar, and punctuation. How did you react when you saw these mistakes? Chances are, not well.

Writing resources

Books

The Elements of Style, Fourth Edition
By William Strunk, Jr., E.B. White, Roger Angell
This book is beloved by English teachers at all levels (including university) for its focus on the fundamentals of writing well.
Get a taste at www.bartleby.com/141.

Hot Text: Web Writing that Works
By Jonathan Price, Lisa Price
Hot Text covers Web writing from several angles, all with a business focus. Its focus on Web delivery may be useful.

English Grammar For Dummies
By Geraldine Woods
If you're feeling the need to brush up on the basics, this book walks you through the mechanics of grammar without making you diagram a sentence.

Web Sites

Merriam-Webster Online Dictionary
www.m-w.com
Look up words and definitions without leaving the computer.

Bartlett's Quotations
www.bartleby.com/100
Offered by Bartleby.com, Inc., Bartlett's Quotations has more than 11,000 searchable quotations. Bartleby's selections include a number of notable reference works, encyclopedias, and dictionaries.

Copyright Law
www.copyright.gov
All authors should know the basics of copyright law, including how to protect their own original work. Pay special attention to the rules surrounding fair use: www.copyright.gov/title17/92chap1.html#107.

Concise, Scannable, and Object: How to Write for the Web
By John Morkes and Jakob Nielson
www.useit.com/papers/webwriting/writing.html
This academic paper written by Internet usability experts in 1997 still does a great job of identifying good online writing practices, many of which play into blog writing.

In most writing, you're trained to regard these kinds of mistakes as careless-ness and a disregard for both the topic and the reader. Some bloggers have chosen to regard this level of informality as a kind of testament to honesty and immediacy — if you're posting without even running a spell checker, the implication goes, you're putting your most honest foot forward. A personal blogger may want to create this valuable impression.

For most business blogs, spelling and grammar mistakes just make your read-ers scoff. At best, they'll think the blog amateurish. At worst, they'll think you don't respect them enough to correct the errors. No one thinks poorly of a blogger who chooses to use complete sentences and keep the split infinitives to a minimum, but many will notice the errors before they pay attention to what you're saying.

Managing a blog with multiple authors

If you're going to be working with several people on one blog, talk over how often you expect each other to post. Having a co-blogger takes some of the stress off you, especially if all the authors contribute regularly, but it can also lead to confusion and repetition. You have several different working strategies you can employ:

- ✔ **Assign each contributor a day of the week for which they're responsi-ble.** Assignments don't preclude others from posting that day, but this practice ensures that someone is minding the store at all times.

- ✔ **Divide duties by topic area.** No doubt each of you has a slightly different area of expertise, and — depending on the focus of your blog — you may have some logical ways to split things up. If you choose this method, it can pay off for you to define those areas quite specifically, both to pre-vent overlap and also to ensure full coverage.

    This division of labor may cause some ego bruising. Keep an eye on con-tributors who post in areas already assigned to someone else.

- ✔ **Appoint an editor.** This person might not have the capability to actu-ally change a posting, but can definitely head off overlap, poaching, and redundancy. An editor can also spot holes in coverage that the bloggers themselves miss when they focus on their dates or areas of expertise.

Richard Scoble's Corporate Weblog Manifesto

Richard Scoble generously allowed me to reprint his oft-quoted advice to corporate bloggers. He blogged in on Wednesday, February 26, 2003, at 11:45 p.m. You can find it online at radio.weblogs.com/0001011/2003/02/26.html.

The Corporate Weblog Manifesto.

Thinking of doing a weblog about your product or your company? Here's my idea of things to consider before you start.

1) Tell the truth. The whole truth. Nothing but the truth. If your competitor has a product that's better than yours, link to it. You might as well. We'll find it anyway.

2) Post fast on good news or bad. Someone say something bad about your product? Link to it — before the second or third site does — and answer its claims as best you can. Same if something good comes out about you. It's all about building long-term trust. The trick to building trust is to show up! If people are saying things about your product and you don't answer them, that distrust builds. Plus, if people are saying good things about your product, why not help Google find those pages as well?

3) Use a human voice. Don't get corporate lawyers and PR professionals to cleanse your speech. We can tell, believe me. Plus, you'll be too slow. If you're the last one to post, the joke is on you!

4) Make sure you support the latest software/web/human standards. If you don't know what the W3C is, find out. If you don't know what RSS feeds are, find out. If you don't know what weblogs.com is, find out. If you don't know how Google works, find out.

5) Have a thick skin. Even if you have Bill Gates' favorite product, people will say bad things about it. That's part of the process. Don't try to write a corporate weblog unless you can answer all questions — good and bad — professionally, quickly, and nicely.

6) Don't ignore Slashdot [an online community that is very active (www.slashdot.com)].

7) Talk to the grassroots first. Why? Because the mainstream press is cruising weblogs, looking for stories and looking for people to use in quotes. If a mainstream reporter can't find anyone who knows anything about a story, he/she will write a story that looks like a press release instead of something trustworthy. People trust stories that have quotes from many sources. They don't trust press releases.

8) If you screw up, acknowledge it. Fast. And give us a plan for how you'll unscrew things. Then deliver on your promises.

9) Underpromise and overdeliver. If you're going to ship on March 1, say you won't ship until March 15. Folks will start to trust you if you behave this way. Look at Disneyland. When you're standing in line, you trust their signs. Why? Because the line always goes faster than it says it will (their signs are engineered to say that a line will take about 15% longer than it really will).

10) If Doc Searls says it or writes it, believe it. Live it. Enough said.

11) Know the information gatekeepers. If you don't realize that Sue Mosher reaches more Outlook users than nearly everyone else, you shouldn't be on the PR team for Outlook. If you don't know all of her phone numbers and IM addresses, you should be fired. If you can't call on the gatekeepers during a crisis, you shouldn't try to keep a corporate weblog (oh, and they better know how to get a hold of you since they know when you're under attack before you do — for instance, why hasn't anyone from the Hotmail team called me yet to tell me what's going on with Hotmail and why it's unreachable as I write this?).

12) Never change the URL of your weblog. I've done it once and I lost much of my readership and it took several months to build up the same reader patterns and trust.

13) If your life is in turmoil and/or you're unhappy, don't write. When I was going through my divorce, it affected my writing in subtle ways. Lately I've been feeling a lot better, and I notice my writing and readership quality has been going up too.

14) If you don't have the answers, say so. Not having the answers is human. But, get them and exceed expectations. If you say you'll know by tomorrow afternoon, make sure you know in the morning.

15) Never lie. You'll get caught and you'll lose credibility that you'll never get back.

16) Never hide information. Just like the space shuttle engineers, your information will get out and then you'll lose credibility.

17) If you have information that might get you in a lawsuit, see a lawyer before posting, but do it fast. Speed is key here. If it takes you two weeks to answer what's going on in the marketplace because you're scared of what your legal hit will be, then you're screwed anyway. Your competitors will figure it out and outmaneuver you.

18) Link to your competitors and say nice things about them. Remember, you're part of an industry and if the entire industry gets bigger, you'll probably win more than your fair share of business and you'll get bigger too. Be better than your competitors — people remember that. I remember sending lots of customers over to the camera shop that competed with me and many of those folks came back to me and said "I'd rather buy it from you, can you get me that?" Remember how Bill Gates got DOS? He sent IBM to get it from DRI Research. They weren't all that helpful, so IBM said, "Hey, why don't you get us an OS?"

19) BOGU. This means "Bend Over and Grease Up." I believe the term originated at Microsoft. It means that when a big fish comes over (like IBM or Bill Gates), you do whatever you have to do to keep him happy. Personally, I believe in BOGU'ing for EVERYONE, not just the big fish. You never know when the janitor will go to school, get an MBA, and start a company. I've seen it happen. Translation for weblog world: treat Gnome-Girl as good as you'd treat Dave Winer or Glenn Reynolds. You never know who'll get promoted. I've learned this lesson the hard way over the years.

20) Be the authority on your product/company. You should know more about your product than anyone else alive, if you're writing a weblog about it. If there's someone alive who knows more, you damn well better have links to them (and you should send some goodies to them to thank them for being such great advocates).

Any others? Disagree with any of these? Sorry my comments are down. Now Hotmail is down too. Grr. Where's the "Hotmail weblog" where I can read about what's going on at Hotmail? So, write about this and link to it from your weblog. I watch my referrer links like a hawk. Oh, is that #21? Yes it is. **Know who is talking about you**.

The tone of a blog written by several people isn't necessary less personal than one written by a single individual, but the overall effect is a collective one. Readers note that different authors have different styles, but think about the blog as a whole. Encouraging participation from these different personalities can be a very powerful technique for conveying the attitudes and styles of a company.

However, you should be careful not to dilute the overall effectiveness of the blog by flitting among too many disparate topics or allowing one personality to dominate. Fast Company, for example, has a history of sharing news articles and Web sites internally as information for its staff. The FC Now blog (`blog.fastcompany.com`) became the external version of that information exchange, and generates high-level discussion between staffers and readers. FC Now, shown in Figure 10-1, is created by multiple bloggers, and sometimes guest bloggers are added to the mix as well. Because each blogger focuses on business issues, the result is varied but still focused.

Figure 10-1: FC Now successfully combines the work of several bloggers.

Practice makes perfect

The best way to improve your blog-writing skills is, quite simply, to practice. Get into the habit of reading several blogs you admire, right when you start your day. As you blog, emulate the style of bloggers you think are using the medium well. When you find a blog entry you think really works, spend some time thinking about why it works.

Perhaps you admire the choices a blogger makes in what they blog about. Perhaps it's the writing style. If you consciously try to identify the factors that make the posting good, you have a better chance at incorporating those elements into your own writing style.

The blogging medium isn't designed for perfectionism. If you spend 20 minutes agonizing over the word choices in a single sentence, then you spend hours formulating a single blog posting. You won't post often, and it's likely that your readers, though they appreciate the quality of your posts, realize the blog isn't updated frequently and stay away.

There's another trap here as well. You will no doubt find yourself rereading your own postings and thinking of ways you could have done a better job with them. Resist the urge to go back in and edit old posts, unless you're making a factual correction. Even then, be sure to leave the original error and indicate the correction. Blog readers are hypersensitive to this kind of editing, and it's almost universally condemned, even when you're changing something simple and fairly inconsequential.

As a business blogger, you have an extra interest in maintaining blog entries as they're posted. Readers can easily assume the worst about why your posting has changed. They may assume you're being censored by corporate lawyers or that the company is changing its message on something. Leave your less-than-elegant postings alone, and work on improving future entries.

Generating Comments

Comments to postings are the way in which blogs allow readers to interact with the blog author or authors: They're buzz on your own blog! When you visit a blog, you often find a comment link underneath the text of a blog posting. Clicking that link lets you read others' comments and submit your own. Sometimes you find that a blogger posts comments to the blog when responding to someone else's comment.

Not all bloggers choose to implement comments, but if you're serious about developing a dialogue with your audience, you should strongly consider doing so. Comments are an easy way to involve your audience in a conversation and to get valuable feedback about what you're doing with your blog. Figure 10-2 shows comments posted to Paul Chaney's Radiant Marketing blog (www.radiantmarketing.biz).

If you do decide to allow comments on your blog, be sure to keep an eye on them. Spammers sometimes take advantage of inattentive bloggers to do a little "marketing" you may not want on your blog. In fact, if you're posting to other blogs to try to drive traffic to your site or your blog, you might be accused of spamming yourself!

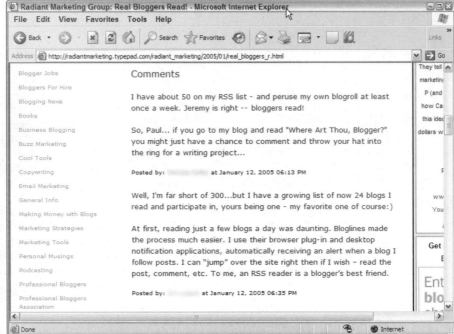

Figure 10-2:
Comments
are a great
way to take
the pulse
of your
readers.

Comments are vitally important to establishing a real dialogue with your customers, but just because you have the technology to offer them doesn't mean readers automatically use them. Especially when you're starting a blog, you may need to encourage your readers to post comments. After you have the blog up and running for a while, and readers start to comment, the commenting usually happens without your help — but most people are reluctant to do something without prompting.

Asking the right questions

To get comments started, you can try asking questions directly of your readers in your posts. Ask for something specific that your readers won't have to research or consider too long, but don't just ask simple yes-or-no questions. You need to get a few thoughtful, useful comments out of people.

Here are some examples of good questions to ask:

- ✔ What was your experience with this?
- ✔ Can anyone tell me more about this?

> ✔ What do you think our company should do about this?
> ✔ How did you solve this problem?

General or trivial questions will probably be greeted with silence — these, for example:

> ✔ What do you think?
> ✔ Do you agree?
> ✔ What's your favorite color?

Calling in a favor

Another way to get some comment dialogue started is to task people directly with reading and commenting on the blog. Look for industry experts, bloggers, and employees who are knowledgeable about your company and its services, and ask them to spend a week looking at the blog and posting comments. You're definitely calling in favor chips, but it may be worthwhile to get the ball rolling.

You don't necessarily want to trick people, but you don't really want to let the world know that these comments aren't "genuine" either. Make sure comments posted this way are on-topic and useful, and not just an exercise in getting a few words onto the page.

If you're feeling extra-cautious, you may even want to post a blog entry to explain that you've asked for some help in getting dialogue started by asking some colleagues to jump in when they find an area they can add to. You have everything to gain by being up-front with your audience rather than fooling them.

Even the appearance of impropriety can get you into trouble in the blogosphere, although it can also get you talked about. Take your pick!

Selecting a Blogger

A blogger is your company's Web interface with the public, someone who represents you to readers, conveys new information, makes amends for company mistakes, and generally makes the company more approachable and friendly. Also, keep in mind that a good blogger is someone who has the time to devote to maintaining the blog. In this section, I discuss how to go about finding a blogger that can get the job done right.

Finding the right characteristics

Your blogger may serve the role of ombudsman, translating customer needs to the company and rephrasing company positions for the public. Or your blogger might serve a more traditional marketing purpose by letting people know about upcoming events, changes in structure, new ventures, and so on. If your blogger manages this task with humor and flair, what is normally dry becomes a way to establish rapport. Try the following ideas to help you choose the right blogger for your company's blog:

✔ **Find a blogger your readers find intriguing.**

Choose a blogger who has the power to provide meaningful information and dialogue. For example, imagine how powerful it would be if your company's president or CEO gave personal attention to every one of your customers — new and existing. Of course, for a company of any size, that's impractical.

But if that person is writing a blog, suddenly the potential for establishing a personal relationship with individual customers is possible. If your company's CEO or president spent 20 to 30 minutes every day writing a blog that explained the company's newest venture, about having difficulty installing antivirus software, or even about buying a new puppy, that person couldn't help but seem more human to the blog's readers, and so would the company. If you can find a blogger that people genuinely want to know more about, whose style is so engaging that even mundane postings are interesting, you've created an enormously powerful tool for communication.

If you want to attract attention and discussion about your blog, hiring someone prominent or famous to blog for you — even for a short time — can definitely earn you eyeballs and recognition. If that person has something a little controversial to say, so much the better for generating buzz!

Mark Cuban, the owner of the Dallas Mavericks basketball team, keeps a blog (shown in Figure 10-3). Though he talks about the Mavs in it, he also discusses his other business ventures and opinions. What makes this blog exciting for fans, however, is the unprecedented access to a team owner's thoughts and opinions — and the ability to communicate with him through comments.

However, depending on what you're trying to achieve with the blog, the CEO might be a completely wrong choice as a blogger. (For more on formulating a goal for your blog, check out Chapter 3.) For instance, if your blog is concerned with keeping readers abreast of the minute detail of your new cellular phone network, the blogger should most likely be someone with real technical knowledge who can speak with authority and answer specific questions — say, a technician or engineer.

✔ **Consider using people who are already talking directly with customers as bloggers.** If the blog is designed to help people use your service (or just better understand it), you might be looking for someone who normally handles customer support or someone who is involved in the day-to-day maintenance of the system. In almost every case, you're looking for a blogger whose everyday job is "doing" rather than managing or communicating.

✔ **Think about asking multiple people to contribute to the blog.** Don't forget that in some cases, more than one blogger is a good idea. For example, Google's official blog (shown in Figure 10-4), intended to keeps its readers current on the "news, technology, and culture of Google," is created by several authors, including product managers, engineers, store managers, and even the VP of operations.

The Google Blog (at `www.google.com/googleblog`) is written very informally, though all its bloggers conform to normal grammar, punctuation, and spelling standards. The overall tone is light, sometimes even self-mocking, but always informative. Several different contributors allow Google to present several different voices and an overall picture of the Google attitude and culture — even while letting folks know about the newly redesigned Google Store.

✔ **Your blogger has to be a good writer!** Whoever you choose to be your blogger — maybe it's even you — you need to find someone who has knowledge but who can also write. The informal, friendly style of most blogs looks easy but can be very difficult, especially for people who are usually tasked with writing company memos and annual reports.

Figure 10-3:
Through the Blog Maverick blog, fans hear directly from Mavs owner Mark Cuban.

Google™ Blog

Insight into the news, technology, and culture of Google.

Get the latest word direct from the Googleplex about new technology, hot issues, and the wide world of search.

Thursday, December 09, 2004

Continuing the mission

Recently we relocated to Japan to take on the challenge of extending Google's global engineering organization by opening a new R&D center in Shibuya, Tokyo (co-located with the existing sales office). We've both been at Google for many years and hope to use our experience to transfer our culture and technical knowledge to a new place with a new group of engineers. It will be an exciting adventure. Just as no two snowflakes are exactly alike, over the years, we expect the Tokyo office will develop its own variation of Google's engineering culture.

Find on this site:

[   ] [Search]

Questions? Suggestions?

Let us know what you think!

Archives

Be sure to flip through Chapter 12 for important information on content, editing, and blog policies. And, in Chapter 3, you find some practical guidance for dealing with some common production issues.

Checking blogging availability

By far the most serious issue in finding someone in your company to write your blog is time. Blogging — at least, blogging well — is a time-consuming activity and not something you should add to an already-full workload — at least not lightly. Think hard before you ask an engineer tasked with meeting a product-launch deadline to add one more task to his list, especially one commonly perceived to be of little practical value. The fact is that even those of your staff who know what a blog is may not have the highest regard for it. Blogs have a reputation for being navel-gazing opportunities for teenagers, rather than serious business undertakings, and you may find your blog treated with similar disdain unless you can make a serious case for its importance. Even after you find someone who agrees with you and wants to write the blog, he or she may unconsciously put the blog at the bottom of the to-do list.

A good blog that attracts readers is one with frequent posts. If your company starts a blog, the blogger should spend some time working on it every day or at least every other day. The blogger should do the following:

✔ **Make a commitment to posting regularly.** It takes discipline for most of us to write, even conversationally.

✔ **Keep the blog in mind.** You may even want to carry a notebook where you can jot down reminders for topics you want to blog about later.

Update the blog on a regular schedule. You may be envisioning a blog that's updated on a regular schedule or is only updated once or twice a month. This can definitely work for some blogs; it just isn't very common.

✔ **Writing shorter is not easier.** Keeping ideas brief and to the point — without losing focus — is stressful. Using too many words rather than too few is often difficult.

If you're really having trouble finding someone with the time to blog, consider using multiple authors. If several people are tasked with contributing regularly, the workload for a single individual is lessened. Someone who simply refused outright to write your blog may be more than happy to contribute as part of a group effort.

Choosing your blogger

Here are some steps you can take to find a blogger that both wants to blog and who will do a good job:

1. Develop a list of expectations and requirements for your blogger — for example, number of posts, and frequency of posts.

2. Make a short list of people you think would be good bloggers. Show them the requirements, and ask if they are interested.

3. Publicize your requirements list, and ask employees to let you know if they are interested in blogging on behalf of the company — or who they think would make an interesting blogger.

4. Ask those who are seriously interested to write a series of sample posts or to blog for a week. Review those posts.

5. Choose your blogger(s) based on their demonstrated writing abilities, and your assessment of whether they can sustain the effort required over the long haul.

If you just can't find the right skill set internally, think about looking for outsiders who can blog for you. Later in this chapter, I talk about hiring freelancers or customers to blog for your business.

Extra pay

One way to make the blog a higher priority for the blogger is to offer extra pay for doing it. Putting a monetary value of this kind of contribution has the guaranteed result of letting people in your company know that you're serious about doing things right — and that the person doing the blogging is doing something valuable for the company.

If you choose to go this route, and I highly recommend that you do, establish some specific guidelines:

- What kind of and how much blogging do you expect this person to do?
- How often do you expect your blogger to post? There's a big different between twice a day and twice a week!
- Are you giving bonuses for posting more than is required?
- Do you expect the blogger to track and respond to comments?
- Do you expect the blogger to keep tabs on internal company happenings to find fodder for the blog?
- If you're using multiple authors, how are you compensating each blogger?
- What if one author produces more entries than the others?

Outsourcing

Some companies have found hiring someone to write the blog useful instead of searching for an internal writer. Doing so has some definite positives:

- Hire a professional writer or journalist, and you get someone with a fresh, curious eye, who knows how to ask questions. Sometimes long-time employees no longer recognize what makes the company really unique and special.
- Hiring outside means you don't have to add the blog to the workload of a current employee, nor must you worry about perceived favoritism within the office.
- Journalists are trained to write accessibly, on deadline, and to cover all the facts — a great recipe for a good blogger!
- Hiring a blogger who also serves as a company ombudsman sends a strong message about your company's willingness to converse openly.

> Readers won't have a perception that the newcomer is an engineer or customer service representative first and a conduit for dialogue second.
>
> ✔ If you're using the blog to heal a business *faux pas,* hiring an outsider to write the blog shows a willingness to be introspective and to change, and your blogger won't be defensive when trying to patch things up with the public.

Some bloggers started such compelling and well-written personal sites that they were then hired by news organizations and other businesses to blog professionally. On the other hand, a person who is an outsider to the company may lack familiarity with people and events, and may not understand the company culture well enough to convey it effectively.

Turning customers into bloggers

One key goal of buzz marketing is to find users of your product or service who can spread the message for you. Hiring an existing customer to be your blogger has some advantages:

✔ **Sometimes customers can be better advocates and experts on services that the company provides than the company can.** This concept is especially true in the technical world, where users of a software product may have better expertise than its engineers because they use the product on a daily basis.

✔ **You send a great message to your customer base.** "We pay attention to who is using our products — and reward them for it."

✔ **You get someone who doesn't have a huge vested interest in the success of the company but who is highly invested in the success of a product.** Who better to address consumer concerns than a consumer, after all?

Microsoft's most famous blogger, Robert Scoble, is a prominent example of this kind of recruiting. Scoble's personal blog was noticed by Microsoft, which then hired him to write the blog as a Microsoft employee. Today, Scoble is a technical evangelist for Microsoft, and the blog Scobleizer (shown in Figure 10-5) has almost singlehandedly decreased industry ire at the software giant. Microsoft doesn't edit Scoble's blog, nor should his postings be taken as official Microsoft positions. Still, Scoble's mix of technical expertise, simple information, kudos to competitors, well-timed criticism (yes, also of Microsoft), and the occasional personal post is a potent concoction read by fans and critics alike. You can read Scobleizer scoble.weblogs.com.

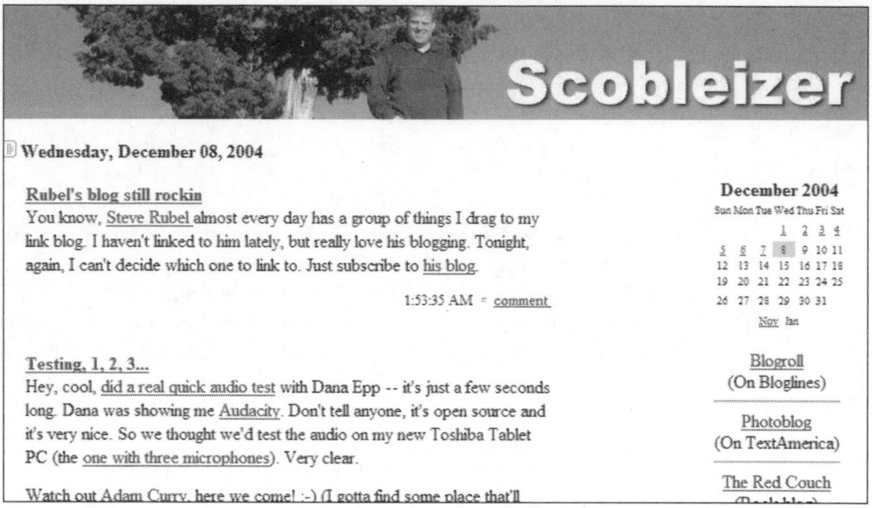

Figure 10-5:
Robert
Scoble,
Microsoft's
technical
evangelist,
writes
the blog
Scobleizer
mainly about
Microsoft's
activities.

If you go this route, you can't censor your blogger's style and opinions about your products. Remember that criticism is most likely based in knowledge — and respond accordingly.

Replacing a Blogger

Staffs change and so do companies; the day may come when your blogger departs for another job or retires. When that happens, you're faced with a crisis — and perhaps a new opportunity.

The biggest problem you should plan for is what to do with those readers whose interest in your blogger means they won't accept a replacement. If the blog has been successful, people know and respect the blogger. The solution: Give them something better.

Customers, as you may already know, are interested in value. Give them that, and they'll continue to appreciate what you're doing. Sure, you have customers who resist change — all those folks who write nostalgic letters about the very first version of your best-selling product — but most folks welcome change if it brings something new and useful to them.

When faced with replacing a blogger, spend some time strategizing. This time is perfect to

▶ Add a new feature

▶ Try a new technology

▶ Change the focus of a blog that was getting stale

If you do make changes, let your readers know what you're doing and why. Sell them the change. And make very sure your new blogger is up to the task.

A great thing to do when you're bringing someone new on board is to ask your readers themselves for feedback on what, if any, changes the blog should undergo during this transition period. They'll tell you what has gotten stale; what could be done better; and (of course) what they want kept just the same.

You might also want to consider the possible value of shutting down the blog, perhaps permanently, perhaps simply in order to launch another with a new focus. Blogs are fairly transitory things, and they tend to evolve over time. Let that natural process tell you whether your blog is in need of an overhaul. Unconsciously, your blogger may have even been bringing your readers to the point of accepting such a thing while contemplating his or her upcoming career move. More likely, however, you simply need to post an explanation and then respond to any comments generated by the closure.

Don't, however, take the blog off the Web — particularly if you created an information blog that people may be using as a resource. Although it takes up room on your Web server, your readers appreciate being able to look things up even after the blog becomes inactive.

Author and journalist Julian Dibbell made his last post to his blog Play Money in April 2004 but has left the site active as a record of the business venture he was chronicling. Play Money (`www.juliandibbell.com/playmoney`) tells the story of Dibbell's fascinations with Internet game Ultima Online, which has the dubious distinction of having a real-world economy as well. Players buy and sell Ultima Online game items on eBay, even going so far as to establish a currency market for Ultima gold pieces. Between December 2002 and April 2004, Dibbell tried to earn a living by selling Ultima Online real estate, weapons, and currency — all virtual items — for real dollars.

In his final entry, Dibbell recaps the adventure by reporting his IRS earnings and says farewell to his readers. In Figure 10-6, you can see part of Dibbell's final post.

Figure 10-6: "Play Money: Diary of a dubious proposition" is Julian Dibbell's now-inactive blog.

Chapter 11

Promoting Your Blog

*Y*ou may have spent a lot of time and some money getting your blog designed and setting it up, but attracting readers isn't a guaranteed outcome. Generating buzz about your blog doesn't have to be painful or cost you money, but it does require some effort.

Because blog promotion is often viral, done right it helps generate needed buzz for your site, bringing you readers, recognition, and maybe even press attention. Of course, you can get all those things for negative reasons as well, but no doubt your CEO won't appreciate critical buzz as much as positive.

Don't put the cart ahead of the horse. If you do a good job designing your blog, post often, and write well, chances are you hook readers and keep them, and your traffic numbers increase as your blog grows and earns links. The conversations occurring on your blog and on others can generate buzz about your company and products naturally. But if things are moving slowly, you can jump-start that growth.

Most of your potential readers won't come looking for you specifically. In fact, they may not even be aware that they need your blog until they find it. It's your job to help them find you. In this chapter, you discover how to attract and increase traffic to your blog.

Promoting a nearly empty blog makes no sense. Be sure that what you're promoting is valuable before you try the ideas I present in this chapter.

Using Technology Effectively

Sometimes getting traffic can be as much about technology as it is about content (but don't tell your blogger that!). I probably don't need to point out that sites that don't display correctly in the browser, contain broken links or nonfunctional tools, or that aren't reliably available don't get read or book-marked. Your technology sends a message about your competence just as much as the quality of your posts. This concept is especially true for a business blog, which can't look as amateurish as ones written by, well, amateurs.

You can use some technological tools to ensure your readers find you. Follow these suggestions:

✓ **Create an RSS/Atom feed.** Make sure you have an RSS and/or Atom feed available on your blog. Some blogging software generates these feeds automatically, or you may have to generate your own feed. I cover RSS in depth in Chapter 13.

✓ **Syndicate your site.** Make sure you're registered with Web sites that syndicate or aggregate blog content. These sites are clearinghouses for people and search engines looking for the latest blog postings, so letting them know when you post or registering your RSS feed with them can greatly increase your traffic.

Many blogging software solutions allow you to *ping,* or notify, blog index-ers automatically at the time that you publish your post, as shown in Figure 11-1. Those that don't may permit you to add HTML or JavaScript to your templates that do the pinging for you. For help, start with the support documentation of the blogging solution you are using. Then move on to `weblogs.com`, `blo.gs`, `blogrolling.com`, and `blogshares.com` for more information about registering your blog or adding ping technol-ogy to your blog.

✓ **Get help from your blogging software.** Some blogging software companies display a list of recently updated blogs that use their software somewhere on their Web site, often on the home page. If yours is one of these, check to see whether you are included automatically or if you need to request that your blog be displayed. Movable Type, for example, has a prominent list of recently updated blogs on the right side of its home page, as shown in Figure 11-2.

If you are using any third-party software plug-ins or tools, they too may have a recently updated list that you can take advantage of. In cases where you are using a popular blogging tool, the traffic to a Web site is probably substantial, and you may be able to benefit.

✓ **Add permalinks.** Sites that use permalinks generally get better traffic, thanks to better search engine indexing and site usability. *Permalinks* are pages that contain a single post, plus any comments associated with it. If you're using blog software that generates a permalink URL using text from the entry title rather than the date, you are even better off, because search engines use words contained in a URL as a way of assessing relevancy.

After you make a permalink for a blog item, don't ever change it. Links to your posts are a great source of traffic, and if you change where your posts live, you're cutting off that traffic. Always change permalinks as a very last resort.

Figure 11-1: Choose to ping indexing sites with Expression Engine.

Figure 11-2: Benefit from traffic by getting on a recently updated blog list.

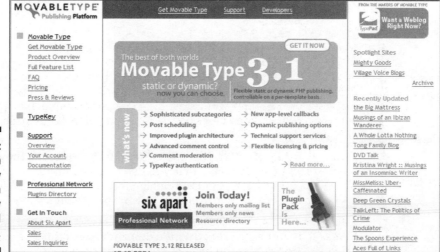

Promoting with Links

Links play a huge part in generating buzz for your site. Get mentioned in an influential blog, and your traffic zooms upward, as that blog's readers come to see what all the fuss is about. From there, these readers may create more buzz by posting on their own blogs, or sending an e-mail, or just talking about what they found at dinner that night. The most dramatic example of this is called the *Slashdot effect*: Getting mentioned in a post on the community Web site Slashdot (shown in Figure 11-3) often brings an unsuspecting server to its knees.

Recently, a novel product called TV-B-Gone picked up some buzz from blogs, and *Wired*'s Web site (www.wired.com) posted a story. The server couldn't handle the subsequent rush of visitors, and visitors were denied access to the site at its peak of popularity. You can have too much of a good thing!

The best way to get mentioned and linked to from another blog is, of course, to post great stuff on your blog. Some other techniques, which I discuss in the following sections, can also help you get and drive traffic.

Figure 11-3:
Sites
mentioned
on Slashdot
sometimes
get too
much traffic
to handle.

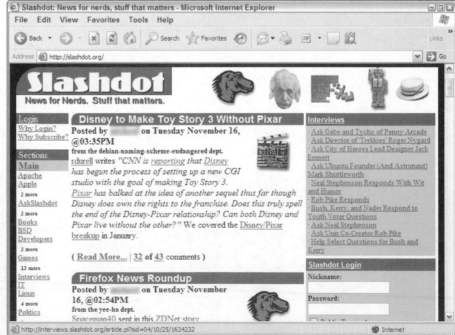

How Trackbacks work

The creators of the Movable Type blog software originally developed the Trackback technology and then opened it up for use by all blogging software. It was designed to be a user service, not a traffic exchange tool, by letting a reader interested in reading everything on a topic see what else was available online. You can get a feel for how this looks in action on WIL WHEATON dot NET, Wil Wheaton's blog is at www.wilwheaton.net and in the figure.

Trackbacks work like this:

1. You come across a great posting on a blog that your readers should see and that you can add a little more information to.

2. You write an entry on your blog and publish it. As it's published, your blog software sends a Trackback ping (notification) to the original post.

3. The blog software used by the blogger you linked to automatically picks up the information in your ping and adds a link back to you, including a summary of your posting.

Because some blog spammers have tried to use Trackback technology as a traffic-generation tool, some bloggers do not allow Trackbacks on their blogs.

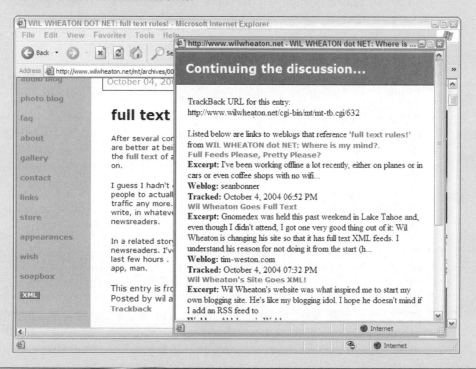

Linking to other blogs

Linking to other sites is useful for two reasons:

- ✔ You establish yourself as a hub for a certain niche, and if you provide people with good information, they come back to you to find more.

- ✔ You can get other people to return the favor and link back to you, thereby increasing your chances of getting buzz and eyeballs from blogs with good readerships.

Many top search engines count links to a site when determining where the site ought to show up in its relevancy rankings. If your blog shows up higher in search engine rankings . . . well, that's a good place to be.

Linking to other blogs from within relevant posts is both a reader service — assuming you are selective and discriminating with your linking — and an established behavior in the blogging world. These links should be to permalink pages — specific postings on that blog that are pertinent to your own posting.

Blog home pages change often, so don't link to another site's home page unless you're only discussing the blog in general terms.

Though you should choose links based on their value to your readers, writing about, and commenting on, postings from prominent, highly trafficked blogs doesn't hurt.

I cannot overstate the importance of adding something to your entry that furthers the dialogue begun in the posting you are linking to. All the content on your blog needs to be useful to your readers, even if you are partly motivated by getting a little more traffic to read that content. Other bloggers also quickly decide if you're contributing worthwhile diablog to the blogosphere, and being bland is far worse than being controversial. Yes, I said *diablog* — that's dialogue in the blogosphere, which has a character all its own.

Here's the word on how to diablog: After you create a link to a blog posting, you need to let the other blogger know that you've contributed to the ongoing conversation. The best, fastest, and simplest way to do this is the use of Trackback technology, which is sometimes available with blog hosting software (check your documentation). See the sidebar "How Trackbacks work" in this chapter for more information about Trackbacks. If you (or they) don't have Trackbacks enabled, you can do one of two things:

- ✔ Add a comment to the blog posting you are linking to. Indicate that you have more information on this topic on your blog, and then link to it.

- ✔ If comments aren't allowed, e-mail the blogger directly and let him or her know that you have more information on your blog — and provide the link. The blogger doesn't have to add the link to the blog (but may do so).

Don't employ *both* techniques. Bloggers pay attention to comments made on their sites (you do, don't you?), and an additional e-mail comes across as pestering rather than informing.

Creating a blogroll

A *blogroll,* or link list, to blogs you read or admire or simply find useful is both a reader service and a potential link exchange. The blogroll should be created for your readers, to show them where you get your information and what blogs you are reading. However, the blogs you link to may be inclined to return the favor by linking back to you from their blogroll. Because many people jump from blog to blog via blogrolls, you may get a few readers this way.

To create a blogroll, follow these steps:

1. **Make a list of the blogs you read most regularly or think highly of.**

2. **Use a blogroll creation tool (see more in Chapter 13) or HTML code to make your list clickable so that every blog is linked.**

3. **Use your blogging solution to add your blogroll list to a right- or left-hand column on your blog.** You may need to know some HTML in order to add this to your blog.

If you do create a blogroll, click each blogroll link yourself for two or three days. This will make you show up in the traffic log files of the blogs you link to and may get you noticed by the blogger. I talk more about how traffic logs work in Chapter 7.

Posting comments on other blogs

Commenting on a posting you find useful or interesting is a great way to increase the dialogue on a topic and gives you a chance to link to your own blog. Even if you don't add a post to your blog on the subject, most commenting systems allow you to enter a URL that is associated with your name when your comment is displayed. If you post a good comment by adding some additional information or politely challenging an opinion, readers of the comments may be interested enough in what you have to say to click the link.

Be careful not to create comment spam! Comments that don't add substantially to the conversation are useless to the blogger and to readers. Unless you have more to say than "I agree!" or "Nice site," resist the urge to comment.

Linking to your old content

Over time you will post a lot of great information, and much of it remains pertinent. If you write a post that expands on a topic you've posted about before, don't hesitate to link back to your original post or posts. By providing this reader service, you give your readers information they might have missed the first time around, and you keep them on your site instead of forcing them to find that information elsewhere.

Steering More Traffic to Your Blog

Still need more traffic? There are more things you can try, from advertising your blog to changing the way you post. In this section, I talk about some common-sense tactics that will get your blog out into the world, as well as some good editorial strategies for advancing your blog.

Making the most of marketing

Here are a few marketing and advertising tips you can use to promote your blog:

- **Get your own domain name.** If you haven't already done so, get a domain name specifically for your blog. An easy-to-remember, easy-to-spell domain name looks better in marketing materials and advertising — and it is easier for people to remember if they see it and can't immediately visit the blog.

- **Tell the world about your blog.** Tell everyone you come across about your blog. Add the URL to your e-mail signature file; put it on your business cards; make sure it's linked to every Web site your company maintains; and for goodness sake, make sure you promote the blog in your company's e-mail newsletters. If you have retail outlets, be sure that the URL is on your receipts and in any promotional material you create. You can create buzz yourself through these simple techniques.

  Don't stop there, either. You can use many traditional marketing techniques to increase awareness of your blog. Try printing up bumper stickers, pens, and other giveaways that tout your blog; hand them out to your customers, business partners, and the person who runs your child's day-care center.

  Some bloggers have added branded merchandise sales to their blogs, which increases brand visibility, sends a message, and makes a few dollars.

✔ **Advertise.** You can also advertise in newspapers, magazines, radio spots, Web sites, and (of course) other blogs. But you don't have to spend a massive advertising budget on your blog. If you choose your advertising space carefully, you can isolate your target audience or aim for the blogosphere at large. Reaching people when they're away from their computer can be less than efficient if you want them to visit you while they're online.

Some blog-specific advertising services can ensure that your advertising ends up on blogs, where it's seen by bloggers and their readers. I mention some blog-specific ad services in the "Advertising your blog" sidebar of this chapter.

✔ **Hold a physical gathering.** Bring your readers and blogger(s) together for an informal meal and discussion in a local coffee house or diner. The event can encourage readers to connect with each other, perhaps by having a focused topic for discussion. Your readers will appreciate the chance to meet you and each other, and of course, everyone likes free food.

You might also want to try hosting a pay-as-you-go event, where you negotiate a group rate at a venue and then ask people to buy their own tickets.

✔ **Enter contests.** You can enter your blog in a number of blog award contests. Clearly, these aren't for the brand-new blog! I recommend that you spend at least six months building up a solid archive of content and comments before you submit your site to this kind of scrutiny. Winning an award, however, definitely brings your blog prominence and a traffic boost — and possibly some press attention!

The most prominent of these award contests is the Bloggies, which is judged in January each year. Visit www.bloggies.com for information (see Figure 11-4) on the latest contest, categories, and nomination procedures, as well as past winners. For a list of other awards, see the "Blog award contests" sidebar.

Advertising your blog

Advertising specific to blogs is still in its infancy, but some early adopters are reporting great successes — both from the publisher's point of view and the advertiser's.

✔ **Blogads** (www.blogads.com): The Blogads service lets you advertise on an impressive number and range of blogs, including Instapundit, Eschaton, and Little Green Footballs. (Advertisers need not be blogs, but sites carrying ads must.) You can see some ads from Blogads on Instapundit.

✔ **Pheedo** (www.pheedo.com): Pheedo is an RSS advertising service. Sign up for an account, provide some keywords, and Pheedo places your creative element in appropriate blogs.

✔ **Textad Exchange** (kalsey.com/textad): As the name suggests, members of Textad Exchange place micro text ads on their blogs. Sign up for an account, and your blog is added to the pool.

Every January, intense campaigning and mudslinging rages among Web celebrities, Trekkies, and the citizens of Dallas. And they do it all for the Bloggie™.

The Bloggies™ are publicly-chosen awards given to weblog writers and those related to weblogs. 90 awards were presented over 2001, 2002, and 2003, and 30 more will be given out this year.

I'm Nikolai Nolan, and these are the...

fourth annual
weblog awards
the 2004 bloggies
2004.bloggies.com

the rules

Figure 11-4:
Find out which blogs took top honors.

Boosting your blog with better content

As you think about ways to generate buzz around your blog, you can also improve the quality of your blog by focusing on your posting techniques. These tips may give you some good promotion ideas:

- **Post about current or controversial issues.** This idea seems like a no-brainer, but it's an easy one to forget. Pay attention to the news, and watch for events and issues that are of interest to your readers. When you find one, create a post or series of posts around the subject. You might want to aggregate blog postings on the subject, sum up opinion articles, or even state your own opinion.

  Don't be afraid to be critical or controversial in what you say, as long as you can defend your opinion. Good blogs don't shy away from confrontation, although they don't create it purely for the sake of argument. Going out on a limb definitely causes people to comment more and probably also result in more links from other blogs to your postings.

- **Post in user groups and forums.** The Web is peppered with user groups, bulletin boards, and forums about all kinds of subjects. If you have set yourself up as an expert and have valuable information to contribute to a forum, you can drive traffic to your blog.

  Be very careful that you don't come off as a spammer or someone who is trying to sell a product or service. Your postings should be on topic and provide information, opinion, or clarification that contributes to the discussion. Let your knowledge sell the blog or your company for you. Don't try to be someone you're not — identify yourself as being associated with a company, because if anyone figures it out and you haven't been up-front, the backlash can overshadow your message, even if you didn't intend a deception.

✔ **Guest blogging.** Invite prominent bloggers, industry experts, and other influential people to guest edit your blog for a day or a week. You may have to provide some incentive to get them to help you out. Other bloggers, however, undoubtedly talk about their guest-blog gigs and bring traffic to the site. The real payoff is in the promotion you can do to bring readers in during that time.

If your blogger is well known, you may be able to offer an exchange: Your blogger for mine. This solution is also handy for those days when your blogger wants to take a vacation or is in some way unavailable to blog. Even an unknown guest blogger is preferable to having your blog go dark.

Be sure to talk with the guest about appropriate topics, writing style, and your expectations on the number of posts to be provided. If you plan to edit the guest blogger, state this up front as well.

✔ **Add photos to your posts.** Say it with images! A blog can be a text-heavy, boring-looking page, even if the writing is scintillating. The addition of photos, charts, and other graphics can add spice and interest to any blog entry — and readers respond well to blogs that use images.

Keep your images to a reasonable size, especially if you have pages that display several blog entries at once.

Blog award contests

The Weblog Awards recognizes blogs in all kinds of categories. Go to `www.bloggies.com`.

The Webby Awards has a blog category: `www.webbyawards.com/webbys/categories.php#webby_entry_blog`

Marketing Sherpa: `www.marketingsherpa.com/sample.cfm?contentID=2729`

Techweb tech blog contest: `www.techweb.com/blogawards/nominate.html`

The Guardian British Blog contest: `www.guardian.co.uk/online/weblogs/story/0,14024,1108883,00.html`

Best Canadian blogs: `www.blogscanada.ca/topblogs/`

Forbes review of the Best Blogs of 2004: `www.forbes.com/2003/04/14/bestblogslander.html`

CyberCatholics held a catholic blog award competition in 2004: `www.cybercatholics.com/stblogs/`

Koufax Awards recognized the best lefty blogs: `wampum.wabanaki.net/archives/000785.html`

Asking others to help

You can do a lot to promote your blog yourself, but don't forget that others will also have good ideas. Think about these techniques for getting employees and customers to talk about your blog:

- **Ask your employees to promote the blog.** Your employees have their own network of family, friends, customers, and business contacts that they can evangelize the blog to. Some may even have personal blogs they can use to promote the company blog, though that should be entirely their choice.

  If you followed my earlier suggestion to have stickers and other merchandise made up to advertise the blog, don't forget to make this material available to your employees, who could hand it out during meetings with clients and business contacts.

- **Ask your customers to promote the blog.** The essence of viral or buzz marketing is in getting others to spread the message on your behalf. What better group to serve that role than your own customers, many of whom may already be bloggers themselves? Satisfied customers are the greatest advocates and the best evangelists for your company you can find. In a manner similar to your employees, make advertising materials available for them to use as well.

  If you have stickers and other merchandise made up to advertise the blog or your company, consider providing some to these customer evangelists to hand out to family members, friends, and colleagues.

- **Ask for ideas!** Other bloggers, your employees, your business contacts, your friends, and — of course — your readers may have some great ideas for promoting the blog. Get them to tell you what they are and then implement them!

Chapter 12

Staying on the Right Side of the Law

As with any communication format, blogging comes with a set of legal issues and worries that many businesses have concerns over. You may be worried that your customers may read promises and guarantees into the text of an informal blog posting or even that a reader may post a libelous comment to your blog.

These are real possibilities but probably less likely to become issues than you think. In most cases, you can easily address these issues — often in advance — by developing a blogging policy and then sticking to it.

Of greater concern to employers are the personal blogs of employees. Few formal employee blog policies are in place, but the part of the blogosphere concerned with business blogging is full of discussion about the need for them.

In this chapter, you find out how to protect your blog and your company from potential legal and public perception problems. In addition, I talk about the pros and cons of developing an employee blogging policy and what such a policy might contain.

Maneuvering Legal Potholes

Companies usually communicate with customers through restricted means: press releases, customer service scripts, and technical support issues. Companies have been conducting this kind of communication for a long time, and both customers and businesses know what to expect from the formats. Becoming an online publisher may mean some new risks for you. Specifically, you can run into trouble by:

- ✔ **Violating copyright:** Make sure you have permission or the right to everything you publish, from text to images to video. If in doubt, assume it's copyrighted and ask permission before using it.

  New online publishers should be especially aware that content created by freelancers or others in the past may not be legal to use online. If your contract with a freelancer only bought you print reproduction rights, for example, you can't use that content online.

- ✔ **Contradicting existing legal documents:** If your company has issues warranties, service agreements, or other such binding documents, make sure you don't inadvertently undermine those documents.

- ✔ **Publishing libel:** The federal Telecommunications Act of 1996 protects online publishers from being held liable for the comments of others on bulletin boards, blogs, and forums. However, there have been some challenges to this act, which means that although you may ultimately be found not responsible for libelous comments, you might still have to defend yourself in a court.

- ✔ **False advertising:** While answering questions or discussing your services or products, be careful that you don't make statements that could be perceived as guarantees or promises.

Because blogs open up a fresh channel for communication in what is essentially uncharted territory, factual errors are easy to make, even while blogs accelerate acquisition of feedback and facilitate interaction. That's worrisome, but it shouldn't be the kind of stumbling block that stops you before you start blogging. These worries should make you cautious, not frightened! In this section, you find out the best way to deal with what you say on your blog before you say it.

Creating a Corporate Blogging Policy

The best defense is a good offense, so the saying goes. Having a blog policy that your readers can refer to can help you deal with promises, corrections, and other messy situations when they do occur.

Think of this policy as your set of operating guidelines, a way to let your readers know the standards to which you're holding yourself and what they can expect from you in terms of reliability and honesty. Knowing just how you handle certain situations may even prevent you from getting into awkward positions to begin with.

Here are some statements you might want to include in your blogging policy:

- ✔ I will be accurate. When I make a mistake, I will correct it as quickly as I can.

- ✔ Corrections will not be edited — I will leave mistakes visible unless they cause harm.

- ✔ I will post only on the following topics: [insert your blog's topics here].

- ✔ You may/may not post comments to this blog.

- ✔ Your comments will/will not be moderated before they are made visible.

- ✔ Your comments will/will not be edited.

- ✔ Comments that contain obscenity, libel, and suspected spam content will be deleted.

- ✔ I will/will not delete criticism of our products, services, and practices.

- ✔ When appropriate, I will link to other Web sites and blogs. I am not responsible for the opinions and content of those sites.

- ✔ I will respond to e-mails and comments quickly.

- ✔ The statements in this blog do not represent any guarantees or override existing product/service warranties, manuals, or user agreements.

Creating a blog policy that contains statements like these may not be necessary, depending on the topic, purpose, and tenor of your blog. In other cases, you may want to develop such a policy as a guideline for your blogger, without making it a public policy.

You can't go wrong, however, in at least thinking through these issues, or in developing strategies for dealing with common blog problems, such as mistakes, corrections, and comment spam.

There is some legal thinking about online publishing that suggest promising to vet comments and delete those that are libelous or obscene makes you liable should any slip through. You may want to consult your legal counsel about the best way to handle comments without incurring liability, but keep in mind that for most business blogs, comments that cross the line will be rare.

Handling mistakes in your business blog

Even at companies where a blogger is edited before entries are posted, the resulting text is very informal and unstructured. It is this very informality that makes the medium so appealing to readers, who feel — rightly — that they are being given new and better access to information. Inevitably, however, this informality leads to mistakes. Some are large, some small, but readers notice most, and you have to acknowledge and correct them. The trick to handling these slips gracefully is to have a plan in place to deal with them when they happen.

Of course, doing your best to prevent mistakes is also a great idea! There are some simple ways to take precautions:

✔ **Use a spell checker.** You can't prevent factual errors, but a spell checker keeps you from making spelling slips. Ultimately, don't forget that spell checkers aren't infallible: "its" and "it's" are both spelled right, but they aren't used the same way!

✔ **Hire an editor.** No matter who is doing the blogging in your company, having another pair of eyes look over copy doesn't hurt before it goes live on the blog. Newspapers have used copy editors for years to ensure that common spelling, grammar, and even factual mistakes don't make it into print (though copy editors aren't infallible, either). Depending on the level of knowledge this person has about your company, he may be able to ask questions and make points that actually add value to the blog postings as well. Once the mistake is made and noticed, you need to make a correction. The blog format is peculiar, and your readers have certain expectations that mean you shouldn't just go in and change the offending information (though technology makes that extremely simple). When you make corrections to a blog, letting your readers know that you've changed something is considered good practice.

The best way to handle these situations is to go back into the posting and, at the bottom, add the text of the new information or fix and clearly label it as an update or a correction. Some bloggers, like Andrew Baio, go so far as to apply strikethrough text to the error as well, to clue readers in that he's made a change. You can see a correction made to his blog (at `www.waxy.org`) in Figure 12-1.

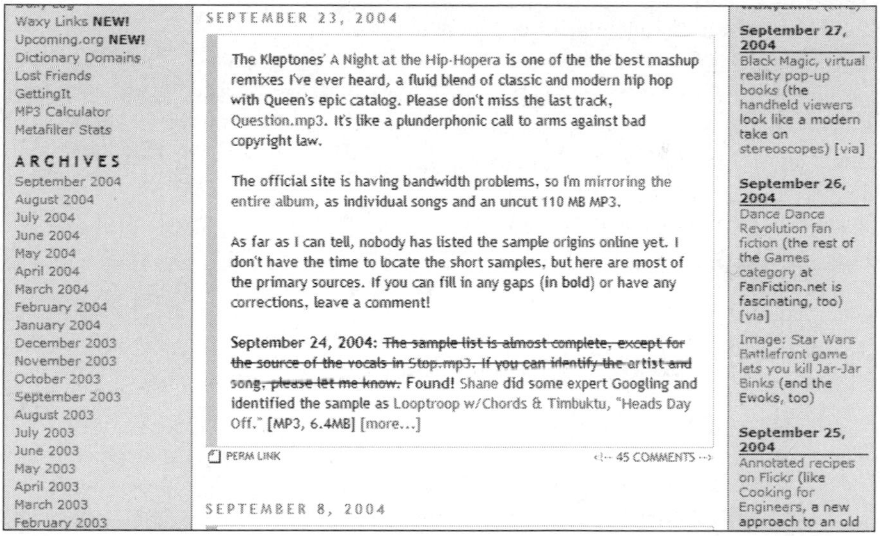

Figure 12-1:
At Waxy.org, Andrew Baio indicates updates and corrections by striking through the original text and then making his change.

If the correction warrants it, consider adding an entirely new posting to your blog. A new post is handy when you need to do some explaining, rather than simply correcting a date or name. Don't forget to go back to the first entry and link to the correction, though!

And, by all means, don't forget to apologize when you really put your foot in it! If you come right out and acknowledge the mistake and put together a graceful note of apology, you immediately diffuse any tension, anger, and ill will engendered by the mistake. If it's worth a correction, it's almost definitely worth a sincere "I'm sorry."

Sometimes, however, you have no choice but to remove text from a posting: If an entry on your blog contains a libelous or damaging — as opposed to just incorrect — statement, take it out immediately. Do include a note about the editing that was done and why, so that your readers understand why the edit was necessary.

Establishing trust

I can sum up nearly every issue you may have to deal with in this way: Your company needs to be able to trust the person authoring its blog.

The reverse also needs to be true: If the blogger doesn't feel that the company backs them up when necessary, he or she doesn't have the freedom necessary to make the blog really sing.

The blogger, whether a customer service person, engineer, or ombudsman, needs to know and understand the culture of the company he or she is working for. Without such an understanding,

the blogger is more likely to make mistakes, reveal secret information, or even jump the gun when deleting critical comments. A blogger who doesn't understand the goals of the blog or the culture of the company can't effectively establish real rapport with the company's customers either.

Trust is, without doubt, the biggest key to making a blog work for your company. No matter how many policies and guidelines you establish, finding the right blogger is the glue that holds it all together.

Making promises

If you make promises on your blog, keep them. These may be small: "I'll ask the tech folks and get back to you," and they may be large: "We'll have that fixed by the time the product hits the shelves." Either way, the blog is such a public forum that your statements can be tracked down, followed up. If you don't keep the promises you make — especially if you're addressing issues about your blog — it can make for some ugly public attention.

That said, not all promises can be kept, in which case you should get online and explain why. Your users appreciate it and respect you more for being open and honest, even if you haven't taken care of whatever the issue might be.

You should also be careful to make clear that whatever is said on the blog doesn't take precedence over other communication from your company, especially that contained in warranties, manuals, service agreements, and so on. The corollary to that, of course, is not to use the blog to make changes in those documents, though you may announce changes and then link to the documents themselves.

Be clear up front about the role your blog plays in your official publications; doing so will help you avoid accusations of false advertising and broken promises. A lawsuit is unlikely but is made less so by posting a disclaimer on the blog that lets readers know just how to judge what they are reading.

Keeping secrets during quiet periods

Depending on the size and nature of your company, you may have to observe a legally mandated quiet period or keep information confidential until a release date. Be sure that you understand what kinds of communication fall into these categories so that you don't accidentally talk about things you shouldn't. When in doubt, choose to err on the side of silence. This concept is especially true of public companies that may be sanctioned by organizations, such as the Securities and Exchange Commission, at certain times.

It goes without saying, of course, that trade secrets and the like should also not be fodder for blog postings. Again, be careful to fully understand just what kinds of information fall into confidential classifications. During a robust conversation, you may be tempted to explain exactly why your product is better than the competition's, in more detail than is usually used in marketing and advertising copy, but don't hand them the secret formula for Coke when you do so.

As well, clients and partners with whom you have business relationships may consider certain information about those relationships to be confidential — sometimes even the existence of the relationship needs to be secret for some period.

You may likely never run afoul of this kind of situation. After all, most employees know what information needs to stay internal to the company and what can be discussed over dinner, and your blog may not even veer into these areas at all. Nonetheless, thinking ahead about what topics you can and can't discuss in the blog pays dividends. When in doubt, consult the company lawyer — or just refrain from posting about the questionable material.

Comment crud

Your blog postings may be squeaky clean, accurate, spell-checked and chock-full of useful information, but that doesn't mean that you are entirely taken care of. Comments, those wonderful interactions that make blogs such a dynamic environment, are an ongoing trouble spot.

For starters, if you blog, you are without question subject to what's called *comment spam*. Comment spam happens when commercial messages, usually for rather unsavory products, are placed in your comments. The message can consist of some advertising copy or a seemingly innocuous line of text, but the links provided send readers somewhere they probably don't want to be. The most common types of comment spam are porn Web sites, pharmaceutical products, online gaming, and unbelievable weight-loss opportunities. You can see how comment spam looks on my personal blog in Figure 12-2.

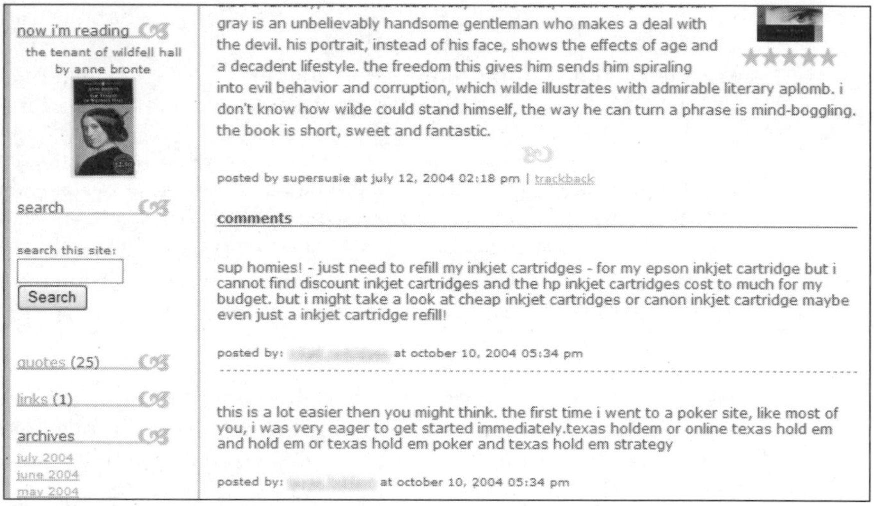

now i'm reading

the tenant of wildfell hall
by anne bronte

gray is an unbelievably handsome gentleman who makes a deal with the devil. his portrait, instead of his face, shows the effects of age and a decadent lifestyle. the freedom this gives him sends him spiraling into evil behavior and corruption, which wilde illustrates with admirable literary aplomb. i don't know how wilde could stand himself, the way he can turn a phrase is mind-boggling. the book is short, sweet and fantastic.

posted by supersusie at july 12, 2004 02:18 pm | trackback

Figure 12-2:
These comments regarding inkjet cartridges and online poker are off topic and inappropriate.

search

search this site:

[Search]

quotes (25)

links (1)

archives
july 2004
june 2004
may 2004

comments

sup homies! - just need to refill my inkjet cartridges - for my epson inkjet cartridge but i cannot find discount inkjet cartridges and the hp inkjet cartridges cost to much for my budget. but i might take a look at cheap inkjet cartridges or canon inkjet cartridge maybe even just a inkjet cartridge refill!

posted by: at october 10, 2004 05:34 pm

this is a lot easier then you might think. the first time i went to a poker site, like most of you, i was very eager to get started immediately.texas holdem or online texas hold em and hold em or texas hold em poker and texas hold em strategy

posted by: at october 10, 2004 05:34 pm

This kind of posting, besides being off topic and distasteful, is probably something that your company shouldn't be associated with. The questionable legality of some online gaming, for example, means that you probably don't ever want to let messages about poker games stick around on your site. Making a good-faith effort to remove such messages should take care of any suggestion that you endorse — or simply don't mind — such activity. There is no current legislation that suggests you are liable for such spam commentary on your blog, but as a responsible publisher it's your job to get rid of it.

I don't mean to sound alarmist — most of your comment dialogue will be valid, fruitful, and useful. You just need to do some policing to make sure it stays that way.

Blogging software that permits comments nearly always permits comment editing, which means that you can delete comment spam when it shows up. Some of the independent blogging software packages include plug-ins and functionality meant to deal directly with comment spam by notifying you when it occurs and letting you prevent future postings that include the offending URL. It's not a perfect solution and requires that you remain vigilant. Because you should be reading all the comments that come into your blog anyway, you can delete spam easily.

Trolls

Other kinds of comments can be termed *spam* — incendiary posts from users meant to stir up trouble rather than dialogue. Such comments are said to be posted by blog *trolls,* and nearly every prominent blogger gets the attention of a few.

Trolls are harder to detect and harder to prevent as well. And not everyone agrees on who qualifies as a troll and who is just raising challenging issues. Offensively phrased dialogue might not be what you are aiming for with your blog, but as long as the comment doesn't include personal insults and off-topic rants, you probably want to leave it alone. As soon as things devolve into name-calling, however, you can safely decide the troll's time on your blog is done. This is true for potentially libelous or damaging statements as well — get rid of them, and get rid of (that is, deny access to) the person who posted them.

Again, most blog software that allows comments also allows you to ban certain users — by e-mail address, and sometimes by IP address. This isn't a fail-safe technique, because obtaining a new e-mail address is hardly a complicated or expensive proposition, but it's your only weapon in this fight.

While your own comments are considered part of the blog's history and should therefore remain in as close a state to the original posting as possible, retaining comments has no such necessity. If you think a comment is offensive, off topic, or spam, delete it with impunity. Do consider coming up with some standard way of judging when a comment falls into one of those categories, however.

Exploring Employee Blogs

When the company has a blog, many employees want to join the party. In fact, some of your employees may already have personal blogs that they post to regularly.

Spend much time in the blogosphere, and you come across bloggers who lost their jobs because of postings to blogs that employers objected to. The quantity of discussion would lead you to believe this happens all the time, but I suspect that the medium simply finds the topic fascinating and that it isn't all that common. Nonetheless, it is true that employees have posted criticism, photographs, and company information on their blogs and then lost their jobs over it. There's no positive aspect to this completely preventable issue: The company loses a valuable employee, and the employee loses a job.

Having said that, no company has actually been sued for content appearing on an employee Web log. Free speech protects the rights of employees to have blogs at all and most of what they post on that blog — but that doesn't mean the company's hands are tied. Consider these situations:

- ✔ Michael Hanscom, then a contract employee of the Microsoft print shop, came across a truck loaded with Apple G5 computers in a company delivery bay, took a photo, and posted it to his blog along with some text, as shown in Figure 12-3. Microsoft objected for security reasons, and Hanscom lost his job over the photo.

- ✔ Joyce Park, then a Web developer working for the social network Friendster, was fired in August 2004 for posting about the company on her personal blog, Troutgirl.

Figure 12-3: Michael Hanscom posted this photo from a Microsoft delivery dock on his blog and lost his job.

Significantly for both bloggers, they both attempted to do the right thing. Hanscom deliberately shot the photo to exclude a view of the building the loading bay was in, and Park claims to have said nothing that wasn't already publicly available. Both companies took a great deal of flack from the blogosphere over the firings, right or wrong, and coverage was extensive in the media as well.

A company blogging policy could have helped prevent both situations or at least provided a set of guidelines under which the personnel actions could have been governed. But no policy can protect you completely.

Microsoft itself has upward of 1,000 bloggers right now, many of whom are blogging about Microsoft technology issues. Take a look at the incredible volume of information being generated by these bloggers at `blogs.msdn.com`. Microsoft has not (yet) formalized a blogging policy, and except in Hanscom's situation, the hands-off approach appears to be working for the company.

Establishing employee blog policies

Even the most velvet-gloved blogging policy means that employers are asking employees to rein in their free speech somewhat during nonwork time and activities.

Many employers are leery of stepping on the free-speech rights of their employees but are also worried about what might be made accessible to other employees, critics, customers, clients, and the press.

Not every company is impacted by public opinion if its employees blog, and in fact many companies so respect their employees' right to free speech that this won't be an issue. But if you're concerned, you can prevent a lot of attention by simply asking your employees to leave identifying business information off their personal blogs. Others have asked employees not to post about company issues and staff.

Businesses with an interest in capitalizing on some of the expertise and personality being displayed by their employees have asked that their employee bloggers note that their opinions are not those of their employers. This disclaimer certainly seems to be the most open, least limiting option available to employers. Figure 12-4 shows an example of this kind of disclaimer on Robert Scoble's blog (`scoble.weblogs.com`).

Some lawyers have suggested, however, that having a blogging policy at all implies a certain level of responsibility for what your employees post on their blogs.

The very best safeguard you can put into place is a mechanism for bloggers to ask questions about what they can and cannot blog about without crossing the line. This person must be available quickly — because blogging is such an immediate medium — and he or she must keep an open mind about advising bloggers. If the knee-jerk response is always "No, don't post that," you are more likely to alienate your employees than help them. As well, this person should be someone who speaks from a position of knowledge, both about the company and about human-resources issues. After all, if you put a person in place to deal with blogging questions and then don't back up his or her calls, you effectively do more harm than good.

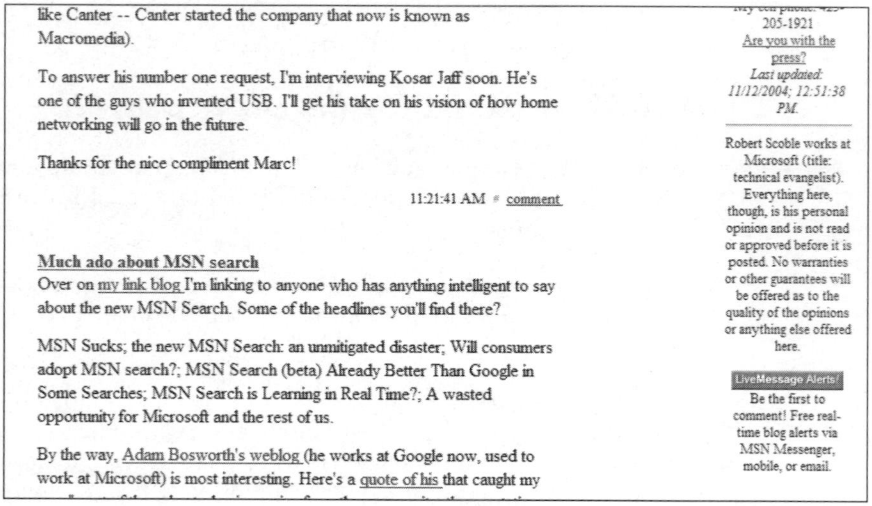

Figure 12-4:
Robert Scoble blogs as Microsoft's technical evangelist but still puts a disclaimer on his blog indicating that he doesn't speak for the company.

Looking at a sample policy

Many companies have embraced employee blogs, even including links to them on the company Web site. Published blogging policies, however, are few and far between. This is due in part to the fact that there aren't many formal business blogs and because many of those that do exist are in smaller organizations that don't need to create such a formal structure. If you're thinking of writing a blogging policy that addresses employee blogs, however, you would do well to look at that of Groove Networks, a privately held software company.

The CEO of Groove Networks, Ray Ozzie, maintains his own Weblog, and there are others at Groove. As you might expect, commitment to blogging at such a high level translates into a policy that reads more like a list of suggestions than a legal document. His company's blogging policy is reprinted here as a sidebar, courtesy of Groove Networks (www.groove.net).

Personal website and weblog guidelines

Some employees who maintain personal websites or weblogs, or who are considering beginning one, have asked about the company's perspective regarding them. In general, the company views personal websites and weblogs positively, and it respects the right of employees to use them as a medium of self-expression.

If you choose to identify yourself as a company employee or to discuss matters related to the company's technology or business on your website or weblog, please bear in mind that, although you and we view your website or weblog as a personal project and a medium of personal expression, some readers may nonetheless view you as a de facto spokesperson for the company. In light of this possibility, we ask that you observe the following guidelines:

- Please make it clear to your readers that the views you express are yours alone and that they do not necessarily reflect the views of the company. To help reduce the potential for confusion, we would appreciate it if you put the following notice — or something similar — in a reasonably prominent place on your site (e.g., at the bottom of your "about me" page):

    The views expressed on this website/weblog are mine alone and do not necessarily reflect the views of my employer.

    If you do put a notice on your site, you needn't put it on every page, but please use reasonable efforts to draw attention to it — if at all possible, from the home page of your site.

- Take care not to disclose any information that is confidential or proprietary to the company or to any third party that has disclosed information to us. Consult the company's confidentiality policy for guidance about what constitutes confidential information.

- Please remember that your employment documents give the company certain rights with respect to concepts and developments you produce that are related to the company's business. Please consult your manager if you have questions about the appropriateness of publishing such concepts or developments related to the company's business on your site.

- Since your site is a public space, we hope you will be as respectful to the company, our employees, our customers, our partners and affiliates, and others (including our competitors) as the company itself endeavors to be.

- You may provide a link from your site to the company's website, if you wish. The web design group has created a graphic for links to the company's site, which you may use for this purpose during the term of your employment (subject to discontinuation in the company's discretion). Contact a member of the web design group for details. Please do not use other company trademarks on your site or reproduce company material without first obtaining permission.

Finally, please be aware that the company may request that you temporarily confine your website or weblog commentary to topics unrelated to the company (or, in rare cases, that you temporarily suspend your website or weblog activity altogether) if it believes this is necessary or advisable to ensure compliance with securities regulations or other laws.

If you have any questions about these guidelines or any matter related to your site that these guidelines do not address, please direct them to the company's Vice President of Communications or its General Counsel, as appropriate.

Part V

Making the Most of Your Blog

The 5th Wave   By Rich Tennant

"We weren't getting the traffic we'd hoped for on our blog, so we're adjusting the servers feng shui and adding a chant into our SEO."

In this part . . .

You started your blog for business reasons, so make it work for you — even while you work to make it better. Better technology and innovative business practices let you do your job better — and bring customers to your blog. In Chapter 13, you take advantage of some exciting blog technologies with funny names. Some blogs even bring in revenue, and I talk about how that's done in Chapter 14. You can turn your readers into consumers and their Web sites into free advertising for your company. Best of all, you can use your blog to conduct your everyday business better by collaborating on projects; find out how in Chapter 15.

Chapter 13

Adding Value to a Blog

One of the things I find most exciting about the blog format is the technological innovation occurring each day. This chapter is devoted to the many exciting and fun tools available for blogs and bloggers.

You don't need to use all of them — in fact, many simply may not be suitable for what you're trying to accomplish — but selecting one or two can really increase the functionality and usefulness of your blog. And they may just keep people reading the blog to see what you do next!

Many blog options actually fall into the category of blog must-haves. A number of tools, such as RSS and surveys, can be invaluable for you and for your readers. Others, such as mapping and *audblogging* (audio blogging), can easily become gimmicks if you don't deploy them properly.

I recommend reading this chapter with an open mind. Think creatively about ways you can do something new to generate excitement about your blog.

Adding Must-Have Technologies

Perhaps the single most important and useful tool available for use on your blog today is *RSS,* or *Really Simple Syndication.* This technology has almost no downside: It's simple and inexpensive to implement, free to use, and virtually guaranteed to increase readership and traffic.

A second critical tool is commenting. Used correctly, comments can also get people to come back to your site frequently and help to generate buzz in the blogosphere and beyond. They can also get you valuable information about your readers that you can parlay into a better blog or better customer relationships.

If your blog software doesn't allow you to permit reader comments, you can still implement them using third-party software. Comments are a defining characteristic of blogs; only the most popular bloggers can get away with not having them, so you need to add this functionality to your blog.

Finally, your readers come to you for information, and one great way you can make your blog more useful is to provide a sidebar of pertinent headlines. Being a clearinghouse for information is one of the strong suits of a blog, and headlines can augment that. (Don't be afraid that people leave your blog to read the stories you feature — they'll be back for more if your blog does a good job.)

What is an RSS feed?

One of your biggest challenges after you start a blog is to generate buzz about it and then not only bring visitors to it, but get them to come back. RSS helps you do both. With RSS, you can actually syndicate your content quickly, easily, and cheaply.

So what's RSS? An *RSS feed* is a XML-based file that contains summaries or the full text of each entry posted on your blog. Another format for updates of this kind is called *Atom.* I say more about this format later in this chapter, but for now, if you see *Atom,* just think *RSS.* RSS and Atom feeds get syndicated in these ways:

- ✔ Picked up by Web sites that syndicate blog content
- ✔ Pulled in by other Weblogs or other Web sites
- ✔ Displayed by newsreader software

In each case, blog content is disseminated around the Internet, increasing the chances that people find and read your blog postings. The advantage to you in providing an RSS feed is that there are more ways that people can find your content, and they are likely to keep reading you over time.

RSS is a technology that pushes your new posts out to other Web sites and to newsreader software automatically, instead of your readers having to remember to come visit you every few hours or days to see if you've got something new.

RSS may also stand for *Rich Site Summary* or *RDF Site Summary.* (RDF is the acronym for *Resource Description Framework.*) Amy Gahran held a contest to come up with a less intimidating name on her blog in early 2004, and the winning entry was *webfeeds,* which seems to be gaining at least some traction. Read more about the contest at blog.contentious.com/archives/2004/04/30/winning-rss-nickname-webfeed.

You need to use RSS as a consumer and a publisher. The following three ingredients explain how it works:

- ✔ A blog automatically generates an RSS feed.
- ✔ Readers of the blog find the RSS feed on the blog or through an RSS syndication site.
- ✔ Readers use a newsreader (or Web site) to display and read the RSS feed.

Reading RSS feeds: The consumption of RSS

As a blog publisher, you no doubt want to create RSS feeds as a user service. But before you get to that point, get acquainted with them as a user.

To figure out how RSS feeds work for yourself, create a collection of RSS feeds that you want to check regularly. As you start your own blog, you benefit hugely from watching what others are doing, even those who aren't writing blogs pertinent to your field or who are keeping successful personal blogs.

RSS helps you gather updates quickly and efficiently. You'll love how much time you save when you're not trying to visit every blog in your bookmark list several times a day. You can use an online newsreader, which works well if you have a constant Internet connection. Or you can install newsreader software that downloads feeds to your computer so that you can read them even if you aren't online.

The easiest way to get started reading RSS feeds is visit to Bloglines. Bloglines is a free Web site that aggregates RSS feeds from blogs all over the Web and allows you to subscribe to and read those that interest you. To get started reading RSS feeds, begin by registering for a free Bloglines account:

1. **Go to** www.Bloglines.com, **and click the Click Here to Sign Up link in the center of the page or the Register link at the top right of the page.**

2. **Provide your e-mail address, select a password, choose your time zone and language preferences, and decide whether you want to receive the Bloglines newsletter.**

3. **Click Register.**

   Bloglines sends you a confirmation e-mail; reply to finalize your registration.

To see which blogs have an RSS feed, watch for an orange button that says XML or RSS on it. The Strong Women Daily News blog, shown in Figure 13-1, includes an RSS feed. Stonyfield Farm, a dairy in Franklin, Vermont, created this blog, and it is one of a series designed to keep interested customers current and informed. Stonyfield Farm has several blogs at www.stonyfield.com.

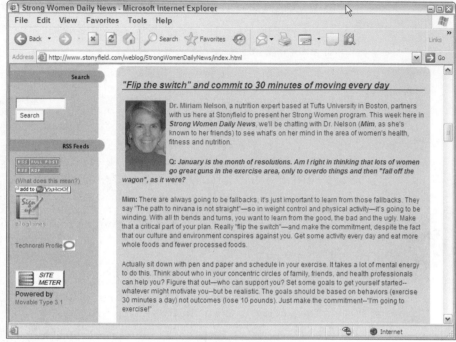

Figure 13-1:
Stonyfield's
Strong
Women
Daily News
provides
RSS feeds
for its
readers.

As you look at the Strong Women Daily News figure, notice the two small RSS badges on the right-hand side of the page. Follow these directions to subscribe to the Strong Women Daily News using one of these badges:

To subscribe to Stonyfield's feed, copy the location of the feed by right-clicking the RSS link and choosing Copy Shortcut or Copy Link Location from the menu. (The wording varies depending on what browser you use.) Then, head back to Bloglines and use the process above to add that feed to your list.

1. **Click the badge labeled "RSS Full Post" and copy the URL from the address bar of the browser.**

   Don't worry if you see what looks like computer code in the browser; you're only interested in the URL.

2. **Go to Bloglines and log in.**

   You are taken to your current feeds or to a page that allows you to sub-scribe to one, if you have no current subscriptions.

3. **Click the Add link in the right-hand area of the page.**

   If you can already see a Subscribe page visible, there is no need to click Add.

   A page appears that lets you add a new feed to your Bloglines account.

4. **Paste the URL of the RSS feed into the Blog or Feed URL box and click the Subscribe button, as shown in Figure 13-2.**

   You are given the chance to organize your feeds by putting them into folders.

5. **Choose to create a folder for this feed and set other preferences, or just complete the subscription by clicking the Subscribe button.**

   Bloglines adds the feed to the right-hand column.

6. **Select the name of the feed to see the blog's postings in descending order on the right side of the page.**

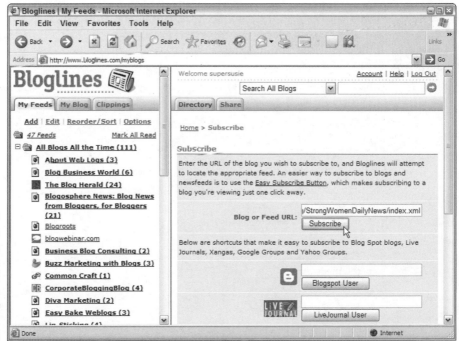

Figure 13-2:
Paste the URL of the RSS feed you want to read into Bloglines.

You can also add feeds by selecting them from the Bloglines directory, which is on the Directory tab, as shown in Figure 13-3. You can use the preset categories — Most Popular Feeds, Most Popular Links, Newest Feeds — to look up a feed alphabetically or do a search to find available feeds.

Selecting blogs to read from the Most Popular Feeds list is a great way to get started — these feeds are some of the most widely read, popular, and successful blogs, and reading some from this category can bring you up to speed on RSS and the blogosphere at the same time.

Even if you can't spot an orange RSS badge on a site you want to track, try subscribing to the site's home page URL anyway. It may be that the blog doesn't advertise RSS but still has a feed.

After you subscribe to an RSS feed, your online service (such as Bloglines) or newsreader refreshes that feed for you, letting you know about a new post, saving you the trip to the Web site unless you actually want to read something.

Two other online RSS readers are Kinja, which also allows you to share your feeds, and NewsGator Online, which is the online companion to NewsGator, a popular downloadable newsreader. My Yahoo! also has RSS reading tools built into its personal home page service.

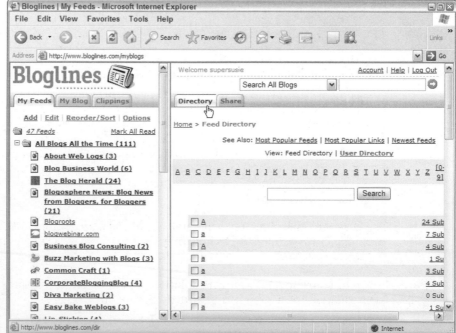

Figure 13-3: The Bloglines Directory lets you search the feeds.

You can also get RSS feeds delivered to on your computer by downloading and installing a news aggregator, such as Feedreader (`www.feedreader.com`) or NewsGator (`www.newsgator.com`). You tell the software what RSS feeds to track, and then use the newsreader to keep current on the latest postings to those blogs.

If you read lots of blogs — and you should, if you're going to be a blogger — using a service such as Bloglines or a newsreader is a big timesaver.

RSS has some downsides:

- Some people claim that users who read your blog via an RSS feed stop coming to your Web site — they miss out on all the extras on the page and your great design even though they're reading the content of your blog.

  My own experience is that the savviest blog readers appreciate the feed and may not visit the site without the RSS prompt to do so. Less-savvy visitors won't use the feed at all. I cover some ways to deal with this problem in the upcoming "Creating RSS feeds: The publishing of RSS" section.

- If you're trying to gather statistics about your blog visitors or if you're using your blog to serve ads that aren't carried by the RSS feed, those who read only the RSS feed and never visit the site won't be counted in your traffic or have the chance to click on your ads.

  Expect to see this situation change as RSS becomes more and more mainstream. In the meantime, the best solution is probably to include only part of each posting in the RSS feed. To get the full text, the reader will then have to come to the blog site.

Creating RSS feeds: The publishing of RSS

A number of different versions of RSS are being used on the Web today — similar to the earliest days of the Web, when different browsers supported different HTML tags. These different RSS versions have frozen at various evolutionary points as the standard was picked up and worked on by different groups for different purposes. Supporting both 1.0 and 2.0 versions is generally considered safest, and most blog software let you generate both types. The 0.91 version is also still popular, perhaps because it's relatively easy to generate.

The Dive Into Mark blog talks in detail about the history of the RSS various versions with a good guide to how they differ at `diveintomark.org/archives/2004/02/04/incompatible-rss`.

Log in to your blogging software solution, and look for instructions on how to implement an RSS feed if it isn't already part of your site.

If your blog software solution doesn't include an RSS solution already, you may be in the unenviable position of having to create your own. As a general rule, any blogging software that uses templates allows you to generate an RSS feed, and while creating the feed is not incredibly difficult, you definitely need someone with some technical skills to help you write the feed. Some good online resources walk you through the process of writing an RSS feed. I find these sites useful and easy to understand:

- **Lockergnome's RSS Resource:** rss.lockergnome.com/resources
- **O'Reilly's RSS DevCenter:** www.oreillynet.com/topics/rss/rss

Newsreader sites and software

The following list covers some of the most well-known offline newsreaders, as well as several online options.

RSS feeds online

BlockTracker (www.dansanderson.com/blogtracker): A browser-based service that works with several versions of Internet Explorer and Netscape on PCs and Macs. Free.

BlogExpress (www.blogexpress.com): Handles all versions of RSS, runs on Windows 98 and better. Free.

NewsGator (www.newsgator.com): Use News Gator to track RSS feeds from blogs and news sites. Pricing begins at $5.95 a month or try the free version. NewsGator Outlook Edition is available, which integrates with your Outlook software. Windows 98 and later. (Both online and offline options are available.)

Pluck (www.pluck.com): Pluck is an Internet Explorer-based newsreader that can be accessed from any computer. Use it to subscribe to RSS feeds and searches, and keep a centralized bookmark file. Free.

Newsreader software to run on your computer

AmphetaDesk (www.disobey.com/amphetadesk): Slightly dated but runs on multiple platforms; displays feeds locally in your browser. For Macintosh, Windows, and Linux. Free.

Feedreader (www.feedreader.com): Feed reader supports RSS and Atom for Windows 95 and later. It's completely free.

Liferea (liferea.sourceforge.net): This newsreader handles RSS and Atom and runs on Linux. Free.

NetNewsWire (ranchero.com/netnewswire): A newsreader for Macintosh OS X 10.2 and greater. Start with a 30-day trial and then pay $39.95. The Lite version is free.

SharpReader (www.sharpreader.net): Handles all RSS versions and Atom. Usable on Windows 98 and later. Free.

Shrook (www.fondantfancies.com/shrook/): Mac software that synchronizes to a main server; handy if you use multiple machines. Updates much sooner than a regular newsreader because of the server integration. OS X, $24.95.

WebGrabit (www.webgrabit.com): A Windows 95 and later Web site and newsreader. Test it for 30 days and then pay $24.95.

FeedBurner is a service that enhances your RSS feed, allowing you to publish in multiple formats, get traffic stats, and enhance your feed's content with photos and links. It's currently free. Find out more at www.feedburner.com.

Once you have an RSS file available on your blog, any site that aggregates Web content can pick it up and display it, though usually only the headlines/titles are displayed (so write good ones!). Users who see the headlines displayed, whether on another blog, a search engine, a news Web site, an e-mail newsletter, or the home page of your company's Web site, can click a headline to go to your blog. Voila! You have made your postings more accessible to more people, and that can't help but generate more blog readers. All these added links also serve to guarantee that your blog postings show up higher in search engine results.

You need to jump-start this process by registering your RSS feed with news aggregation Web sites.

You must set your blog software to *ping,* or notify, some important sites when you publish a new post. Again, many blog software solutions include functionality to let you ping automatically. If yours doesn't, visit the following sites, and look for directions on how to register with them:

- ✔ **Blo.gs:** www.blo.gs
- ✔ **My Yahoo!:** my.yahoo.com/s/publishers.html
- ✔ **Weblogs.com:** www.weblogs.com

These sites require that you visit and submit your blog, usually only once, in order to be included in the RSS index:

- ✔ **Bloglines:** www.Bloglines.com
- ✔ **BlogRolling:** www.blogrolling.com/ping.phtml
- ✔ **BlogStreet:** www.blogstreet.com
- ✔ **FeedBurner:** www.feedburner.com
- ✔ **Feedster:** www.feedster.com
- ✔ **Popdex:** www.popdex.com
- ✔ **PubSub:** www.pubsub.com
- ✔ **Syndic8:** www.syndic8.com
- ✔ **Technorati:** www.technorati.com

I also advise you to embed, on each page of your site, a Meta tag that explains in a uniform way the location of your RSS feed. A Meta tag allows autodetection of your feed by several tools and by crawlers.

Modify this tag to point to your own RSS feed, and add it to the head tag of each HTML page, if it's not already in the template of your blogging software:

```
<link rel="alternate" type="application/rss+xml" title="RSS"
        href="url of your feed here" />
```

Upgrading to Atom feeds

Atom is a format that serves many of the same functions as RSS, though it's slightly more complex to implement for syndication purposes. Actually, it's a lot more complex! The format provides a universal XML interface for posting with blog tools, editing blog entries, and publishing a blog feed.

Atom is a newer format than RSS, and though it has many supporters, many news aggregators don't yet handle Atom content. It may be a sign of things to come, however, that Blogger currently only provides feeds in the Atom format.

For your own use, look for a newsreader that lets you read both RSS and Atom feeds. On your blog, though, I recommend you definitely provide RSS 1.0 or 2.0 and Atom if your blog software includes it already.

Adding comment functionality

Want to use comments on your blog but can't because your blog software doesn't have the functionality? You have two options:

- ✔ **Migrate your blog to blogging software that does offer comments:** If you've been blogging for a long time or have thousands of entries, changing software can be a huge task.

  Chances are, however, that if you're using a blogging system that doesn't offer comments, you may want to upgrade anyway; you're probably missing out on other useful technology.

- ✔ **Use HaloScan:** You can integrate this leading comment system into almost all the existing blog software solutions.

  HaloScan (www.haloscan.com) is free — and requires that you copy and paste two lines of code into your Web log to get started. You can edit and delete comments, as well as ban offensive commenters.

  You can use HaloScan on any Web site, not just a blog. What are you waiting for? Go sign up!

Creating a blogroll

Most bloggers like to read blogs as much as they like to blog themselves. They have favorites, and they're happy to share them with you in the form of a *blogroll:* a list of links that the blogger regularly refers to. Blogrolls are also a way for bloggers to share blogs they admire with their readers.

Of course, bloggers also create a blogroll for other reasons:

- It never hurts your search engine rankings to be linking to highly traf- ficked Web sites.
- The blog you link to may return the favor, especially if your blog is send- ing it traffic.

Blogrolls are usually sorted alphabetically and placed in a column on the right or left of the blog content, as shown in Figure 13-4.

You can easily add a blogroll to your blog, but you do have to spend some time researching available blogs to find those that are most appropriate for you and for your audience. People reading your blog while they are at work don't appre- ciate being sent to something X-rated or frivolous just as the boss walks by.

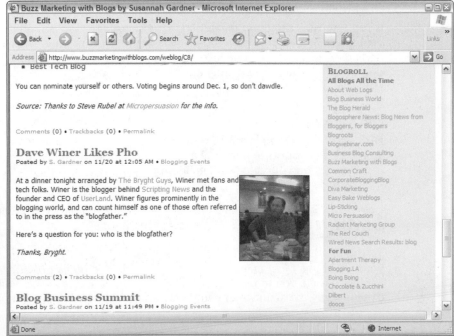

Figure 13-4:
The Buzz
Marketing
with Blogs
blogroll
is on the
right side of
the blog.

Blogrolls are also usually fairly organic — expect to add and remove blogs over time, especially if you're actually using your blogroll to detail what blogs you are reading. Blogs come and go, so be sure to check the blogs you include in your blogroll regularly to make sure they are still active.

To get your blogroll online, check to see if your blog software has a mechanism designed specifically to create it. Some do; some don't. If you don't have built-in blogrolling or linking functionality and can't just write the HTML for it yourself, take a look at BlogRolling and Bloglines, both of which can generate a blogroll for you.

If you're a chronic link surfer, and you want to share many interesting links on your site each day, consider setting up a second blog. If your blog software lets you create multiple Web logs, you can just create another blog and alter your templates to display the link blog alongside your main blog.

BlogRolling

BlogRolling is a free Web-based tool was designed to give you an easy way to create and use your blogroll. Simply visit www.blogrolling.com and register for a free account. You have to handle a little bit of copying and pasting to get the necessary code onto your blog, but once that's done, adding and editing your blogroll are fairly simple.

Bloglines

If you are using Bloglines (www.Bloglines.com) to read RSS feeds, you can generate a blogroll based on those feeds to put on your blog. You have to copy and paste a snippet of code into one of your blog's templates, but once that's done the blogroll is completely automatic. Follow the blogroll instructions on the Share tab.

Furl

Furl (www.furl.net) is a Web tool that lets you save bookmarks and actual Web pages in your own personal archive. It also has a way to place your latest saved pages on your site (and, incidentally, in a daily e-mail newsletter).

Scanning news headlines

You can add headlines from any site that provides an RSS or Atom feed to your own blog. Most major news organizations and blogs provide RSS feeds and encourage you to put a list of headlines on your site — after all, you are driving traffic to them when you do so.

Do check the terms of use for any RSS feed you want to display, however. Some organizations put restrictions and requirements on the use of their content that you need to comply with.

You can find usable RSS feeds for your blog in two ways:

✔ You may already have a source in mind, perhaps an industry publication or local news outlet. Visit the Web sites of these organizations to see if they provide RSS feeds.

✔ Search several sites that index available RSS feeds for headlines that will work for you. These sites catalog and index RSS feeds, and you can search them to find pertinent feeds:

• **Syndic8:** `www.syndic8.com`

• **BlogStreet's RSS Directory:** `www.blogstreet.com`

When you have an RSS feed, go to Feed2JS (`jade.mcli.dist.maricopa. edu/feed/`), and create a small snippet of JavaScript that displays the RSS feed as a set of headlines on your site.

Feed2JS also has a list of other Web sites that provide this service; look around to find the one that suits you best.

Several blog search engines also let you display a feed of their most popular or newest search results on your site:

✔ **Daypop:** `www.daypop.com`

✔ **Feedster:** `www.feedster.com`

✔ **BlogDigger:** `www.blogdigger.com`

Useful Technology

Imagine living in a time when you can send pictures and sound from anywhere to anywhere, even if you're on the move. Now imagine you're there already — and you are, if you've caught up with mobile blogging, photoblogging, and audblogging.

Mobile blogging

Mobile blogging, or *moblogging* as it's usually called, is the fine art of posting to your blog from your phone (mobile or land line), PDA, digital camera, or via e-mail. Moblogging is a favorite tool of bloggers who also have camera phones, but its real strength is that you can post to a blog even when you're not sitting down in front of a computer with an Internet connection.

Moblogging is designed to keep you blogging on the run, in airports or during your commute. (Please, don't moblog while you're driving!) It's often used to *photo blog* or *audblog* (audio blogging).

Moblogging software

Azure (web.vee.net/projects/azure): This free phone and PDA blog client supports Movable Type blogs and may expand that in the future. You can use it to create new posts and edit posts remotely. You need a Java J2ME phone, PDA, or device that uses CLDC/MIDP 1.0 and can connect to the Internet, as well as a Movable Type blog.

PocketBlog (www.pocketblog.com): Use PocketBlog with any Pocket PC device that has Internet connectivity. Add and edit blog entries with Blogger, Movable Type, and Radio UserLand. It is currently free.

AvantBlog (www.dentedreality.com.au/avantblog): AvantBlog lets you post to your Blogger.com blog from a Palm or WinCE device equipped with the default Palm browser AvantGo and an Internet connection. It is currently free.

Pocket SharpMT (www.randyrants.com/sharpmt): Pocket SharpMT lets you post and upload images to your Movable Type blog via your Internet-enabled Pocket PC. This is *donationware,* where the software developer requests a donation if you decide to use it.

BlogPlanet (www.blogplanet.net): Write, edit, and delete posts to several different blog hosts from your phone or Palm PDA. Some hosts and devices also support uploading camera phone images in your posts. The software will set you bakc 10 euros.

HBlogger (www.normsoft.com/hblogger/): This Palm device software lets you send posts and images to quite a few blog hosts. Your Palm must have Internet connectivity and run OS 3.5 or later. Buy it for $14.95.

Airblogging (www.airblogging.com): Post pictures and text to your LiveJournal, Blogger, or Movable Type blog mobile phones that can send e-mail or SMS (Short Message Service) text messages.

Kablog (www.kablog.org): Kablog is a photo/moblogging tool for phones and PDAs with Internet connections. Kablog supports quite a few blog hosts, including TypePad, Blogger, Movable Type, and Radio UserLand.

Unless you tell them, your readers never know that you're moblogging, so don't count on this tool to build traffic to your site or get you any blogosphere tech credit; moblogging is really about making your own life easier and ensuring that your blog is regularly and frequently updated even though you don't have a computer at hand.

Many hosted and independent blog software solutions have built-in moblogging support, but if your solution doesn't include moblogging, some Web-based services act as middlemen, receive your e-mails or photos from your remote device, and pass that data long to your blog software. See the "Moblogging software" sidebar for some examples.

Most moblogging is done through e-mail — sign up for a moblog service, or configure your blog software to accept your moblogs, and then use your phone, PDA, or other Internet-connected handheld device to send text, images, and video via e-mail to your blog. The blog software translates the e-mail into a new blog posting. Usually, the subject line of the e-mail becomes the posting title, and the body of the message is placed in the post. Attachments, such as photos, are saved to your Web server and linked to from the new post.

Photoblogs

Photos add excitement and interest to your blog — assuming they are reasonably good photos — and are also a great way to give your blog a more human feel. In a photoblog, each posting is usually a single image, with a caption and headline — if only for the purposes of making it findable in search engines — because the purpose of the blog is to display images.

Most photoblogs also include comments. You can use a photoblog to record events, trips, conferences, and even products. Chronicling the development of a new car design may be especially exciting in a photoblog, or you can give your readers an inside look at the construction of your new headquarters building.

What makes a photoblog different from a slide show or photo gallery? Don't forget the fundamental definition of blogs — chronological entries labeled with a date and time. Lose those elements, and you probably have created a slide show rather than a photoblog. Photos that work best on a blog have a spontaneous, captured-moment feel to them and stand on their own — they shouldn't need to be viewed as a series to make sense.

Moblog hosting

If you want to start a blog that is solely created from moblog posts, you need moblog hosting:

Moblog UK (`www.moblog.co.uk`): Moblog UK is a moblog-hosting service that permits to you to post audio, video, and photos via any device that can send e-mail. Currently the service has no advertising, and pays its bills by asking its subscribers for voluntary donations and subscriptions.

textamerica (`www.textamerica.com`): Post text, video, and images from your phone for free with textamerica. textamerica provides a selection of blog designs, the ability to edit your template code, comments, captions, RSS, and a blogroll. The service is free.

Also, don't confuse a photoblog with simply adding images to your text blog postings. Adding photos to text blogs is a great technique to make your postings more appealing to your readers, but the blogosphere thinks of photoblogs as a blog comprised primarily of images. Text, if any, plays a supporting role on a photoblog.

Although many primarily text blogs include a photoblog as a sideblog — an accompaniment to the main blog — a number of blogs on the Web today are solely photoblogs, many of them created by amateur photographers. Joi Ito includes photos in this fashion on his blog (joi.ito.com) shown in Figure 13-5.

Blogs that use a photoblog as a sideblog often display the photoblog postings as thumbnails in a column to the right or left of the main blog.

You can create your photos for a photoblog in a number of ways:

- ✔ A digital camera or camera phone.
- ✔ A standard point-and-shoot camera. Request that your photo lab provide you with a CD of digital images when they develop your file.
- ✔ A scanner. Although using this device can be time-consuming and require you to take extra pains, it turns your printed photographs into digital images.

Figure 13-5:
Joi Ito supplements his blog with a photo blog.

Photoblog hosting

Buzznet (www.buzznet.com): Buzznet is a social network for photographers that lets users share photos online. Use Buzznet to host photo-blogs with comments, moblogging, different blog designs, and RSS feeds. Free accounts have fewer uploads than paid accounts.

Expressions (www.my-expressions.com): Expressions calls itself a "visual blogging system" and offers versions in several languages, online photo editing tools, and a blog template builder. Accounts start at $3 after a 30-day free trial.

Flickr (www.flickr.com): Flickr, shown in the following figure, is an online photo management and sharing service with some great built-in support for bloggers, including moblogging, captions, and RSS feeds. It's also a community-based service designed to connect photographers. Free accounts get you started; paid accounts get more space and other features. (For more about Flickr, flip over to Chapter 12.)

Fotolog (www.fotolog.net): Fotolog is a free online photoblogging tool. You're limited to one photo upload per day using the Fotolog site or moblogging. The blog pages have some customization preferences, and visitors can post to a guestbook.

Fotopages (www.fotopages.com): A free service, the Fotopages photoblog services allows moblogging, text entries, captions, comments, and a blogroll.

Fotothing (www.fotothing.com): Fotothing is a free photoblog service offering comments, captions, and RSS.

Ploggle (www.ploggle.com): Ploggle hosts photo and video files online and lets you moblog or post from your computer. It includes captions, some photo editing tools, some page design preferences, and many other features. Start with a free account, and get extra space and features by paying an annual fee.

Next, you need to get your photos into the photoblog. Good independent blog software, such as Movable Type or Expression Engine, allows you to create multiple blogs and upload images, so using your main blog engine to set up a separate photoblog if you are using one of these solutions is logical. Many hosted blog solutions also offer the ability to upload images and can be used to create photoblogs or albums.

Audioblogging solutions

Audblog (www.audblog.com): Send audio to your Blogger, Radio UserLand, Movable Type, or LiveJournal blog via any phone. Audblog offers a free trial. A $3 monthly subscription gets you 12 four-minute audio posts.

Audioblogger (www.audioblogger.com): This service of Blogger is available for all Blogger blogs. Post an unlimited number of audioblogs for free. The following figure shows a button labeled "Play this audio post" that takes you to an Audioblogger posting.

Audioblog.com (www.audioblog.com): Record over the phone or over the Web, or upload an MP3 or WAV file. You can use Audioblog.com with Movable Type, TypePad, Blogger, and LiveJournal blogs. Basic service is $4.95 a month.

Userplane AV Blogger (avblog.userplane.com): Create audio and video messages you can use on your blog or e-mail. The media is saved on Userplane servers while you copy and paste some code into your blog. First 10 messages are free.

VoiceAlizeR (www.voicealizer.com): Record audio using VoiceAlizeR and then copy and paste the resulting code into your blog postings. Accounts used to start at £9.99; check to see what the current rate is in euros.

A photo blog uses up more space on your server much more quickly than text! If you post lots of images at high quality, you may need to invest in some additional disk space with your Web host. Also, if you're using a camera phone to photoblog, try to get one that takes decent pictures. Most camera phones produce grainy, dark images that won't impress your readers — though the technology in this arena is rapidly improving.

For more information on photoblogs, and for resources, examples, and software recommendations, visit `www.photoblogs.org`.

If you want to create a photoblog to use as a sideblog and can't do so with your blogging software, look into using a third-party photoblogging service such as Buzznet or Flickr. Both let you display your photoblog postings on an external blog or Web page.

Audblogs

Audblogging is blogging with audio, usually over mobile phones. Some bloggers simply use audblogging as another remote blogging tool; others are using the medium to conduct short interviews and other radiolike experiments.

When you audblog, remember that your posting are only as good as your sound situation. Audblog in the middle of a crowded restaurant, for example, and you're as hard to hear online as you are when having a phone conversation in similar circumstances. If you try to use your phone for interviews, you may want to experiment with phone placement and different headset microphones in order to increase the quality of your postings. The point is not to get broadcast-quality sound, but there's no point in creating audblogs that can't be heard or understood!

Most of the audblog services turn your audio into MP3 files that are then downloadable from your blog posting.

Fun Technology

You can have a lot of fun with some of the new blogging technology available. Just think — if you could post video blog entries, what would you say? And what could you do with mapping technology on a travel blog?

The technologies in this section add spice and excitement to your blog, but don't worry if you can't incorporate them. Save them for a rainy day when you need to try some new.

Vidblogs

Vidblogging, or video blogging, is relatively uncommon still, thanks in part to bandwidth requirements and the relative complexity of producing video clips. Nonetheless, some bloggers hail vidblogging as the hot blogging tool of the future.

Although she doesn't call it a videoblog, Ellen DeGeneres uses the format to present the daily monologue from her talk show at `ellen.warnerbros.com/galleries/video.html`. Figure 13-6 shows the site's daily monologue page.

If you want to vidblog, you can either set yourself up with a digital video camera and video editing software to produce your clips, or you can look for a service that records via a Webcam or video camera attached to your computer. If you don't already have the hardware necessary to record video or the software to edit it, be prepared to spend some time and money getting set up.

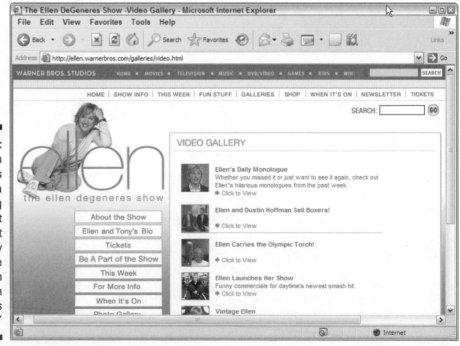

Figure 13-6:
Ellen
DeGeneres
uses a
videoblog
format
to present
the daily
monologue
from
"The Ellen
DeGeneres
Show."

One service to consider using is Userplane AV Blogger (`avblog.userplane.com`), which lets you record a video clip through your computer's Webcam and then post it on your blog. The media is saved on Userplane servers, and you copy and paste some code into your blog posting to make it display. The first ten messages are free.

For more details on the evolution of video blogging, visit `www.me-tv.org`.

Blogmapping

Do you travel a lot and blog from the road? Do your posts have to do with different geographic locations? Is your location — or that of what you're blogging about — of interest to your readers? You need to check out blogmapping.

A *blogmap* provides a geographic interface to your blog entries: Each time you post, you indicate the location you want to associate with the post. A map on your blog then shows — usually graphically — a post on the map, and your readers click the locations that interest them. Blogmaps can be great for journalists or for blogs that are tracking the geographic appearances of objects — think an interactive map of sign locations for a sign company or of public art installations on a city's Web site.

If you post often in the same location, your map may be hard to read and use, as dots build up on the same location. As well, blogmapping provides only one bit of information about a post — the geographic location — and no other clues to what the post is about, so don't use blogmapping as your only point of access to your blog postings.

If this idea interests you, visit Blogmapper at `blogmapper.com` to find out how you can add this functionality to your blog.

Keeping Readers Hooked with a Killer App

One technique for catching and keeping readers is to create something so cool on your blog that they will be astonished by your ingenuity, creativity, and skill. This is the *killer application* (or *app*). The best killer app in the blog world is one that is always useful and fresh, as it keeps visitors coming back for another look again and again.

The example I show here isn't from a business blog, but from a personal blog that has been incredibly successful at building a diverse and dedicated readership and traffic. The Trixie Update may be a very personal blog, but it commands traffic and loyalty to which any business blogger can aspire.

The Trixie Update (`www.trixieupdate.com/`) chronicles the life of Beatrix MacNeill in minute and astonishing detail. Trixie has been a blog star almost since her birth on July 31, 2003.

The killer app on this blog is the Trixie Telemetry system displayed at the top of the blog, shown in Figure 13-7. It tracks Trixie's sleeping and waking schedule and records a daily and lifetime diaper change count (3,392 as of 10:45 a.m. January 19, 2005). Before she began eating solid food, the Trixie Telemetry session also detailed her bottle feedings, right down to the amount of milk she consumed each day. Another important component of The Trixie Update is the TPOD (Trixie Picture of the Day). Trixie's growth from Day 1 is visible by tracking back through more than a year of photos.

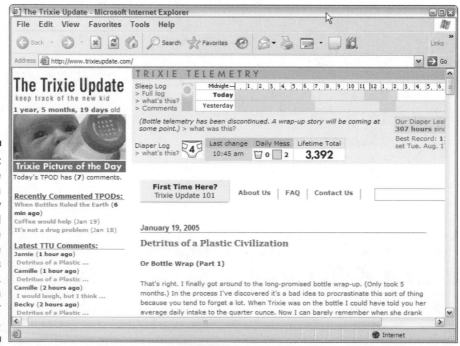

Figure 13-7:
The Trixie Update is a fabulously detailed chronicle of Trixie MacNeill's infant life, right down to a Diaper Log.

The Trixie Update is maintained by her dad, Ben. He started the blog because Trixie's mom, Jennifer, had to go back to work and wanted to stay connected during the day. The Trixie Update also has text postings, sometimes accompanied by images, that are sorted into categories such as Behavior, Day-to-Day Minutiae, Inner Workings, Milestones, and Site News.

The Trixie Update is updated every couple of days, and Ben's writing style is engaging, personal, and informative. The site's comments often include advice and commiserations from other parents and responses from people who have simply become fans of Trixie and her doings. The most interesting aspect of The Trixie Update may simply be its popularity among people who don't know Trixie personally and never will; this site attracts many more readers than just her grandparents.

The data tracking Trixie Telemetry system (numbers of diaper changes, feedings, naps) has been spun off into software called Trixie Tracker, subscription software currently in beta testing. Ben MacNeill plans to offer three-month subscriptions for $10. You can visit www.trixietracker.com to get more information.

Chapter 14

Making Money with a Blog

Most of this book gives you ideas for a blog that markets your existing business, products, and services. However, you can employ some strategies to earn money directly from your blog. Most of these ideas are intended for individual bloggers seeking to promote themselves, but that doesn't mean you can't use one or more of these techniques on a business blog.

If your blog exists purely for business reasons, be careful about adding too many additional commercial messages to it. Your readers may resent the attempt, and ultimately your blog needs readers to be at all useful for your business.

Having said that, these tools are fast and easy to implement. Done right, advertising, affiliate programs, and merchandising may even be of service to your readers!

Putting Advertising on Your Blog

If you've ever looked at a Web site, you're familiar with the most common Web advertising formats: banner ads, vertical skyscrapers, buttons, boxes, pop-up ads, and even animations that open over page content. The problem with all these formats? They haven't proven to be greatly successful. In fact, many consumers claim to be actively annoyed by this kind of advertising and less likely to use the services of the advertiser.

Even Web sites that offer generalized content, such as newspapers and magazines, encounter problems with advertising. Imagine how much less successful this kind of advertising would be in a niche publication like a blog! Some bloggers are experimenting with using *targeted* advertising instead of mass-market advertisements.

Imagine visiting your favorite blog about, say, knitting, and seeing ads for wool and knitting needles alongside a pattern you just love. The likelihood that you see these ads as valuable rather than intrusive and irrelevant changes dramatically. Blogs are in a great position to take advantage of targeted advertising of this kind, because the content of a blog is generally so focused and specific; readers are nearly guaranteed to be interested in the topic of the content (they wouldn't be at your blog otherwise) and much more likely to appreciate ads that are also on topic.

A number of enterprising businesses have sprung up to take advantage of this affinity and developed advertising programs specifically for blogs. Google is by far the largest organization to develop a program, and if you've spent any time visiting blogs recently, you have probably seen its contextual ads in action. Blogads also lets advertisers target your blog specifically and lets you choose whether to accept the advertising.

Advertising with Google AdSense

Google AdSense advertising is extremely common on any site with changing content — especially blogs. Google's service is free to use, easy to implement, and provides advertising based on the keywords Google finds on your pages: Write a post about fried chicken, and you might get Google AdSense ads for cooking supplies and restaurants. And these ads are contextual on a page-by-page basis, so every permalink page on your blog has its own set of topic-appropriate ads.

Each time a reader clicks a link in one of these ads, you earn money. You choose where the ads are on your pages, what they look like, and even what kinds of advertisers to display. You can see Google AdSense ads on the Apartment Therapy blog (`www.apartmenttherapy.com`) in Figure 14-1.

You can also include a Google search box on your blog. Users who use the search box from your blog get targeted Google ads in their search results — and you receive money from any ads they click.

Figure 14-1:
The Apartment Therapy Blog uses Google AdSense contextual ads to add value to its content and earn revenue at the same time.

You can sign up for Google AdSense by following these steps:

1. **Open a Web browser, and go to** www.google.com/adsense.

2. **Click the Click Here to Apply button, shown in Figure 14-2.**

3. **If you're new to Google, fill out the New to Google form with your e-mail address and a password of your choice. Users of Google's AdWords or with a Google Print account can simply log in.**

4. **Select whether your AdSense account is an individual or business account and then click Continue.**

Figure 14-2:
Sign up for Google AdSense advertising to place content-related ads on your blog.

5. **Provide the account information.**

   You need to provide your name, address, phone, fax, URL, and Web site language.

6. **Decide whether you want to receive a periodic newsletter.**

7. **Sign up for AdSense and/or AdSense search (optional).**

8. **Review the FAQ and Program Policies, and click Submit.**

9. **Review your information.**

   To make corrections, click the Edit Account Information button.

10. **When you're sure everything is correct, click Continue to complete the application process.**

After you finish the application, Google reviews your blog, and if it approves your application, you have to provide some additional information: Social Security number, Employer Identification Number, and so on. The review Google conducts ensures that the Web site the ads are placed on meets Google's editorial guidelines (for example, no obscenity).

After Google completes its review, you receive instructions on how to customize and place the ads into your blog templates. You may need a little help from your technical staff or some HTML skills of your own.

The ads appear automatically on your pages based on the content of your blog after you add the code to your templates. Visit the Google AdSense site to customize the look of your ads, check your earnings, and remove certain advertisers (such as your competitors!) from the ads that appear on your site.

Advertising your blog on other blogs

You probably have realized that other blogs are a great place to find readers who may be interested in your blog. That being the case, Blogads, AdBrite, and other services are great ways to advertise directly to that audience. The open nature of the blogosphere means that other bloggers may welcome your advertising, if your site is useful to their readers, even though you may be competing for the same eyes. Try using one of these services to advertise the launch of your blog or to drive traffic during a lull. Be sure to target blogs whose readers are likely interested in your topics that also get good traffic.

Using Blogads

Blogads, a service created by former journalist Henry Copeland, is a service that puts ads on blogs. Advertisers select blogs they want to target; bloggers choose whether to accept the ads on their sites.

Advertisers using Blogads can put together an ad that uses an image, text, and links, and then select blogs they want to reach. They also choose the length of time they want their ads to appear and can pay extra for better placement in the queue of Blogads on a site. The blogger then gets a chance to approve the ad and the terms of its display before it goes live.

You can see an example of Blogads on Utterly Boring (`www.utterlyboring.com`), a blog by Jake Ortman in Figure 14-3.

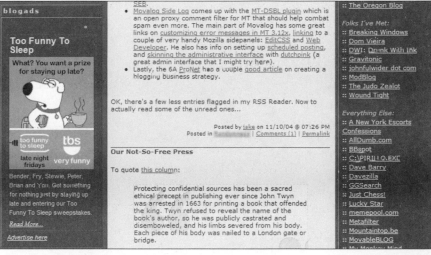

Figure 14-3: Blogads in action on Jake Ortman's Utterly Boring blog.

© Utterly Boring.com

The Blogads service is designed to match up advertisers and bloggers. Participation is free to bloggers; remuneration obviously depends on what kind and how many readers your blog attracts. Blogads itself keeps a percentage of your earnings in exchange for serving the ads and managing the relationship with the advertiser. If you want to sign up for the Blogads service, visit `www.blogads.com`.

Using AdBrite

AdBrite is a similar service to Blogads that lets you place text ads, banners, and skyscraper ads on your blog. (*Skyscrapers* are those tall, thin vertical ads you see on many newspaper Web sites.) Businesses visiting your blog have a chance to click a link and purchase advertising directly from your site. You, the blogger, choose what advertising opportunities to offer, whose advertising you accept, what to charge, and how long the ad appears.

The popular Gizmodo blog (www.gizmodo.com) runs AdBrite text links in the right-hand column, along with a Buy a Link Now opportunity for potential advertisers, as shown in Figure 14-4.

AdBrite manages the relationship between blogger and advertiser, serves the ads, and facilitates billing. In exchange, AdBrite keeps a percentage of your ad earnings. Visit www.adbrite.com to sign up and begin accepting advertising on your blog.

Figure 14-4:
Gizmodo uses AdBrite to serve targeted text link ads.

Making Use of Affiliate Programs

Many online retailers — and some service providers — have begun to offer affiliate programs. The basic idea of most affiliate programs is that the publisher, or blogger, can earn money from recommendations made on a Web site. It's seen as a win-win-win scenario. The consumer gets a product they want, the blogger gets a commission from the sale, and the retailer makes sales without having to spend advertising dollars.

To use most affiliate programs, you must register with the retailer, who provides you HTML code or other mechanisms for linking the products you mention on your site to them. Your readers can then click directly from your site to the retailer's product page, put the item in a shopping cart, and check out. Because the reader clicked the link on your blog to get to the product, the retailer can then credit you a commission on the sale.

One of most commonly used affiliate programs — and one of the earliest in existence — is that of Amazon.com. I tell you how to use it in the following sections.

Using the Amazon.com Associates program

Amazon.com sells books, electronics, games, hardware, and more, and most of these products are included in the affiliate program. Interested? Here are a few ways to use Amazon.com's Associates program:

✔ Ever recommend a book, CD, or DVD? Got a cool new gadget that your customers can also love? Link directly to the product page from your blog.

✔ Can your product or service be used in conjunction with something Amazon sells? Create a list of these items as a resource your users can use to get information and then make purchases.

✔ Does a category of product appeal to your audience? Tell Amazon the types of products you want to display, and let it do the work in selecting, updating, and displaying them.

✔ Let your customers search Amazon directly from your site and earn money from anything they purchase from the search results.

Many bloggers use Amazon's affiliate program to add value to the discussions on their blogs or to promote specific products. Not surprisingly, the affiliate program is especially popular with book authors. You can see an example of the program in action through the blog of author, actor, and blogger Wil Wheaton (yes, *that* Wil Wheaton), WIL WHEATON DOT NET (`wilwheaton.net`), which is shown in Figure 14-5.

You may be able to use an affiliate program in some creative ways so that you earn a little money and also provide your readers with a service that gets them information they need. If you're feeling adventurous, you can even sign up for an affiliate program with your competitors and link to their products. If you're going to lose customers to these companies, you may as well still make a little money!

things like this. I don't feel like I need to run away from the stuff I used to do (or the person I used to be) anymore. I feel like I spent the first thirty years of my life building this complicated foundation, and now I'm living in a wonderful house atop it.

I'm off to prepare my presentation for ApacheCon on Monday in Las Vegas. Have a great weekend, everyone.

This entry is from the *Just A Geek* department.
Posted by wil at 09:56 AM | Comments (61) | TrackBack (1)

November 06, 2004

throw the goats

A few weeks ago, the evil geniuses at goats.com started a story called "a dish best served delicious (or, invoking godwins law)". In the story, I play an important part in the untimely death of the Pork-o-tron 5000.

Figure 14-5:
Wil Wheaton uses an Amazon Associate account with his book, music, and DVD recommendations.

With so many affiliate programs out there, you can probably find one to suit your needs. When you visit the sites of companies you want to affiliate with, scroll directly to the bottom of the home page — most of them place an affiliate link there somewhere.

Be careful not to come across as money-grubbing when you implement affiliate links. Most people understand that clicking a product link on your site might result in profits for you, and if the entire blog starts to look like a way to earn money off your readers' purchases rather than a way to communicate and inform them, they won't stick around. And they certainly won't click your affiliate links.

Signing up for Amazon Associates

To sign up as an Amazon Associate, open a Web browser, and go to www.amazon.com/associates. Be sure to read over how the program works before you sign up!

1. **Click the Join Now button.**

2. **Provide your primary e-mail address, and select a password, and then click Submit.**

3. **Review the Operating Agreement and then provide the information necessary to open your account.**

   Necessary info includes payee name, address, phone number, tax ID number, and tax classification, and let Amazon know how you want to be paid.

4. **Provide your blog's URL, a description of your blog, and the kinds of products you want to list. Click Submit.**

5. **Depending on how you want to receive your earnings, you may need to provide your bank account information.**

6. **Review your information to confirm that you entered everything correctly!**

   To make corrections, click the Edit button. To go to the next step, click the Submit button.

7. **Check each category that your Web site falls into, as shown in Figure 14-6.**

8. **Select the number of employees at your company and the method you usually use to send people to Amazon.**

9. **Click Submit to finish.**

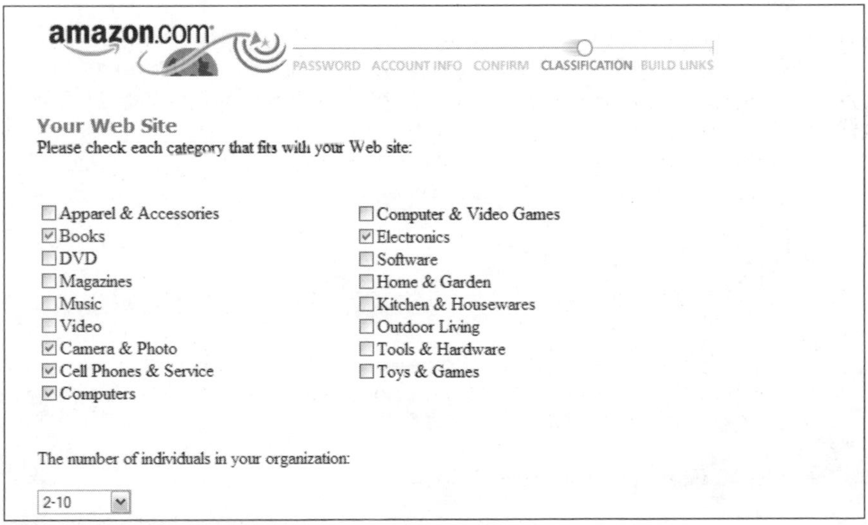

Figure 14-6:
Use the Amazon.com Associates program to earn money from your product recommendations.

Amazon takes a few days to approve your application while taking a look at the content of your Web site, but you can begin building links and sending people to Amazon from your site right away.

Putting Out a Tip Jar

Depending on what kind of business or organization yours is, a tip-jar approach might be one way to solicit monetary contributions from your readers. Some blogs use these donation appeals for a short time to fund specific activities (a shortfall in Web hosting funds or to purchase a new piece of software), and others keep the links active all the time.

Of course, if you are Sears, keep in mind your customers likely won't feel compelled to drop money in a tip jar! This strategy works best for nonprofits, educational institutions, political campaigns, and other service-oriented organizations.

Quite a few online donation services target nonprofits directly, but two popular options for nonprofit and for-profit institutions are the Amazon Honor System and PayPal Donations. Any type of organization can use both to solicit donations for any purpose.

Little Green Footballs (`www.littlegreenfootballs.com/weblog`), an incredibly popular political blog run by Charles Johnson, appeals to visitors for donations using both PayPal and Amazon donation services. Figure 14-7 shows links to PayPal and Amazon.

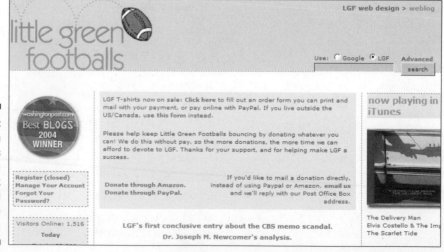

Figure 14-7:
Little Green Footballs has a donation link front and center on every page.

Here's how it all works:

1. You sign up with a donation collection service such as Amazon or PayPal.

2. You place HTML code and a graphic on your blog (you choose the location), and explain to your readers why they should give you money.

3. Your generous reader clicks the link and is taken to the donation collection company to complete the transaction.

4. The service provider collects and disburses funds that come in for you, keeping a percentage to cover its own costs.

You can use the tip-jar technique to ask outright for financial support — and if you are truly providing a unique and valuable service, you may just get it. For an entirely commercial organization, this idea probably won't fly unless you write a very clever appeal.

However, a for-profit business can use this technology to generate revenue for specific purposes:

✔ Ask readers to make donations toward the cost of hosting an event where readers can get together and talk face-to-face. (Don't forget to attend!)

✔ Ask for donations to accomplish a charitable purpose. Promise to match or even double any contributions that come in. Don't forget to follow up with information on how the money was used to generate some great good will from your readers!

✔ Ask readers for donations to use as prizes for a contest in which you involve the readers.

Accepting donations with PayPal

To get started with PayPal Donations, open a Web browser, and go to www.paypal.com. Then follow these steps to sign up:

1. **Click the Sign Up Now button.**

2. **Select business account and the country in which you're located. Click Continue.**

   You can only use personal accounts to send money, so you definitely need to choose the business account to handle incoming donations.

3. **Provide information about your business, and click Continue.**

   You have to divulge your name, category of business, address, customer service contact information, URL, and the contact information of the business owner.

4. **Provide an e-mail address, choose a password and security questions, and agree to the terms of the User Agreement and Privacy Policy.**

   The security questions are just in case you ever forget your password.

5. **Fill out a visual security check, and click the Sign Up button.**

6. **PayPal sends a confirmation e-mail to your e-mail account.**

   Use the information in the e-mail to activate your account and sign into PayPal.

To obtain the code that allows you to add a PayPal button to your blog, follow these steps:

1. **Click the Merchant Tools tab. Look for the Accepting Website Payments header, and click the Donations link.**

   To specify an amount for the donations: Add the amount to the Donation Information section and then go to the Choose a Donation Button section.

   To leave the donation amount open for users to determine: Keep the Donation Information section blank, and jump right to the Choose a Donation Button section.

2. **Select one of several PayPal buttons, as shown in Figure 14-8, or enter the URL of a button on your own site.**

3. **Click Create Button.**

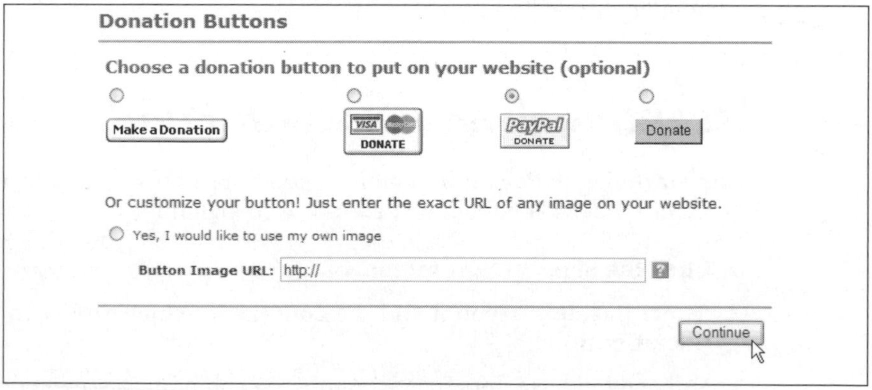

Figure 14-8:
Select a
button from
several
offered
by PayPal
Donations,
or use your
own image
to solicit
funds.

4. **Copy the resulting HTML code into your blog templates.**

   You may need the help of a technical person if you don't have the ability to edit the templates yourself. If that's the case, copy the code carefully and provide it to your technical person, along with information about where to place it on the page and any information to use alongside it.

Accepting donations with Amazon Honor System

Sign up for the Amazon Honor System by opening a browser and going to www.amazon.com/honor.

If you already have an Amazon Associates account, you can simply add the Honor System to your existing account. If you are an Amazon customer, you can also sign in with your regular account to use the Honor System, but make sure that you don't use a personal account to solicit funds for your business or non-profit!

Follow these steps to begin using the Honor System:

1. **Click Join Now or follow the directions to start a new account.**

2. **Enter or select an existing credit card Amazon can use to verify your identity. Click Continue.**

3. **Select the billing address to use or enter a new one.**

4. **Review your info for accuracy.**

   You need to verify your address, credit card information, and your phone number.

5. **Choose the name your readers see when they donate to you through Amazon.**

6. **Indicate your acceptance of the Participation Agreement.**

7. **Choose whether to enter your bank account information now or later. Click Continue.**

   If you chose to enter your bank account information at this time, follow the directions to do so.

When you complete the sign-up process, Amazon directs you to a Getting Started page that walks you through the process of creating an Amazon PayPage through which donations are made. Follow these steps to customize that page:

1. **Click the Create Your PayPage button.**

2. **Edit the text of the PayPage and any thank you e-mails your readers receive after making a donation. Click the Edit button next to the item you want to customize or Continue to accept the text and images as is.**

   You can also edit information being displayed about you, add an image, and decide whether your readers can set their own donation amounts. If you're working to collect funds toward a financial goal, you can also customize the Goal Chart and Payment Counter, which let your readers see progress toward the goal.

3. **Check the Preview page carefully for errors.**

   Click the Go Back button to make corrections or Continue to move on to the Paybox Style page.

4. **Select Use this Style next to the Amazon donation link you want on your blog from the Paybox Style page.**

   You are moved on to the Create a Paybox page.

5. **Create the message you want to use in the Paybox, and click Continue.**

   Click Edit to make corrections. If the preview looks the way you want it to, click Save and Continue.

6. **Copy the provided HTML code, and paste it into your blog templates.**

   You may need the help of a technical person if you don't have the ability to edit the templates yourself. If that's the case, copy the code carefully and provide it to your technical person, along with information about where to place it on the page and any information to use alongside it.

Figure 14-9 shows an Amazon PayPage.

Figure 14-9: Readers can reach an Amazon PayPage by clicking the Amazon Honor System link on your blog.

Selling Blog-Branded Merchandise

Does your business have a popular brand, cute logo, or catchy slogan? If so, you may be able to generate sales of branded merchandise from your blog. If you already have a retailer who handles this kind of merchandise for your company, check to see whether the retailer can handle online ordering. You can also contact your Web host about setting up a shopping cart, secure connection, and merchant account, and sell items directly from your Web site or blog.

Selling tangible items online can be a problematic and expensive process, however, so think hard about whether you're likely to sell enough product to make back the time needed to produce, package, ship, and bill for your merchandise.

If all that sounds like a headache — or too expensive to be worthwhile — but you're still interested in the idea, visit CafePress.com, an online retailer that lets you create branded merchandise and then handles production, orders, transactions, and even shipping for you.

CafePress.com charges a base price for its stock of T-shirts, mugs, bumper stickers, calendars, mouse pads, bags, lunch boxes, buttons, magnets, posters, books, CDs, and more. But it doesn't charge anything for you to create a store with CafePress (unless you would like to fully customize the look and feel of shop pages to match those of your Web site). Anything you choose to charge over this base price is pure revenue.

To use CafePress.com effectively, you need to create some high-quality versions of your logo (or other elements you want to use), upload them to CafePress.com, choose which products to put them on, and then advertise their availability on your blog.

You can order items from your own shop to use as giveaways, prizes, and gifts.

To get started selling hats with your logo today, visit www.cafepress.com and open a shop! Figure 14-10 shows the CafePress.com shop I set up for my Web design company, Hop Studios.

Figure 14-10:
You can use CafePress.com to quickly and easily sell branded merchandise through your Web site or blog.

Chapter 15

Going Beyond Blogs

*B*logs are a powerful communication medium that you can use to facilitate dialogue among groups of all kinds on almost any subject. The heart of this strength lies in the powerful software applications that produce blogs. Though a specific, authoritative definition of blogs may be elusive, one thing is certain: Blogs are made possible because of the existence of this blogging software. These software programs are perfect for blogging, but they can also be adapted and used for other Web projects. The possibilities may surprise you.

Businesses and individuals seeking reasonably priced content management software, especially publishers, have discovered that blog software can be used for everything from e-commerce applications to corporate intranet systems. With a powerful blog software package and a savvy technical developer, the possibilities for using blog software for nonblog purposes are wide open.

Blog software is especially useful for organizations that want to launch a Web site *and* a blog — purchasing a good blog software package fulfills both needs and makes updating your site much easier. It's easier on the pocketbook, too.

In this chapter, I walk you through some ways in which you can use blog software to go beyond blogs or to produce both blog and nonblog content for the Web.

Using Blogs for a Whole Web Site

Most of this book assumes that you're adding a blog to an existing Web site, but if you don't have a Web site yet or need to redesign, consider using blog software to build the entire package. It takes some work, so you should have a good Web developer close at hand or be one yourself, but you may just find that the end result is easier to update and organize than a Web site made up of individual HTML pages.

Web sites (that aren't blogs) built with blog software don't need to look or feel like blogs at all — remove the timestamps, comments, and chronological arrangement of posts, and you start to have a collection of material like any other Web site. Start thinking of categories as Web site sections, permalinks as pages, and blogs as organizing principles, and you're on your way.

Many of the Web sites built with blog software actually combine multiple blogs in the same page. For an example, take a look at Alaska Science Outreach (www.alaskascienceoutreach.com), a science information clearinghouse site run by freelance writer Sonya Senkowsky. Alaska Science Outreach, shown in Figure 15-1, runs on pMachine's ExpressionEngine, but very little of it looks or acts like a blog. Each section of the site is actually a separate blog.

The Online News Association used Movable Type to build the Web site for its 2004 conference (shown in Figure 15-2), and it too is made up of several different blogs. Visit the site at journalists.org/2004conference, and you see that the site's polished look reads more like a news Web site than a blog. Click around, however, and you find ONA making great use of blog functionality, such as comments, to enrich the site.

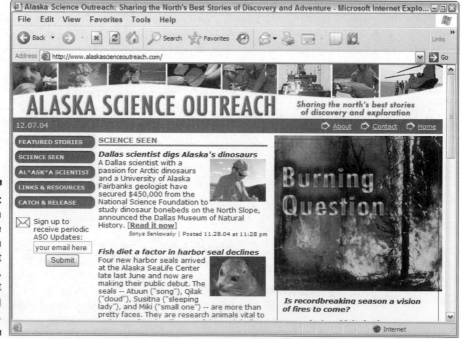

Figure 15-1:
Alaska Science Outreach doesn't act like a blog, but it is built with blog software.

Figure 15-2:
The Online
News
Association
used blog
software to
build the
conference
coverage
Web site.

During the conference, ONA ran a blog for participants: Any conference attendee could add content during (and after) the conference. Instead of registering every attendee as a blog author — a major headache fraught with forgotten passwords and incorrectly typed e-mail addresses — ONA created a single post and allowed participants to post comments to it. By tweaking the design of the page, the result looks and feels like a blog created by multiple authors, rather than a huge list of comments.

Using Blogs for Project Management

Before I move on to the more creative applications of blog software, take a moment to note that blogs themselves are a natural tool for collaboration and project management.

You can use a blog to keep together a group of team members to do the following:

- Organize a conference, retreat, or company event.
- Track bugs and fixes in a process.
- Help shift workers coordinate progress and schedules.
- Share meeting notes.
- Alert each other to new tools and tips that can speed up tasks.

    ✔ Create checklists and tasks, and assign workflow.

    ✔ Build consensus.

    ✔ Keep noncore employees in the loop with fewer monotonous meetings.

    ✔ Solicit feedback on decisions in a low-pressure environment.

This list is only part of the daily communicative encounters that happen during the course of normal working life.

Using blogs instead of e-mails, memos, and endless meetings has the added benefit of creating a electronic archive of the ongoing conversation — going back to figure out what people were thinking when a decision was made or keeping tabs on progress is easy to do.

If a new member joins the project midway through, instead of having to forward a dozen e-mails and files, the new member can see the evolution of the discussion and the efforts of each member — if not perfectly, hopefully a little more easily than sifting through someone else's old e-mails.

Will using a blog to track progress increase productivity? There's no evidence that it does, but adding more accountability to your workflow may have the effect of making people feel more engaged, involved — and more publicly responsible for the work they do.

Organizations such as Google, InfoWorld Media Group, Microsoft, Sun, Disney, and others are reportedly using blogs for workplace collaboration and communication. How many companies use blogs this way is hard to know, because naturally these blogs are not open to the public!

The price tag for letting your employees add a blog to their communication tools is certainly reasonable as well. Many basic blog packages start at rates much, much lower than larger project tracking software, and their easy-to-use interface encourages people to use the product. In the long term, your needs may outgrow blogging software, but in the short term, you can be up and going in minutes.

Blogger (www.blogger.com) lets you create a blog with multiple contributors for free, although the blog is public. Turn to Chapter 5 to find out more about Blogger.

Creating Intranet Web sites

An *intranet* is a private Web site or network of a company or organization used to maintain internal information, manage projects, provide employee information, and distribute common forms and files. They are especially important for large organizations with employees in multiple locations who need access to the same data — think of a headhunting organization with a database of employers, for example.

Organizations commonly have pages on an intranet site for sections, departments, even individuals. Kept updated, these sites can be a great way for employees to stay in touch and on the same page. Allowed to grow stagnant, the organization gets little to no benefit from an intranet. So if the intranet keeps everyone else informed, the question is: Who keeps the intranet updated?

In the best possible world, the intranet would be updated by the people who use it and know the information best. Typically, these are people who don't have the time or need to learn HTML and code Web pages; they have jobs to do! Centralizing updates in a technical department is one solution but one prone to failure in times of technical crisis or sheer work overload. On the other hand, training dozens of people in the details of FTP and HTML is difficult and less than efficient.

The best solution is to run the intranet using a content management system, or Web publishing tool, that puts intuitive, simple updating tools in the hands of employees. Sound familiar? Part of what is so revolutionary about blog software, after all, is the ability of nontechnical folks to publish and keep publishing powerful, functional Web sites.

Intranets and blog software are a close fit, which many companies have realized and taken advantage of. Some have turned off the more "bloggy" features, such as timestamps and comments, and focused on simply having announcements with headlines and text; others have incorporated these features into the functionality of the intranet and increased the communication abilities of staff at the same time.

The Children's Hospital and Regional Medical Center in Seattle is one such organization. The hospital has had an intranet since 1995 that connects its (approximately) 3,000 employees, referring physicians, University of Washington students, and other partners.

When looking for a more robust way to manage the intranet a couple of years ago, the technical team initially considered using a more traditional content management system. It proved to be hard to customize pages for different departments and was very difficult for would-be updaters to get the hang of. Plus it was expensive. Keith Robinson, then the lead Web developer (he has since left to pursue another job opportunity), had been using Movable Type to publish a personal blog and wondered whether it might be something the hospital could use for the intranet.

Christian Watson, eHealth Program Manager, says they built a test intranet site using Movable Type with news and announcements and trained some key staff to update it. The hospital invested six months in testing the system to see if it would really work and in the end converted nearly its entire intranet to Movable Type.

There are seven sections to the intranet, which is shown in Figure 15-3. It contains these sections: home page (news, events, calendar), policies and procedures, staff resources, clinical resources, education and development, an about section, and approximately 70 department pages. The Web team also maintains a How To blog to help staff use the system.

Figure 15-3: The Children's Hospital and Regional Medical Center, Seattle, runs its intranet site using Movable Type blog software.

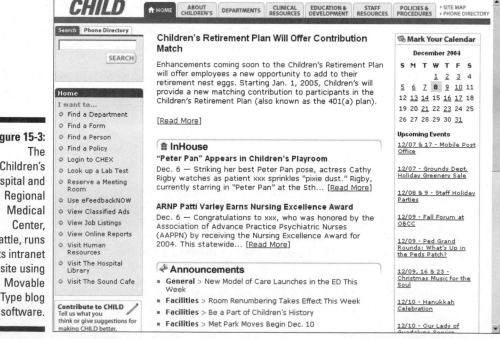

© Children's Hospital and Regional Medical Center

There are about 50 different employees who update the site themselves; infrequent updates from smaller department are still usually handled by the Web team. Overall, Watson says, the usability of the system has greatly increased, and users like the increased control they have over their content.

Not all departments were converted; those with specialized applications continue to use older systems.

Testing of the site and development of the system took almost a year; the hospital had some difficulty in finding the right combination of tools and servers. Today, adding sections to the intranet is relatively easy, even for those who want a customized look and feel. Users are updating more often, employees can find things more quickly, and the Web team workload has dropped. The Web team, with its eye on the future, appreciates that Movable Type generates static pages that could — if need be — be ported to another application or just edited.

Using Blogging Software to Build a Store

You can easily adapt blog software to any content that contains multiple sets of information that must be formatted in the same way. Think of news stories (always have a headline, author, and story), library catalogs (books always have titles, authors, publication dates, and publishers), and products (name, description, and image).

Although no blogging software that I know of (yet) includes an e-commerce tool (though I expect that to change soon), many can be adapted to display products information with links to an external shopping cart.

Blanca's Creations

To launch this site, I adapted blogging software for use as an e-commerce site for a Los Angeles-based artist who wanted to sell her work online without learning how to build HTML pages herself.

Blanca Lee of Blanca's Creations (www.blancascreations.com) sells hand-crafted key chains, pendants, bracelets, pillows, and other objects she makes through eBay but wanted to be able to showcase all her merchandise on one Web site, which is shown in Figure 15-4. I adapted the pMachine ExpressionEngine to integrate her products with the PayPal shopping cart system.

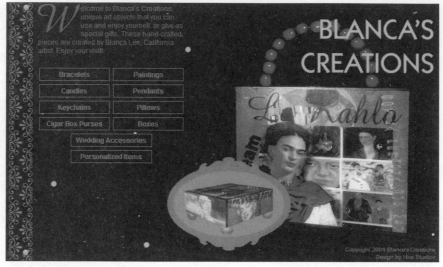

Figure 15-4:
Blanca
Lee uses
blogging
software to
add prod-
ucts to her
e-commerce
Web site.

Here's how it all works:

1. When she has a new product to add to her Web site, Blanca launches the Expression Engine back end and begins a new "blog" entry.

   Expression Engine allows users to customize the interface fields. Blanca can enter the description of a new piece of art in a Description field, instead of a Body field.

2. In the new entry page, shown in Figure 15-5, Blanca enters the name, cost, shipping cost, and description, and selects a category for the product.

   While blogging software is easy to use, it doesn't have the same error checking capabilities as e-commerce software. If Blanca enters the price as "sixty-five dollars" the software doesn't tell her she needs to enter it as numerals, and if she leaves the decimal point out, it doesn't alert her that her cost is too high.

3. Using Expression Engine's built-in image upload tool, Blanca uploads the image and creates a thumbnail image for the product.

   Expression Engine handles storing the files in folders, and the creation of smaller versions of the pictures.

4. Blanca clicks Submit, and the product is automatically published to her Web site in all the appropriate categories.

   The templates that generate the pages themselves include the code necessary to make the Buy Now buttons and add selected products to the PayPal shopping cart.

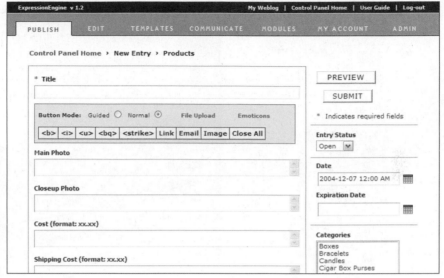

Figure 15-5:
Entering a
new prod-
uct is as
simple as
publishing a
blog entry.

You can find out more about PayPal's free shopping-cart system by visiting
www.paypal.com and clicking the Merchant Tools tab. You can use PayPal to
process credit card payments from customers without acquiring a merchant
credit card account or other expensive e-commerce software.

Because this site is created using blog software, Blanca neither needs to learn
HTML nor bother with file transfer software to get new products onto her
site. The process is simple and streamlined, and Blanca can quickly and
easily remove out-of-stock items from the site, update product information,
and upload photos without the help of a Web designer or technical team.

T-Shirt King

The online t-shirt retailer T-Shirt King also uses blog software in conjunction
with e-commerce, but in a slightly different format: By posting informative
blog entries about what is on the T-shirts, T-Shirt King entertains, informs,
and sells products at the same time.

In the past, T-Shirt King created short essays to accompany popular T-shirts
and promote sales. A T-shirt with John F. Kennedy's image on it, for example,
was accompanied by a timeline of his life. For a *Goonies* T-shirt, T-Shirt King
produced a collection of trivia about the movie. These short essays were
entertaining to read and gave each T-shirt some context. They proved to be
a successful technique for increasing sales as well.

In 2003, T-Shirt King began posting these essays (previously delivered by e-mail newsletter) on a blog at blog.t-shirtking.com, shown in Figure 15-6. Readers of the blog get both content and a fairly low-key sales pitch, and some do choose to buy.

The integration of the e-commerce Web site and blog isn't seamless but nonetheless serves to convert some blog readers into T-shirt customers.

Figure 15-6: The T-Shirt King blog entertains while promoting sales.

T-Shirt King.com ™

Pros and cons

Using blog software to produce an e-commerce site isn't a solution for every would-be online retailer. If you have thousands of products or products that aren't easily categorized, you will want to consider some of the more advanced shopping cart and transaction systems available. Still, you can get started or run a test store quickly and inexpensively by adapting blog software for the purpose.

You may find *Starting an Online Business For Dummies,* by Greg Holden, useful if you're thinking of starting an online store.

With some small modifications by a good programmer, you can fairly easily modify the blog software to allow:

- Product customization (sizes, colors, and so on)
- Display of related products

Unless you do a lot of modification or integrate your blog software with a robust shopping cart, you won't get:

- Inventory control that tracks sales against product availability
- Invoicing, sales confirmation e-mails, and other common customer communication features — unless they're part of your shopping cart, as with PayPal (see Chapter 14).

Building Customer Service FAQ Lists

Businesses with online customer service and support Web sites deal with managing customer questions and comments in several ways: forums, e-mail, documentation, and frequently asked questions lists (FAQs).

Each tool comes with its own set of limitations, and for a really effective support system, some combination of two or more of these is likely ideal.

Blogs can certainly come into effective use in this area, especially in the creation of a really useful list of frequently asked questions. Here's how to make customer support work with blog software:

1. Users submit a question via e-mail or a Web site.

2. A customer service person (or whoever handles these incoming "How do I . . ." type issues) identifies issues that are likely to be useful to several customers — those that are or will be "frequently asked."

3. Once identified, the question and its answer are posted to the FAQ blog, which you can refine to allow questions organized by topic.

4. Customers looking for answers to that question can search for it, read it, and if they have follow-up questions can post them as comments.

What's a wiki?

Wikis are collaboratively created Web sites that allow any user to add, edit, or delete content. They are an exercise in group content creation, with no software-imposed limitations on contributors or content. The concept and name originated with Ward Cunningham, who also created the first one — the Portland Pattern Repository — in March 1995. Wiki is Hawaiian for "quick."

The most well-known example of a wiki is Wikipedia, which is shown in the following figure. Wikipedia (www.wikipedia.org) is a free encyclopedia created by anyone who cares to contribute, maintained and edited by anyone who wishes to take that role. Some popular wiki engines are UseMod, TWiki, MoinMoin, PmWiki, and MediaWiki.

The rules governing how a wiki works are set by the person who initially sets up the wiki, but generally wikis are open to the public. Any visitor to the wiki can choose to add or edit a page — presumably to provide useful content — or even to delete one. Wiki software tracks and saves all additions and changes, allowing content to be rolled back or recovered if needed.

Sometimes "contributors" provide wrong information (consciously or not) to a wiki. The whole philosophy, however, assumes that wiki members self-police, self-censor, and self-edit; inaccurate contributions are caught and removed quickly and with little effort.

Wikis are great for creative projects involving large groups who bring lots of different expertise to the table. Use them for project management, planning, content, and more. They are better at collecting information that grows and keeps its value over time — a daily weather report isn't a good candidate for a wiki, but an earthquake-monitoring and experience-collection wiki might be quite interesting.

If you do allow comments, be sure to scan them promptly or moderate them to ensure that your FAQ is accurate and useful.

By using Blogger, you can even create a FAQ of this kind for free. I created a FAQ about *wikis* in about 20 minutes, which you can see in Figure 15-7. (See the sidebar in this chapter or visit the FAQ at `whatsawiki.blogspot.com` to discover what a wiki is.)

Figure 15-7: I created The "What the Heck is a Wiki?" FAQ using Blogger.

Because FAQs are typically organized somewhat differently from a blog, you probably need to spend some time customizing the HTML templates that build your pages. For instance, I removed the timestamp information from my FAQ because this information is *evergreen* — that is, it stays current for some time to come. I also prevented Blogger from creating a monthly archive, because a date-based archive doesn't make sense for this short FAQ list.

Keeping Track of Resources

Almost any collection — whether it's intangible code or shop tools — lends itself to easy cataloging via even the most basic blog software. Use comments to track everything from use to location, all within a framework that allows "borrowers" to see just who has overdue items.

If you keep a small library or resource center, consider using blog software to maintain a catalog of your books, CDs, and other materials. Especially in circumstances where these resources are shared by collaborators, you can use the comment functionality to share reviews or post notices about wear and tear and service records.

Human resources groups that maintain staff Web pages or an employee directory can use blog software to easily add, update, or remove employees from the directory. Blog software that lets you sort postings alphabetically instead of by publication date is especially useful in this case.

Part VI
The Part of Tens

The 5th Wave   By Rich Tennant

"You can smirk all you like, but I know wearing this helps keep the entries in my Squash Lovers blog authentic."

In this part . . .

Good things come in tens — at least in a *For Dummies* book! This chapter proves the rule. Chapter 16 is a collection of 10 great ideas you can turn to when you're having a hard time coming up with blog posts. In Chapter 17, count how many of the 10 traits of a good blogger you have, and get some ideas on how to improve your blogging. Finally, in Chapter 18, take one more look at blogs that make the grade with great writing, beautiful design, and fabulous user-interface. If that's not enough, I throw in some blogs that push the technology envelope in astonishing and inspiring ways.

Chapter 16

Ten Dry-Spell-Breaking Ideas

*O*ne of the nice things about blogs is that you can post whenever you want, from wherever you want. It's convenient, but it's no guarantee that you have something to post about. There are times in every blogger's career when ideas run dry, but you still have to produce fresh content. Other times, you feel like you've been cooking the same meal over and over, and you need a dash of spice to liven things up.

In this chapter, I share ten ideas that may help you when you've hit a dry spell and need some inspiration. Don't use them all up at once!

Don't forget that blog entries can be created and stored. On days when you feel incredibly creative, why not write a blog post or two that are *evergreen* — that is, can stay useful for some time — and stockpile some posts for the days when you are really casting about for content.

Holding a Contest

Everybody likes a winner, and everyone wants to be one! Put together a quick competition. You can call on your readers to be contestants, and make the community part of the judging as well. Every contest generates excitement and discussion, no matter how small the stakes.

Some topics that work well

- Name This Product/Service.

- Assign a topic, and have people post entries on your blog or on their own blog and link to yours.

- Guessing games are always fun. For example, put a super-close-up photo of one of your products on the blog, and get readers to guess which product it is. Or show a tool used in the creation of your products, and ask readers to guess its use.

- Have your readers submit creative ideas for using your products or photos of your products in use.

- Ask readers for predictions on a sales number or news event.

For inspiration, take a look at the immensely popular community forum Fark (www.fark.com), a site that frequently runs amazingly creative Photoshop contests. The site has a lot of nonwork safe links, but look for a Photoshop logo and then click the Comments link to see people's entries.

Giving out prizes of value can be tricky — maybe you're on a limited budget, and maybe your legal department would have a fit if you tried to offer "wonderful prizes." But public acknowledgement in an active community can be a nice prize, or you can send a company-branded item to the winners (even if you didn't promise them a material prize).

Posting Reader Photos

Let your readers send in pictures of themselves with your product or service, or your logo, or of your company's local presence. Post pictures in an online gallery, and let the audience rate them. Blog about the best or most interesting ones. (This could also be a contest.)

Photos have proven to be very popular with blog readers, who also respond well to being included in the creation of blog content, so a photo gallery is almost always a win-win situation.

For an example, visit iPodlounge's iPods Around the World at gallery. ipodlounge.com. For a more elaborate example of a user-generated photo gallery, visit Lomography at www.lomography.com.

Describing Where You Work

A blog post about what's on your desk is likely to be too boring for even your mom to read. (I'm just kidding. Your mom will read everything.) But the rest of your readers might like to know a little about the more general setting of where you do your blogging.

Take a tour of the company break room. Show the amazing quantity of Twizzlers your programmers go through. What's the lobby look like from the receptionist's point of view — most people always see the lobby from the couch, never from the commander's chair.

What can you see from your roof? What does your building look like from the place across the street? Use common sense — don't post pictures of someone punching in the security code on a keypad, for instance. But give readers a feel for where you work. Is there construction going on? An occasional update on progress is always nice and gives you a chance to talk about the benefits of a new facility.

Posts like these are a great way to show readers the person behind the blog without getting too personal or off topic.

Opening Your Mail

Several journalists blog about the worst or most inappropriate press releases they've received or about the promotional trinkets and swag that comes in the mail. But you can also post traditional mail — the best or most interesting customer service letters, for instance, especially if you think the topic being addressed is useful for others.

Be sure to ask permission first. Customers who correspond by mail with your company expect their letters to be read but may be unpleasantly surprised to find that anyone can read it on your blog.

Wired and *Games* magazines often display the most interestingly addressed envelopes on their letters page; you can do something similar online.

Creating a "Best of" Collection

After you blog long enough, reward yourself. Take a day or a week, and post the best of your blog postings. Update them where appropriate, but in general, you're just giving your best material a chance to see the light again and helping future visitors to find the best of the early days.

Your blog isn't your press release section. Bringing attention to an old press release is odd, but it's quite normal to refer back to a particularly valuable piece of writing you did.

Author Seth Godin did just this in his blog in late 2004, as you can see in Figure 16-1, or at `sethgodin.typepad.com/seths_blog/2004/12/ the_best_seth_g.html`.

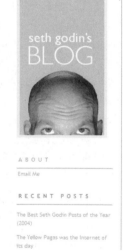

Figure 16-1: Help your readers find gems they might have missed by pointing out old posts that are still current.

< The Yellow Pages was the Internet of its day | Main

The Best Seth Godin Posts of the Year (2004)

Easier than checking the archives! More efficient than wading through inane banter.

If you're only going to read 2 of my posts a month (that's 24 for those of you without a calculator) then this is where I'd have you start:

Seth's Blog: Sleeping at night.

Seth's Blog: A Little Like Francisco Franco.

Seth's Blog: What happens when it's all on tape?.

Seth's Blog: Beware the CEO blog.

Seth's Blog: Three kinds of blogs.

Seth's Blog: Lies to protect the status quo.

Seth's Blog: Trust and Respect, Courage and Leadership.

ABOUT

Email Me

RECENT POSTS

The Best Seth Godin Posts of the Year (2004)

The Yellow Pages was the Internet of its day

Taking the Show on the Road

You don't have to get too far away from your regular haunt to get a little perspective and maybe some fresh air to boot. You can probably blog from a nearby library, a coffee shop, the local college, and even some city parks if you have a WiFi-enabled laptop.

Leave work behind when you're on vacation, but if blog topics occur to you after you unwind, you'll feel glum if you don't jot them down for future use.

Besides, your audience gets a certain wow factor simply from your posting from a novel location. For example: "I'm in a taxi speeding to our investors' meeting today, and I'll have a lot of new information for you tomorrow when I return" is a lot more interesting than "I'm out of the office for corporate reasons. Please come back tomorrow."

Making Yourself Heard

For a change of pace, how about blogging in audio format instead of in text? Readers (now listeners) are interested in hearing the speaking voice of someone they have read for a while.

Audio posts work best with content that you can read dramatically — let your listeners really hear that sarcasm drip, if that's the way you're going. You can also use an audio post to record sounds in your current environment that your readers might find interesting — the chaos of the trading floor, the sounds of traffic on the street, or the Muzak in the company elevator.

Don't forget to pay attention to the conditions in which the audio is recorded; too much background noise can drown you out and make you hard to hear.

Don't lower your usual standards, but realize that the novelty of speaking your post does take some of the emphasis off the content of it. As well, some people won't or can't listen to audio postings, so don't choose this post as the occasion to make a huge news announcement.

Some good software packages are designed to let you create audio postings from a phone, so you can take this technique on the road with you as long as you have a mobile phone. Check out audioblog.com for one audioblogging service, and read more about other audblogging tools in Chapter 13.

Questions, Please

Q: Does the Q & A format draw people in? Does it seem to interest people more than a regular, bland post?

A: Yes; yes, it does. Find someone in the hall, detain them for five minutes, and ask them what they're working on and why. That's all you need for an interesting post. Repeat as needed.

These mini-interviews give people who aren't normally part of the blog a voice and presence, and make them known to readers as well. Use these to recognize unsung heroes, reveal little-known areas of expertise, or to capture the jokes of the hilarious guy down the hall.

Making Someone Up

I'm not advocating that you lie about the facts. However, consider writing a blog entry, or series of entries, from the point of view of a made-up character.

Faced with covering Lance Armstrong's sixth Tour de France, the *Austin American-Statesman* decided to have a little fun. It created a blog to cover the race and typed up a fun, funny take from the point of view of Armstrong's *bike*. Lance's Bike blogged his dissatisfaction with his current paint color, confessed his gambling problem, and discussed the after-race celebrations in the bike storage trailer. The blog is at `www.statesman.com/sports/content/custom/blogs/tourdiary` and shown in Figure 16-2.

Of course, creating a false persona to blog in is a little risky — you may sound corny rather than funny, and it can be hard to sustain for long. For some blogs, it may not be appropriate at all, depending on the usual tone and style. Still, this technique can garner a lot of attention when done right.

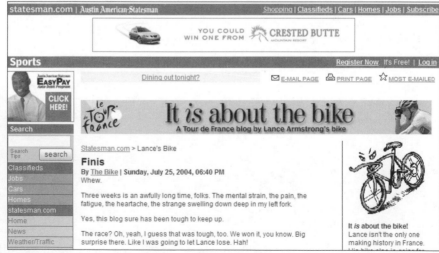

Figure 16-2:
The *Austin American-Statesman's* Tour de France blog by Lance Armstrong's bike.

Building a Widget

Not every blog post has to be static. You can quite easily find a nifty, free JavaScript program and adapt it for your own use. Coming up with the idea for a quick little Web widget can be a fun way to increase traffic to your site and interact with the readers.

As an example, visit the Cyborg Name Generator (`www.cyborgname.com`). This application allows readers to enter their name and choose an avatar image, and produces a small graphic displaying the avatar and a reasonably humorous robot acronym based on the user's name.

Your program doesn't have to be a super-well-designed program. In fact, it doesn't have to be programmed at all; it could be something as simple as a "Choose Your Own Adventure" style series of linked posts.

On the other hand, you could start with a simple idea, and it could grow beyond your blog. After all, the best way to get yourself out of a rut is to build a road to somewhere else.

Chapter 17

Ten Traits of a Good Blogger

*B*logs that get traffic and repeat readers do so not because they use a particular style of writing or stick to a particular topic — in fact, almost all of them are wildly different, and most can't be easily categorized or explained. Some blogs allow comments; others don't. Some are beautifully designed; others use the cookie-cutter templates of a blog software package. Some post short, some long; some are personal, some clinical.

So what is it that makes a blog successful? What brings readers back over and over again? What makes them post comments and tell their friends about it? What all these blogs have in common is pretty simple — they're written by a really good blogger.

With that in mind, this chapter pulls together the traits of a good blogger whose chances of creating a blog that get people interested are high.

Feeling Passionate about the Topic

> "Love. Fall in love and stay in love. Write only what you love, and love what you write. The key word is love. You have to get up in the morning and write something you love, something to live for."
>
> — Ray Bradbury

While writing this book, I spoke with many bloggers. To a person, they all had a genuine love for the topics they blog about. They really, really care, and that enthusiasm can't help but show in the quality of their writing, dedication to their readers, and nose for news. Given the choice, most of them would talk about the topic of their blog all day, including to perfect strangers on the bus.

Readers put up with many faults if your passion for the subject matches their own.

Having passion for a topic does not mean forgoing critical thinking and posting. In fact, those bloggers who care passionately about what they blog about are in the best position to make astute criticisms of people and events, and they should never shrink from doing so.

Writing Wonderfully

"Read, read, read. Read everything — trash, classics, good and bad, and see how they do it. Just like a carpenter who works as an apprentice and studies the master. Read! You'll absorb it."

— William Faulkner

"I don't want to be studied in English classes. I want to be read."

— Tim O'Brien, novelist

The blog style has, so far, been conversational, casual, and usually somewhat humorous in tone. Not everyone can write this way, and of course not every blog has to follow this method, but a well-written blog almost invariably is a well-read blog. A great blogger can probably interest you in a topic you never thought you cared about and make you a devoted visitor to a blog whose topic you are already interested in. Every habitual visitor to a blog got hooked somehow, and a sharp, interesting turn of phrase might just be what reeled them in.

Write a blog much like you write an e-mail — direct, to –the point, and meant for a specific reader. You should be compelling to read because of your enthusiasm, not because you throw in four adjectives when one does the job.

With writing, practice does make perfect, so a blogger who has the requisite passion but is weak in the literary department can benefit greatly by simply sticking with it. Of course, a good dictionary, spell checker, or editor can move this process along.

Posting Often

"The more a man writes, the more he can write."

— William Hazlitt

It's been said before, but I have to say it again: Blogging isn't for those who are already overscheduled. Posting doesn't have to be a lengthy task, especially if you keep things short, but even the shortest post takes some time to research, write, and publish. Adding images makes the process even longer. Really dedicated bloggers usually post several times a day, depending on what they blog about, so starting a blog requires that you devote at least an hour to reading and writing every day.

A blogger who doesn't love the topic and feel compelled to evangelize about it, or one for whom writing is a terrible chore, doesn't last long. Frequent posts keep readers coming back often, raise your traffic numbers, and attract the attention of other bloggers — so posts are by no means optional.

A flagging blog that doesn't get the feedback and kudos discourages the blogger, so infrequent posting can be an ever-deepening spiral.

If you haven't posted for a while, don't get hung up on making your next blog post really sharp to make up for a long silence. Just do a post right now, and worry about your *next* one.

Developing a Nose for Information

"True genius lies in the capacity for evaluation of uncertain, hazardous, and conflicting information."

— Attributed to Winston Churchill

Part of what makes blogging so time-consuming is the need for content. If you want to post four times a day, that means you have to find four new things to talk about every day. Political bloggers in the 2000 and 2004 elections never lacked for fodder, but most bloggers constantly scramble for news and information to talk about.

A good blogger was an avid news consumer long before becoming a blogger — blogging means always being on the lookout for the latest information. If you're already reading everything you can get your hands on about the topic you want to blog, your task is that much easier. If you're thinking of blogging about something you don't know much about and don't already watch for information about, get ready for a lot of research time before you ever get to the business at hand — posting to your blog.

If you find something on the Web, you may be the first to spot it, but the odds are against you, and others will eventually link to the source, not you. A more valuable service to your readers is to take some relevant bit of information from the analog world and present it to them via your blog.

Looking Outward

> *"Why wouldn't you write to escape yourself as much as you might write to express yourself? It's far more interesting to write about others."*
>
> — Susan Sontag

> *"Writing is communication, not self-expression. Nobody in this world wants to read your diary except your mother."*
>
> — Richard Peck

Good bloggers know who they are blogging for and are mindful that what they're posting is of interest. The bad reputation blogs have earned among many (especially media critics) is associated with bloggers who post solely about themselves and their activities; they're usually mocked as being narcissistic navel-gazers. It is unfortunate that blogs developed this reputation early on, because a good blog is anything but an exercise in narcissism.

A great blog has the potential to be a Web site that feels like it was made just for each reader, tailored to each reader's activities or life., A great blogger is someone whose interest in the topic of the blog creates an immediate resonance with others who share that interest.

As long as you keep in mind that the blog is *for* the reader, your blog can be successful.

Staying Open and Accessible

> *"Difference of opinion leads to enquiry, and enquiry to truth."*
>
> — Thomas Jefferson

Most bloggers allow readers to comment on their posts, and most readers read and value those comments in relative proportion to the posts themselves. The spirit of a blog is all about interaction and dialogue, and with few exceptions, a huge portion of the value a blog has for readers is the access they have to the blogger.

Genuinely wanting to hear what your readers have to say (even when it's critical) allows you to reap the benefits in several ways:

- ✔ The blog is more attractive to readers.
- ✔ Readers offer more information, including what they want more of or dislike.
- ✔ You become better-informed about the topic.
- ✔ Readers are more likely ask about problems or mistakes, rather than attack.

The good blogger makes a point of providing a way for readers to get in touch via the Web or e-mail, or even by providing a phone number. These folks are taking the spirit of blogging to heart, and their readers know it.

Moving Forward with Creativity

"You can't wait for inspiration. You have to go after it with a club."

— Jack London

Your ideal blogger is not a stenographer; you're not posting court transcripts. Much of a blog's value is in interpreting information that probably is available elsewhere. So you need to spot and react to small trends, and keep the blog fresh by trying new experiments as the medium grows and matures.

Whatever blog tool you use, you will eventually find some limitations and bugs in it. You need to think of a way to get around these blocks and grow and develop as your blog grows and develops. The format and technology is too young for you to keep your blog static.

Handling Criticism Gracefully

"To avoid criticism, do nothing, say nothing, be nothing."

— Elbert Hubbard

Interaction on a blog isn't all positive — all bloggers are criticized on their own blogs, and businesses are especially subject to criticism as customers experience problems.

Good bloggers are prepared for criticism; in fact, many welcome it. Besides indicating that the community around a blog is thriving, critical feedback spawns further dialogue and ultimately, better understanding. Well, it does if handled right! Good bloggers don't react with knee-jerk defensiveness but use criticism as an opportunity to assess whether change is needed or opinions are actually off base.

Better bloggers admit when criticism is warranted. If you do so in a complimentary fashion, you just may earn the admiration of the original critic.

The best bloggers might actually take action based on that criticism, if it is warranted, and even involve readers in deciding what changes to make. This is an unusual stance for most companies to take in such an open forum but one that earns a business loyalty and respect when handled well.

The worst thing you can do, except in cases where abuse is more like spam and is flooding your blog from one source, is to delete the criticism. Doing so just opens up more questions from other bloggers about what else you're hiding.

Being Honest

"If the writing is honest it cannot be separated from the man who wrote it."

— Tennessee Williams

So many of the bloggers I spoke to talked about the necessity of honesty in business blogs. The blogosphere is full of whistle-blowers and watchdogs, many of whom are also sensitive about the use of blogs for commercial purposes. Spin, damage control, and lies (even white ones) have no place in this medium, and the best bloggers know that.

I don't mean to imply that communication is by nature dishonest, but the blogging philosophy is something wholly different than traditional marketing. Blogging requires a level of openness and transparency that most companies just haven't needed to provide in the past. Good bloggers are scrupulously honest, acknowledging when a competitor is doing something better, when the company has made a mistake, or just when the facts were wrong in a post. Without that honesty, your readers will go elsewhere, either to ignore you or to read something they think is honest.

To put it another way — if your readers are going to learn about you, wouldn't you rather it was the truth from you rather than the imaginative interpretations of someone else?

Knowing Where You're Going

"If you start with a bang, you won't end with a whimper."

— T. S. Eliot

It might sound obvious, but a blog needs to have a mission. Measuring success is awfully hard when you don't have any goals in the first place!

Good bloggers set out with some goals in mind and are always thinking about new ones. Perhaps the blog needs to accomplish something for the company — rehabilitate a less-than-popular brand image or help increase awareness around a hard-to-understand product. Maybe the blogger wants to establish credibility for the company within the industry. Maybe the blog is an internal one and needs to create better morale within a department.

No matter what the goal is, you must have a strong understanding of it and how to address it. Many a blog has run into trouble when the blogger lost sight of the original goal and got sidetracked by unrelated topics. Ultimately, the goal for the blog must be related to the readers to be achievable; if the goal of your blog is to generate advertising revenue, think again! Advertising revenue is the result of readers, and readers reward a blog that is providing a genuine service, not one that is smoke and mirrors.

Chapter 18

Ten Blogs You Should Know

1 have featured some great blogs in this book, but there are many more whose authors have worked out the formula for success and deserve to be recognized. This chapter introduces you to a small fraction of those: ten blogs I think you should know about, especially if you're serious about understanding and being part of the blogosphere. The blogs in this chapter span the gamut in terms of topics, style, and philosophy, but each bring something unique and special to the blogging community.

I can't include every blog — I trust you to explore the blogrolls of each of these blogs to unearth more gems!

Dan Gillmor's Blogs

```
dangillmor.typepad.com
weblog.siliconvalley.com/column/dangillmor
```

Up until January 2004, Dan Gillmor wrote a blog about technology, economics, policy, and politics called Dan Gillmor's eJournal. Since then Gillmor has begun blogging about grass-roots journalism on a new blog. It's worth taking a look at the popular eJournal and then checking out Gillmor's new blog to see how he's maintaining his momentum in the new space.

Gillmor was with the *San Jose Mercury News,* the publisher of SiliconValley.com, since 1994. The eJournal blog dates from October 26, 1999. Gillmor wrote both the blog and a column for the *Mercury News.* The column was his outlet for extended analysis and thoughtful commentary; the blog let him focus in on short, timely tidbits. He sometimes solicited feedback or information in the blog while researching his column.

The new Grassroots Journalism blog, shown in Figure 18-1, covers many of the same topics that Gillmor covered in eJournal, and Gillmor appears to be succeeding at keeping his readers.

Of blogging, Gillmor says, "Use a human voice, not a corporate one. This is the only absolute rule I would follow."

Figure 18-1:
Popular blogger Dan Gillmor blogs about grass-roots journalism.

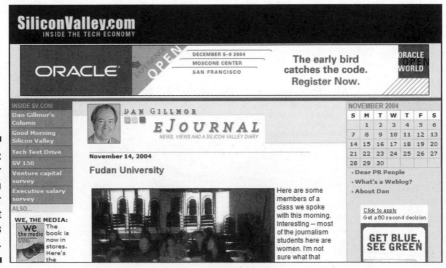

BuzzMachine

www.buzzmachine.com

BuzzMachine is the personal blog of Jeff Jarvis, the president and creative director of Advance.net. Jarvis has a bee in his bonnet about blogging's potential to revolutionize media and business, and he isn't shy about letting you know just why you should care, too.

Jarvis often breaks with blogging tradition by posting very lengthy entries on his blog. He posts about the news media, freedom of speech, and — as do most bloggers — unpredictable topics he happens to find interesting. His opinionated and reasoned posts attract comments from readers and other bloggers. Jarvis began his blog during the early spike of blog creation in response to the attacks of September 11, 2001. In it, he chronicled his transformation from pacifist to war supporter. He is unapologetically in thrall to blogs and their potential. If you are looking for passionate explorations of blogging issues, look to BuzzMachine, shown in Figure 18-2.

Jarvis's past credentials include some heavy media resume lines: TV critic for *TV Guide* and *People,* creator of *Entertainment Weekly,* Sunday editor of the *New York Daily News,* and a columnist for the *San Francisco Examiner.*

Figure 18-2: Buzz Machine, the personal blog of Advance.net President Jeff Jarvis.

BuzzMachine

by Jeff Jarvis

December 05, 2004

The First Amendment gets its day in court

: Fox – bless 'em – has decided to fight the FCC's record fine against its Married by America, getting the first court test of the FCC's censorship in more than 25 years.

Fox Broadcasting Co. is appealing a record-setting $1.18 million fine for airing racy fare on a show called "Married by America," saying the government's indecency rules for broadcast television are unconstitutional because they don't apply to cable and satellite television.

Fox said the show was not indecent, and it argues that over-the-air broadcasters are now treated as "second-class citizens" by a Federal Communications Commission that unfairly holds them but not their rivals to decency standards.

If the FCC upholds the fine, Fox could take the case to court, creating the

: HOME ... : Email me ...
: RSS/XML ... : About me
: Rules of engagement

ISSUES2004
: All posts
Intro
Comments | Links
: Health care
Comments | Links
: Iraq
Comments | Links

InstaPundit

www.instapundit.com

Glenn Reynolds is a law professor at the University of Tennessee and the prominent blogger behind InstaPundit, shown in Figure 18-3. Reynolds also writes a column that looks an awful lot like a blog for MSNBC. Reynolds blogs about politics on the right, law issues, the presidency, and anything else that strikes his fancy.

In his FAQ, Reynolds warns readers that InstaPundit is a hobby, not a news site, and admits that he can't explain the blog's popularity: "Other than e-mailing a few journalist-types early on, I've done nothing to promote InstaPundit; it's all been a function of links and word-of-mouth. Well, word-of-e-mail, anyway. It's just the magic of the Internet." Reynolds started InstaPundit in August 2001.

Unlike most bloggers, Reynolds does not allow readers to post comments on his site.

Figure 18-3: InstaPundit is a popular right-wing Web log created by Glenn Reynolds.

Power Line Blog

`powerlineblog.com`

In late 2004, the right-leaning Power Line blog was named Blog of the Year by *Time* magazine, which said that Power Line was the blog most responsible for turning blogs into a major media resource in 2004.

Power Line, shown in Figure 18-4, is the work of three attorneys: John Hinderaker, Scott Johnson, and Paul Mirengoff. Together, the three are credited with turning the controversial *60 Minutes* report about President Bush's National Guard service records on its head. Readers of the blog pointed out inconsistencies with the documents revealed by *60 Minutes,* and the Power Line authors pulled it all together. Ultimately, the documents were shown to be forgeries, *60 Minutes* and CBS were left with mud on their faces, and Dan Rather chose to retire. Power Line — and its highly vocal readership — get much of the credit for forcing the issue to the forefront. (If you're interested in reading the post that got it all started, go to `powerlineblog.com/archives/007760.php#007760`.)

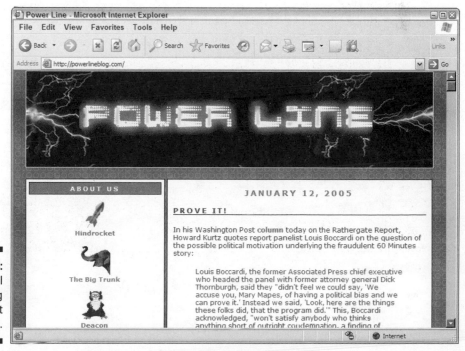

Figure 18-4: Get your fill of right-wing politics at Power Line.

Doc Searls Weblog

doc.weblogs.com

Doc Searls has been blogging since November 1999. Searls is the senior editor of *Linux Journal,* a co-author of The Cluetrain Manifesto (www.cluetrain.com), and advisory-board member of several tech companies.

Searls originally intended the blog to be a companion of the book version of The Cluetrain Manifesto, but it quickly became more personal. Today, he sees the blog (shown in Figure 18-5) as an ongoing conversation, a place to bounce ideas off interested readers and refine his thinking. Searls blogs on all kinds of topics, from the weather to technology. His entries are typically short, link-filled, and personal. He frequently mentions his activities and family.

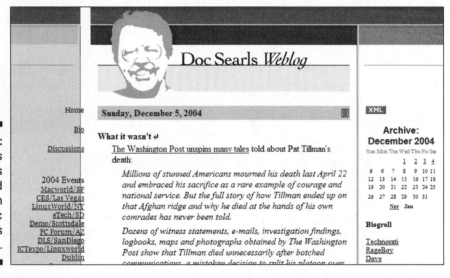

Figure 18-5: Keep tabs on all kinds of news and information on the Doc Searls Weblog.

Scripting News

`www.scripting.com`

Dave Winer may actually be the blogfather (the title gets thrown around a lot). Winer is the founder and CEO of Userland Software. He created his Scripting News blog in 1997 but was doing bloglike things as early as 1995. He's helped establish a number of technologies and conventions that underlay blogging technology today.

Scripting News is his personal blog, and Winer posts about technology, business, blogs and bloggers, and his own activities. Winer is known for posting needle-sharp criticisms in order to prompt discussion, which makes him interesting to read and someone to be a little leery of as well. His readers may not always agree with him, but he has nonetheless developed a hefty following. His background and success as an early computer software programmer means he knows of what he speaks, technologically. Readers may not post comments on Scripting News (which is shown in Figure 18-6).

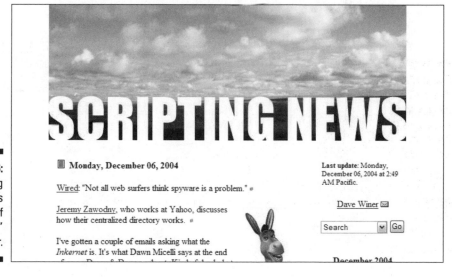

Figure 18-6:
Scripting News is the blog of "blogfather" Dave Winer.

Gizmodo

www.gizmodo.com

Are you in the market for the hippest mobile phone, best digital camera, or sharpest monitor? Attractively packaged and well written, gadget blog Gizmodo keeps you up to date on the latest in consumer electronics.

Gizmodo serves in the neighborhood of 200,000 pages a day and boasts 1,130,768 unique visitors a month, an impressive figure for any site, let alone a blog. Gizmodo made its debut in June and July of 2002 with posts about the Hewlett-Packard Jornada and the world's largest hard drive (200GB). Technology has improved, and the public has developed a huge appetite for knowledgeable, well-written product reviews.

Gizmodo, shown in Figure 18-7, is part of the Gawker Media network of blogs run by Nick Denton.

Figure 18-7: Gizmodo dishes all the news about consumer electronics you can handle.

Anil Dash

www.dashes.com/anil

Anil Dash is currently a vice president at Six Apart, the company behind popular blogging software Movable Type and hosted blog tool TypePad. Anil is the quintessential blogger — highly technical, ubiquitous online, tireless, and an interesting writer. Like Dave Winer and Jeff Jarvis, Dash is convinced that blogging is a revolutionary publishing format. He contributes to several blogs and apparently never sleeps.

Dash's blog is by intention an aggregation blog that brings together tidbits from around the Web — there's a lot here about blogs themselves and plenty more for those looking for unusual photos of Japanese storm drains and the definition of the word *spadia*. (Look it up.) He splits his posts between short, link-only items and longer entries with more thought and explanation. Dash isn't the biggest blogger in the pond, but he's exceptionally well connected. Whither goes blogging innovation, goes Anil.

Dash's blog, with its tongue-in-cheek tagline "taking the 'daily' out of 'daily links,'" is shown in Figure 18-8.

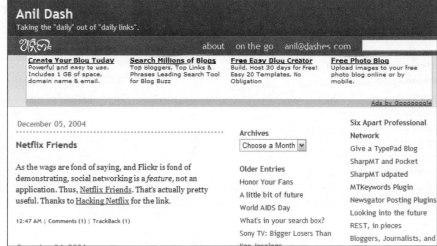

Figure 18-8: Get a Dash of Anil at www. dashes. com/anil.

Blogging.la

www.blogging.la

The brainchild of minor media magnets Sean Bonner and Jason DeFillippo, Blogging.la brings together the collective insights and interests of several major Los Angeles–based writers. Together, they blog for and about Los Angeles, creating community and connecting far-flung residents. There are currently 20 L.A. bloggers contributing as the mood strikes them, but usually several times a week each. During any given week, the blog contains posts about upcoming events (exhibits, parades, performances), new clubs, the weather, and — it *is* L.A. — traffic.

Blogging.la, which is shown in Figure 18-9, is one of several Metroblogging efforts put together by Bonner and DeFillippo. Twenty-five other cities have similar blogs, including Atlanta; Chicago; London; Tokyo; Vienna; and Washington, D.C. Plans are in the works for Paris, Dublin, and Istanbul (www.metroblogging.com).

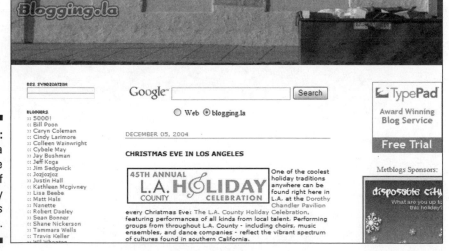

Figure 18-9: Blogging.la gives hope to the idea of community in Los Angeles.

Chocolate & Zucchini

www.chocolateandzucchini.com

Chocolate & Zucchini is the blog of cook Clotilde Dusoulier, a computer engineer considering a career change to food journalism. Chocolate & Zucchini is beautifully designed, thoughtfully written, and mouth watering. Dusoulier cooks, but is not a cook, and readers of her blog discover the joys of the Parisian food markets as she does.

Her unassuming joy in describing food makes each blog entry great reading for even the most kitchenphobic reader and inspires others to try new recipes and techniques. Dusoulier blogs about new recipes, cooking tools, great food in restaurants, wine, and simple descriptions of eating something delicious. The blog boasts an e-mail newsletter, forums, a glossary of French cooking terms, a recipe index and a picture gallery. She began the blog, shown in Figure 18-10, in September 2003, and it now reaches an audience of about 100,000 visitors a month. But allow me to warn you: This blog is guaranteed to make you hungry.

Figure 18-10:
Head for the kitchen after reading Chocolate & Zucchini.

Part VII
Appendixes

The 5th Wave   By Rich Tennant

DataSuk
Service & Support

"Answer the following survey questions about our company's performance with either, 'Excellent', 'Good', 'Fair', or 'I'm Really Incapable of Appreciating Someone Else's Hard Work'."

In this part . . .

In these appendixes you find information that supplements what you read in the chapters, from the blogging glossary in Appendix A, to the great case studies in Appendix E. In Appendix B, learn how to make use of the companion blog for this book, and in Appendix C, get the scoop on all the hosted and independent blog solutions available to you as you search for the right one for your business. Use Appendix D to refresh your memory about just how domain names work.

Appendix A

Glossary

• •

aggregator: A collector of information about a topic or idea. An aggregator can be a person, blog, or Web site. Technologically speaking, RSS is an aggregation format for individual blogs. Google News is an example of a Web site that aggregates news for many sources.

Atom: An XML-based file format that produces a list of recent posts on a blog that can be read by newsreader software. The Atom "feed" can contain titles, text, information about posts, and links.

blog: A chronological log of information kept by an individual, group, or business. The term *blog* is a merging of the words *Web* and *log*. On a typical blog, the most recent post appears at the top of the page, usually timestamped. Scrolling down the page takes the reader to older posts. Each post usually offers an opportunity for readers to interact by adding their comments and might also display Trackback information about other blogs that have linked to this post. Blog content is determined entirely by the author of the blog; so many are personal journals, but others are focused aggregations of news or commentary.

blogger: The author of a blog.

bloggerati: The intelligentsia of the blog world — the people recognized by the blogging community as experts or celebrities.

blogging: Producing blog posts is called blogging. A blogger blogs on his or her blog.

blogmapping: The practice of tagging blog entries with location information and then showing entries on a geographic map. Blogmapping isn't appropriate for all blogs, but it's ideal for those about travel. This term has also been used to describe the practice of tracing the flow of information across the blogosphere.

blogosphere: The community of blogs and bloggers around the world.

blogroll: A collection of links used or recommended by an individual blogger. A blogroll is usually shown in a column on a blog.

blogware: Blog software.

buzz: A highly intense and interactive form of word-of-mouth communication.

buzz marketing: A no- or low-cost method of marketing associated with people telling other people about a company's products or services. Buzz marketing is based on people's direct experiences with specific products or on the experiences others have related to them.

comment: A piece of feedback left by a reader on a blog post.

CSS: This acronym stands for *Cascading Style Sheets,* an advanced HTML technique that permits fine control and layout of a Web site and quick changes in formats across the site.

entry: A publication to a blog, possibly containing text, images, and other media. An entry may also be called a *post.*

feed: *See RSS* or *Atom.*

fisk: Critically rebutting a news article or essay point by point, usually by quoting and then commenting. The term is derived from the name of journalist Robert Fisk, whose stories have been frequently fisked in the blogosphere.

FTP: *File Transfer Protocol* is the mechanism that allows transfer of files and data from one computer to another.

HTML: *Hypertext Markup Language* is the computer coding used by Web designers to create Web pages.

linkroll: *See blogroll.*

meme: *Memes* are ideas that evolve virally. As bloggers post, comment on other blogs, post about posts on other blogs, and add their own thoughts, a meme spreads across the Internet, changing as it goes. Some groups spread memes consciously by participating in answering a set of questions or posting on a topic, but most memes are a natural byproduct of interesting topics.

moblog: *Moblog* is short for *mobile blog,* and *moblogging* is short for *mobile blogging.* Moblogging is simply the practice of posting content to a blog while not in front of a computer (from a PDA, phone, or camera, for instance). A moblog is a blog that is the result of mobile blogging.

permalink: Short for *permanent link*. This is a page of a blog that contains a single blog posting, which is easy to link to when referencing that post.

photoblog: A blog composed entirely of images, sometimes with caption information.

ping: A *ping* occurs when one computer asks another whether it's there; the second computer confirms its presence. In the blogosphere, many bloggers ping blog-aggregation Web sites to update that site when posting a new entry.

post: A publication to a blog, possibly containing text, images, and other media. A post may also be called an *entry*.

RSS: *RSS* stands for *Really Simple Syndication* and, like Atom, is an XML-based feed of a blog's postings that's picked up by blog-aggregation sites or software.

sideblog: A less important blog that appears within another blog. Many bloggers include a sideblog of photos or links. The name derives from the location of the sideblog: to the side of the main blog.

Trackback: *Trackback* is a mechanism that tracks references to a blog posting that occur on other blogs. Trackbacks are designed to help readers find other blogs discussing the same topic. They also let bloggers know that another blogger has blogged about and linked to a post.

vidblog: Short for *video blogs,* these blogs are made up of short video clips (in lieu of text or photo entries); creating the entries of a vidblog is called *vidblogging*. Bloggers sometimes include video in a mostly text blog, and this is also referred to as vidblogging.

viral marketing: A strategy that encourages individuals to pass on a marketing message to others. Viral marketing creates the potential for exponential growth, depending on the message's influence on, and exposure to, its target audience. Like a virus, viral marketing is based on the premise that growth will spread exponentially.

word-of-mouth marketing: Word of mouth is the person-to-person passing of information, especially recommendations, in an informal manner, rather than by mass media, advertising, organized publication, or traditional marketing. Word of mouth is typically considered a spoken communication, although Web dialogue, such as blogs, message boards, and e-mails, is now included in the definition.

Weblog: *See **blog**.*

XML: *XML* stands for *eXtensible Markup Language* and goes beyond HTML to allow publishers to build their own structures into markup languages. XML can be used for any kind of structured information and is intended to allow information to be passed to any computer system, regardless of the platform that the computer uses.

Appendix B

Using the Book Blog

I've created a companion blog for this book that you can visit at `www.buzzmarketingwithblogs.com`. Stop by today and make use of these handy features:

- ✔ Get up-to-date news and information about what's new with business blogs, from tips to new ventures.

- ✔ Reference lists of useful blogging tools that will help you make better use of blog technology.

- ✔ Read profiles of new business blogs — find out what the competition is doing, and improve your own blog.

- ✔ See several practical applications of the technologies that I discuss in this book, including the Amazon Affiliates program, Google AdSense, Bloglines, and more.

- ✔ Weigh in on the ongoing discussion about the utility of business and marketing blogs.

- ✔ Let me know about your blog so that I can add you to the growing list of businesses that are taking advantage of blogs.

If nothing else, stop by and let me know how to make the book blog useful for you as you start your blog and after you've been running it for some time. I really want this book and the book blog to be valuable resources for you, so don't hesitate to let me know when you need more information or when you're thinking about trying something new with your blog. I can't wait to see what you put together!

Appendix C

Hosted and Independent Blog Solutions

• •

*T*his appendix provides a list of possible hosted and independent blog solutions to help you while you research the right tool for you. It is by no means comprehensive, as more blogging services come online all the time.

Many blogging solutions reflect the early roots of blogs as personal diaries and cater to social networking situations. They may not all suit your business blog purposes.

Table C-1	Hosted Blog Solutions
20six	www.20six.co.uk
aetheri	www.aetheri.com
Blog-City	www.blog-city.com
Blogger	www.blogger.com
Blurty	www.blurty.com
Diaryland	www.diaryland.com
Diary-x	www.diary-x.com
Digital Expressions	www.digitalexpressions.nu
Easyjournal	www.easyjournal.com
eBloggy	www.ebloggy.com
LiveJournal	www.livejournal.com
Pitas	www.pitas.com
Radio UserLand	www.userland.com

(continued)

Table C-1 *(continued)*

TypePad	www.typepad.com
UpSaid	www.upsaid.com
Userland Hosted Manila	www.userland.com
Xanga	www.xanga.com

Table C-2	**Independent Blog Solutions**
b2	www.cafelog.com
Blosxom	www.blosxom.com
boastMachine	www.boastology.com
Drupal	www.drupal.org
ExpressionEngine	www.pmachine.com
Geeklog	www.geeklog.net
Greymatter	www.noahgrey.com/greysoft/
Movable Type	www.movabletype.org
Nucleus	www.nucleuscms.org
Pivot	www.pivotlog.net
pMachine Pro	www.pmachine.com
Roller	www.rollerweblogger.org
Serendipity	www.s9y.org
Textpattern	www.textpattern.com
Wordpress	www.wordpress.org

Appendix D

How URLs Work

URL, or Web address, has three parts:

- ✔ **Protocol:** This is the part that tells a computer to look for a Web page and is, by default, part of every Web address. The vast majority of Web addresses use `http://` as the protocol. Most browsers don't require that you type in the `http://` — they automatically add it for you.

- ✔ **Domain name:** This is the unchanging root of your Web site's address. Two domain names you're sure to be familiar with are `www.yahoo.com` and `www.google.com`. The first portion of a domain name is usually `www`; this is actually the name of the Web server. Some browsers allow you to skip typing the `www` — they automatically add it for you if it's needed. The domain name (`yahoo`) and suffix (`.com`) are the parts you register.

- ✔ **The suffix is appended to the domain name and is intended to identify its purpose.** A `.edu` suffix, for instance, indicates that the URL is that of an educational institution. Most businesses choose to use their business name as the domain name and follow it with the `.com` suffix.

  Anything that follows the suffix indicates the location of the file you are viewing on that Web server.

If the domain name you want to use isn't available with a `.com` suffix, check and see whether you can get another suffix, such as `.biz` or `.us`. You can find suffixes for every country, and other domains that were used by computer networks (`.net`), non-profit organizations (`.org`), government institutions (`.gov`), educational institutions (`.edu`), and so on.

Remember that domain names are not case sensitive, and that they can't contain any punctuation other than a hyphen. Even hyphens aren't a great idea because they aren't pronounced and will prevent users from reaching you if they hear about your domain only verbally. You also can't use spaces. When you advertise your blog, you can add capital letters to make the domain more readable without affecting its usefulness. For example, you can type BuzzMarketingWithBlogs.com or buzzmarketingwithblogs.com into a browser, and they both take you to the same Web site. For that matter, you could type BuZzMaRkEtInGw . . . you get the idea.

Appendix E

Case Studies

• •

*T*o help you negotiate building your own business blog, I talked to many bloggers — both professional and personal — who are running successful blogs. In this appendix, you find tips and advice from these bloggers, many of whom have added a blog to a set of other offerings, or customized the blog to meet particular needs of their readers.

Use these case studies to inspire your creativity about what can be accomplished with a business blog, and to get some great ideas for building thriving online communities. These folks are doing it, and doing it right.

Scobleizer

URL: `scoble.weblogs.com`

Created by: Robert Scoble

Date of birth: December 15, 2000

Numbers count: 2,500–4,500 unique visits most days (or 8,000–10,000 "on a good day")

The Gist: Scobleizer is a place where Web geeks meet to talk about the bleeding edge of computer hardware and software development and to see what Microsoft employee Robert Scoble thinks of them. Begun as a way for the then-conference planner to communicate with Web builders and software developers, the blog soon morphed into a home for rants and raves about all things high-tech — and helped Scoble secure his current job as a Microsoft "technical evangelist." Now, as a sort of official unofficial spokestech, Scoble continues to maintain the site on his own time. It doesn't include a newsletter or membership, but readers may post (unmoderated) comments or e-mail him directly.

The Technical Details: Scobleizer runs on Radio UserLand, a subscription-based, site-building tool. A one-year membership for $40 includes a license for blog-building software (installed and maintained on your own computer) and remote hosting.

The Financial Details: "My blog doesn't cost much money," says Scoble — and it's a bargain compared to official Microsoft advertising or promotion: "For an investment significantly less than $1 million, it has a major PR win on this, and it came from putting a human face on the company."

What's Cool: The blog is written by a Microsoft employee, but it's not the company line, which increases reader trust. *Scobleizing* means praising the good — and prodding for better when software or service (even Microsoft's) don't meet expectations. Also cool: Scoble offers sneak peeks at the newest Microsoft technologies and offers a forum for geek dreamers to pitch their own requests.

Plans for the future: "I'm just looking for hot things, trends, things I can get excited about and play with. I will be buying a media center and cell phone this fall; those will be the hot things of the next six to seven months. Three years ago, if you told me I'd be working at Microsoft, blogging, I'd be, 'What?' So it's hard for me to look farther into the future than that. One of my friends might invent a technology that completely changes my worldview. And I want to be there." Scoble also continues to work on the other official part of his job, interviewing software developers for the Microsoft official video-blog insider site, "Channel 9" (`channel9.msdn.com`).

Business Advice: "If you're starting a blog, read 50 for at least 2 weeks before you think about writing one. Just active reading can get you going. If you read them for two weeks and you're not fired up, either you're dead or it's not for you. I read 800 blogs a day. Usually, somebody is going to fire something off in my brain. Suddenly, you have this conversation going.

"Blogs are all about passion, what drives you, you know. If you're a skier and all you think about is how to make the perfect turn, write about that; that's going to make a great blog; or politics, if all you think about is these issues, one party versus another, write about that. That's what makes a great blog."

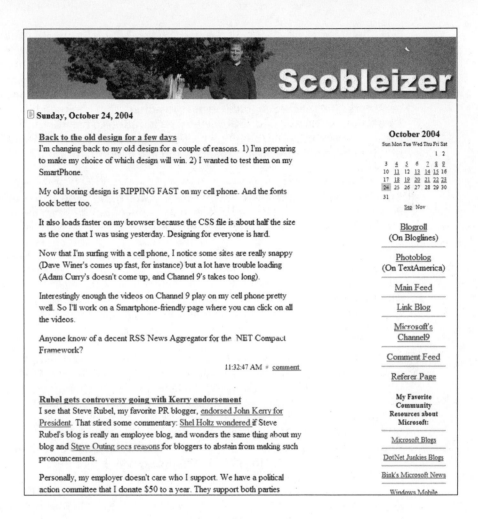

Media Kitty

URL: www.mediakitty.com

Created by: Heather Kirk, Laura Serena, and Kurt Mang

Date of birth: September 5, 2001

Numbers count: 2,729 members; 2,398 total member posts; 20,000 to 40,000 unique visits per month, with around 20 page views per visit; 10,000 e-mail subscribers to the free newsletter

The Gist: Media Kitty is a blog designed to facilitate information exchange and build connections between journalists and public relations professionals working in the travel industry. Members make content contributions in the form of press releases, story pitches, requests for contact, event information, and more. Media Kitty staff track members and facilitate introductions between members. Staff also encourage posters to adhere to a common level of excellence and usefulness, and review every registration to ensure that members are journalists or public relations professionals working in the travel industry. Membership is free for journalists and $49 a month for public relations professionals.

The Technical Details: Media Kitty runs on proprietary software running on an ASP.Net SQL server. The system boasts some common blogging functionalities: tools for posting in HTML without knowing HTML, search, and entry expiration dates. It also has some unusual aspects: 120-bit encrypted user authentication and e-commerce. The system was designed for simplicity and can be maintained by a single part-time person.

The Financial Details: Revenue comes from subscriptions. Media Kitty has conducted very little advertising or marketing, relying on word of mouth to make its target audience aware of the service.

What's Cool: Members of Media Kitty keep current via e-mail alerts and can even search for job opportunities and media trips via the site. Media Kitty launched just before September 11, 2001, but survived the depression in the travel industry that followed that date — a testament to the usefulness of the site and the value of its content.

Plans for the future: Media Kitty plans to launch an affiliate program and a syndication service and to spend some time developing a serious sales pitch to build the site's membership. In addition, it's looking for ways to help journalists sell their stories through the site. In the long term, Media Kitty plans to apply the knowledge it's gained serving this niche market to other industries.

Business Advice: "Protect your investment by earning a good reputation and coveting it. For example, build a loyal customer base and serve them in a personal way by looking out for opportunities they can benefit from. Ask them often about their needs and respond to those needs." — Heather Kirk

Technical Advice: "People should buy whatever they can off the shelf. Only develop custom code for what you can't buy out of the box. Also, be sure to design for all browsers and platforms — don't make your users jump through hoops." — Heather Kirk

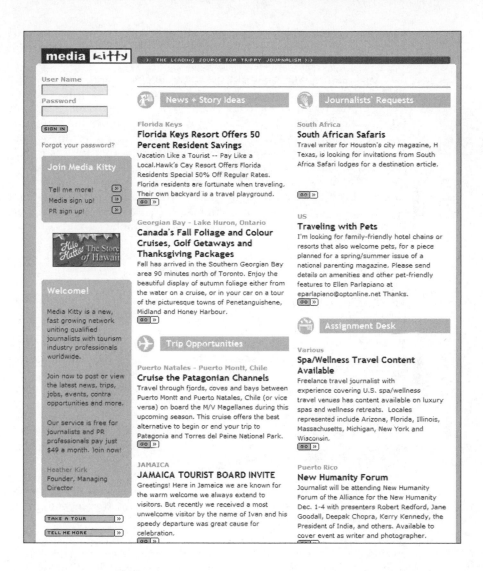

Blog Maverick

URL: www.blogmaverick.com

Created by: Mark Cuban

Date of birth: March 12, 2004

Numbers count: Blog Maverick gets about 300,000 unique visitors per month, and at times the count can be as high as 100,000 unique visitors a day.

The Gist: Mark Cuban is an entrepreneur; investor; and, since January 2000, owner of the Dallas Mavericks basketball team. Blog Maverick gives Cuban direct contact with fans and a way to tell his story without the traditional filter of the media getting in the way. Cuban also enjoys his ability to throw out ideas and get responses online. Blog Maverick is a forum for Cuban to post about his business ideas, new projects, and other interests. Cuban founded Broadcast.com and MicroSolutions, early and successful Internet companies. In November 2004, Cuban was fined by the NBA over comments made in his blog about the timing of the NBA's opening night. (Opening night was election night in the United States.) Blog Maverick is part of Weblogs, Inc. (www.weblogsinc.com), a network of blogs in niche markets.

The Technical Details: The blog runs on the Weblogs, Inc., software package called Blogsmith and is hosted by Logicworks.

The Financial Details: Cuban is a Weblogs, Inc., blogger (and an investor in the company).

What's Cool: Cuban's personal prominence and reputation in the business world, combined with his spirited cheerleading for the team, have been a winning combination in getting the blog traffic and repeat visits. Fans get specialized insight from a person they wouldn't normally have access to and can speak directly back to Cuban via the blog. You can see the success of this blog in the number of comments provoked by every posting; it's not surprising to find 50 comments on a post. Combined with the prominent "Contact Mark Cuban" link at the top of every page, the blog provides a remarkable level of access to Cuban himself.

Plans for the future: For the present, Cuban is happy with the format and interaction made possible on the blog. Maintaining that level of dialogue is key to keeping the site successful in the future.

Business Advice: "Limit blogging activity to the person in the company who sets the vision, and people who are enabled to discuss factual items, like technology. You don't want multiple employees sending different corporate messages."

Technical Advice: "Make *full* use of the software you buy."

Photo Friday

URL: www.photofriday.com

Created by: Marc North and Nick Feder

Date of birth: December 11, 2002.

Numbers count: Photo Friday gets "in the neighborhood" of 50,000 visitors a week.

The Gist: Marc North, a programmer living and working in Northern California, met Nick Feder (then a teenager) online, and the two began exchanging instant messages about photography. Eventually, the collaboration produced the idea for Photo Friday: a site where photographers respond to a weekly conceptual challenge, and exemplary photos are recognized as noteworthy. The most popular challenge was "clouds," with 660 submissions. The site has become hugely popular amongst aspiring and working photographers looking for encouragement and traffic to their portfolios. Initially North and Feder selected images for recognition, but the task became daunting as Photo Friday grew in popularity. Today, visitors vote on submissions, and the results are tallied automatically.

The Technical Details: The site began with an installation of Movable Type, but Marc North has significantly altered it, adding the Link Viewer and the voting mechanism that allows users to select noteworthy images. North has also created tools to help eliminate ballot stuffing and other system abuses to keep Photo Friday fair.

The Financial Details: North reports that the site pays for itself through advertising, which covers the $100 monthly hosting costs. His own time is donated.

What's Cool: The custom Link Viewer built by North allows visitors to keep a list of submissions open on one side of the browser while viewing individual submissions on each photographer's own Web site on the right. During the 12:01 a.m. Friday to 11:59 p.m. Sunday CST voting period, visitors can also vote for noteworthy images while they use the Link Viewer.

Plans for the future: North anticipates rebuilding and redesigning both the front and back ends of Photo Friday in the next 6 to 12 months. Ultimately, the site will a powerful user community with built-in communication and linking tools.

Business Advice: "It really is about understanding acceptable barriers to entry. You don't necessarily want everyone and his mother participating on your site, so build your community around minimal acceptable requirements for participation. It's about listening to the users and giving them some limits and rules in which to function. Listen seriously to criticisms and understanding what their needs are. Anticipate growth.

"Be ethical about the trust that people are placing in you. Establish an aggressive privacy policy and then live by it. You have to be impeccable in your trustworthiness, and don't ever violate that by selling mailing lists. It takes forever to establish that trust, but only a single incident to lose it all. It has be all about the users."

Technical Advice: "At the end of the day, if you're a one-man shop, you need to be brilliant. There are so many ways to screw up on the Web. Building a flexible schema and system out of the gate is critical. If you can't build it yourself, make sure that you have someone who can."

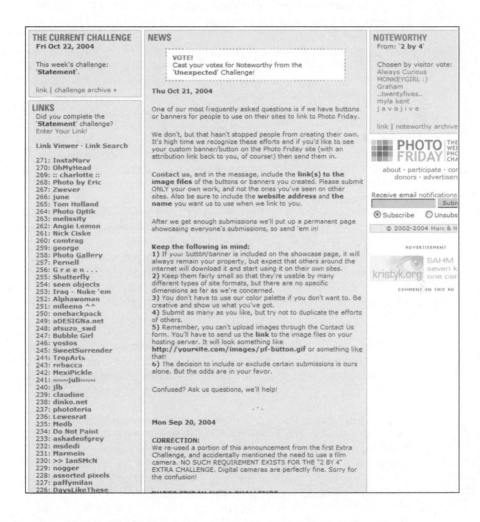

Fast Company Now (FC Now)

URL: blog.fastcompany.com

Created by: Rob Roesler created the blog; Editorial and Community Director Heath Row is the lead contributor.

Date of birth: August 5, 2003

Numbers count: The blog has gotten a lot of traffic but hasn't been tracked reliably. Fast Company has recently switched to a different tracking system to eliminate hits by robots and spiders. In general, however, traffic has trended upward since the blog was launched, with peaks around certain posts.

The Gist: Fast Company has published a business magazine focusing on revolutionary business practices and its impact on the world since 1995. In print and online, the magazine now has a print distribution of 725,000 and 3.2 million readers. In 2003, Fast Company decided to launch a team blog that multiple Fast Company writers, designers, and production staff could take part in. It was the first business magazine to launch a blog and one of the first magazines to do so. The blog gives Fast Company the ability to alert readers to issues that aren't being covered by a full story in the magazine — software that wouldn't be reviewed but might still be useful, a trend that was fully formed enough to merit 800 words or a quick opinion or stance. It is also a great way for Fast Company to ask questions of its readers and get a better idea of where trends and interests lie. Contributors also use the blog as a way to direct readers' attention to old stories suddenly current again or Web-only offerings that they might otherwise miss. The blog's major themes are leadership, innovation, and change, which reflects the general editorial direction of the magazine as well. On any given day, 3 to 5 people are assigned to blog, but as many as 20 may actually do so. There are 8 to 10 core contributors who post frequently and one staff member who comments regularly on posts.

The Technical Details: FC Now is run on Movable Type. Fast Company also uses RSS to display the most recent entries on the home page of the magazine Web site. They use the MT-Blacklist plug-in to monitor and remove spam comments.

The Financial Details: Fast Company used in-house technical and design staff to set up the blog and purchased a multiple-author Movable Type license. Staff time used in producing the blog varies, depending on the frequency of posts. Lead contributor Heath Row says that by far the biggest staff time is spent in removing spam comments from the site, sometimes up to 1.5 hours a day. The site makes revenue from advertising.

What's Cool: FC Now is remarkable in the journalism industry generally for its demonstration of openness and transparency in the organization. For instance, FC Now has frequently opened its doors to bring guest bloggers aboard. At the time of the blog's one-year anniversary, Fast Company held the FC Now Blog Jam and invited more than 30 readers to guest blog over the course of 2 days. Authors of books reviewed by the magazine are frequently invited to guest-blog for a week on topics of their choice.

Plans for the Future: Fast Company is looking for ways to integrate FC Now content more fully into the rest of the magazine Web site, beginning by pulling FC Now posts onto topic-related pages of the magazine Web site and by automatically generating topic newsletters from blog posts. As Fast Company expands its Readers' Network — an on- and offline social network of readers — it plans to offer a blog to every member (there are currently 10,000) and then help members with related interests meet and exchange ideas.

Business Advice: Heath Row: "Be part of the broader community. Don't approach a business blog as a stand-alone blog. Figure out how the Web and the blog world works before you get started. Wade in the water for a while before launching."

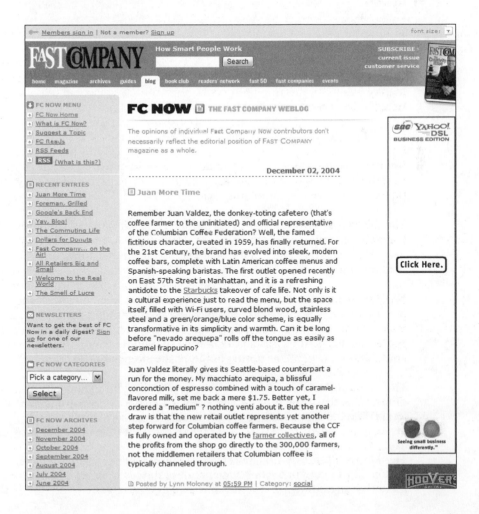

The Fast Company linking policy came under fire for its limitations and difficulty of use; the company was slammed in the blog world. The company reevaluated its policy, changed it, and participated in the online discussion on its blog and on others. Heath Row says the company got a lot of negative attention, but "had I not been part of the community, it would have been so much worse. I wouldn't have been able to respond. People who came to our defense did so because we had connections with them."

Technical Advice: Heath Row: "Be sure you have the time to keep comments clean, even if it's just responding to criticisms within the comments. If you don't allow comments, what kind of feedback mechanism do you offer? Reverse flow as well as outward flow. Keep it up to date."

Dunstan's Blog

URL: www.1976design.com/blog

Created by: Dunstan Orchard

Date of birth: August 20, 2003.

Numbers count: Dunstan says he doesn't have a good count but estimates that the site is visited about every 3 seconds, though that changes depending on what his most recent posting is about.

The Gist: While "stuck in a field" in Dorset, England, Dunstan Orchard grew frustrated reading about the technical happenings in San Francisco and decided he needed to be there. The route he decided to take in reaching San Francisco was through a blog. He also knew he needed this blog to do and be pretty special and that it needed to demonstrate his programming and design skills effectively to be noticed. Dunstan's approach was to create a personal blog with some intense programming that makes use of the latest Web standards and technology. A year after it launched, Dunstan has met the goals he began with: He's living in San Francisco, and he has a job offer in the technical industry. Moreover, he says, all the work he has gotten in the past year has been through the blog.

The Technical Details: Dunstan built nearly everything himself, including the blog engine that runs the site, using mySQL and PHP, lots of JavaScript, CSS, and XHTML. The blogrolling script was adapted from Python, but everything else is pure Dunstan.

The Financial Details: Because Dunstan wrote all the software himself, he had no startup costs beyond Web hosting. However, he notes that it took him a year of full-time work to create the blog.

What's Cool: The feature that has gotten the most attention on Dunstan's blog is the panorama that is displayed at the top of every page. This image is a real-time reflection of the weather and time of day in Dorset. The view is from the top of Dunstan's parents' house. There are more than 90 different versions of the panorama to reflect all possible weather conditions, times of day, and phases of the moon. Dunstan has even gone so far as to make the sheep behave appropriately for the current conditions — they huddle together at night and spread out during the day. Weather information is obtained from `weather.com`.

Plans for the future: Dunstan's blog is doing well, and beyond the occasional tweak he doesn't have big plans to change it. He has begun to post more photos and is thinking about trying to integrate his photography portfolio (currently at `www.1976design.com/photo/`) into the blog.

The last seven posts on Dunstan's blog

Die photos, die!
22nd October 2004, late morning | Comments (18)

If you've ever written me an email you'll know that I'm not very good at keeping up to date with my correspondence. My stock defense is that I receive more than my fair share of emails and it usually takes me a while to answer them all, but in truth I'm just rather lazy...

View this post in full (349 words, 1 image).

Skim-surfer on Stinson Beach
20th October 2004, mid-afternoon | Comments (12)

Photo of a skim-surfer on Stinson Beach, California.

View this post in full (No words, 1 image).

Hitler who?
19th October 2004, mid-afternoon | Comments (45)

On IM:

Dunstan: I've just seen something called "The Nazism Exposed Project"

that's, like, old news... surely?

View this post in full (58 words).

Anyone out there work for the INS?

Business Advice: "Be as friendly as you can possibly be and as genuine as you can possibly be. People really seem to like the fact that I refer to my mum. You've got to style yourself slightly on what your business is — Rolls Royce might not want to sound too chummy — but generally people like *human* text to read. I don't think they really like marketing talk. Be human. Use your name whenever you can."

Design Advice: "Make sure the blog looks nice. It doesn't have to be beautifully designed, and you don't have to hire some guy who will charge you a fortune and make it look like a work of art. I always think of trying to make things look classy. Good writing can overcome bad design, but I personally judge businesses by their Web sites, and if it looks horrible, I don't want to have much to do with them. Elegance above all."

Technical Advice: "Use software that people know. Demonstrate that you know what you're doing by choosing good, recognizable software."

iPodlounge

URL: www.ipodlounge.com

Created by: Dennis Lloyd and Dennis Martin

Date of birth: October 23, 2001

Numbers count: iPodlounge has 36,000 registered members in the forums and 19,000 registered users of the site (some people are registered in both places). The site serves 7 million page impressions a month — about 1.2 unique users a month.

The Gist: When Apple announced the iPod in 2001, long-time Apple fan Dennis Lloyd jumped on the product and enlisted the help of friend Dennis Martin. iPodlounge began its life as a very well-done fan site, a hobby that Lloyd maintained around his full-time job. From the first, it was beautifully designed and sought out relationships with the many iPod accessory manufacturers. By January 2002, iPodlounge had launched its most popular feature, the iPods Around the World photo gallery, which got the site noticed by iPod users in a big way — and by Apple. Apple linked to iPodlounge in April 2002, giving it an enormous boost. Over time, Lloyd (the publisher of iPodlounge) added features that turned the site into a community, giving users ways to comment and interact. He also stayed on top of new products, creating an unrivaled iPod accessory review collection. Today's offerings include news, editorials, reviews, special reports, user guides, forums, and software downloads.

The Technical Details: iPodlounge started its life as a collection of HTML pages, but Lloyd switched to pMachine Pro in early 2003, benefiting from the blog functionality and comments the software enabled. The site uses vBulletin for the forums and Coppermine Photo Gallery for the photo collections. Ads are served by phpAdsNew.

The Financial Details: iPodlounge now earns enough revenue through advertising to pay freelancers, one full-time salary, and several part-time staff.

What's Cool: Users love the breadth of the iPodlounge accessory reviews — Lloyd takes care to review new accessories as soon as they become available (and sometimes before). The iPods Around the World photo gallery was a huge hit when it was launched and remains one of the highest-trafficked areas of the site. For a peek at the current thinking of the iPodlounge staff, visit the Backstage blog, where editors ask for reader feedback, prerelease new reviews, and generally have fun: www.ipodlounge.com/backstage.

Plans for the Future: By the time this book is published, iPodlounge will have released a comprehensive guide to all things iPod. Thanks to advertiser support, the book is free to the site's readers. iPodlounge is also looking at adding more editorial content and staff.

Business Advice: "You need to connect with your readers. You can't talk down to your readers the way old-school business has. They become part of the business; that's inherent to the Internet. Businesses have a new responsibility to add a new voice to their business. It's not about brochures and salesmanship. Blogs let you get direct feedback on things if you're not afraid to have comments — both good and bad. People really like companies that respond to their feedback. We see that in our forums."

Technical Advice: "Our site is heavily designed, and people reacted well to that. A lot of blogging software comes with templates, but using a template means you'll look like a cookie-cutter. Take some time to create a design that reflects the personality of the company and differentiates you from other Web sites. Take your time, learn some CSS, get in there and get your hands dirty, and make your site reflect your personality. People will see the difference between your site and others, and it will strengthen your written voice as well."

Dennis' iPod mini color: Silver.

Courtesy of iPodlounge.com

Weblogs, Inc.

URL: www.weblogsinc.com

Created by: Brian Alvey and Jason McCabe Calacanis

Date of birth: January 1, 2004

Numbers count: Weblogs, Inc. had 65 blogs as I wrote this book and plans to add more. Several of the Weblogs, Inc. blogs have hundreds of page views monthly, some with millions.

The Gist: Co-founders Jason McCabe Calacanis and Brian Alvey believe traditional journalism is broken and that blogs are a way to make news meaningful again. In 2003, Calacanis and co-founder Brian Alvey decided they needed to be involved in blogs but that it would take a network of blogs to be a viable business. Weblogs, Inc., is that network. Weblogs, Inc., partners with individual bloggers, who get to concentrate on writing (and not on software or advertising). Weblogs, Inc., provides the blogger with software to blog with and sells advertising that appears on the blogs. Depending on the blogger, Weblogs, Inc., either pays a salary or splits advertising revenue with the blogger. The blogs range from the popular electronics blog Engadget (shown in the figure), to Blogging Baby, to the Documentary Film blog. Weblogs, Inc., has no particular content agenda — as long as a blogger brings passion for a reasonably marketable subject to the table, Weblogs, Inc., is likely to take on the project. Since starting the network, Weblogs, Inc., has only shut down one blog, after it became difficult to find new content for it. Calacanis stresses that the single biggest requirement for a potential blogger is they love what they are blogging about. The quality that results, he says, creates its own momentum, marketing, buzz, and revenue — Weblogs, Inc., spends nothing on marketing.

The Technical Details: Weblogs, Inc,. has developed its own proprietary blogging tool called Blogsmith that is used by each of its bloggers.

The Financial Details: Weblogs, Inc,. was funded by Calacanis and Mark Cuban, owner of the Dallas Mavericks.

What's Cool: Individually, each Weblogs, Inc., blog maintains its own flavor, personality, and focus, usually within the context of a unique design. Weblogs, Inc., has maintained a hands-off attitude toward its blogs — no editing, posting requirements, or influencing the content. Calacanis says, "Because we let the writers do what they want, they do a better job."

Plans for the Future: During 2005, Weblogs, Inc., will make its in-house blogging tool, Blogsmith, available to the public for free. After users reach a certain threshold of traffic, they will have the option to pay for the blog account or serve up Weblogs, Inc., advertising.

Business Advice: Calacanis: "Be honest. Participate in the blogosphere. Comment on other people's blogs; comment on what other people are saying. It's about relationships and conversations. Remember that blogs are conversations. You want to get out there and meet the people running the other blogs."

Technical Advice: Calacanis: "Post often."

Search »

Saturday, December 04, 2004

Pyrophone, the propane-powered flaming organ >

Related entries: Misc, Gadgets

It's a organ. And it plays music, alright. But it's powered by burning propane. What, you think there's something funny about that? Buddy, this is *art*. Actually, gas/heat powered organs (pyrophones) aren't really anything new, but Eric Singer and the Madagascar Institute's (a Brooklyn art combine, whatever that is) created a flame-belching, MIDI controlled, MAX/MSP software-enabled hunkahunka burning love (er, music) monster of a pyrophone. See the video now, before Ozzy (or maybe Mr. Quintron?) buys the thing and all the rights. Man, would those be some wicked solos.

Read   Permalink | Email this | Comments [4]

Samsung edges out Motorola in cellphone sales >

Related entries: Cellphones

Do you care that Samsung and Motorola have been locked in a heated battle to be #2 in the $100 billion dollar a year cell phone market? Maybe not, but can we say that the fact that this quarter Samsung's (finally) inched ahead of Motorola with 13.8 percent market share, compared to Motorola's 13.4 percent, is sort of a big deal given that Samsung hasn't been a major player for all that long? Their next target: Nokia.

Read   Permalink | Email this | Comments [5]

When are US trains gonna get WiFi? >

Related entries: Transportation, Wireless

Index

• N •

• O •

• P •

BUSINESS, CAREERS & PERSONAL FINANCE

0-7645-5307-0

Grant Writing For Dummies

Home Buying For Dummies

0-7645-5331-3 *†

Also available:

- Accounting For Dummies †
  0-7645-5314-3
- Business Plans Kit For Dummies †
  0-7645-5365-8
- Cover Letters For Dummies
  0-7645-5224-4
- Frugal Living For Dummies
  0-7645-5403-4
- Leadership For Dummies
  0-7645-5176-0
- Managing For Dummies
  0-7645-1771-6

- Marketing For Dummies
  0-7645-5600-2
- Personal Finance For Dummies *
  0-7645-2590-5
- Project Management For Dummies
  0-7645-5283-X
- Resumes For Dummies †
  0-7645-5471-9
- Selling For Dummies
  0-7645-5363-1
- Small Business Kit For Dummies *†
  0-7645-5093-4

HOME & BUSINESS COMPUTER BASICS

Windows XP For Dummies

0-7645-4074-2

Excel 2003 For Dummies

0-7645-3758-X

Also available:

- ACT! 6 For Dummies
  0-7645-2645-6
- iLife '04 All-in-One Desk Reference
  For Dummies
  0-7645-7347-0
- iPAQ For Dummies
  0-7645-6769-1
- Mac OS X Panther Timesaving
  Techniques For Dummies
  0-7645-5812-9
- Macs For Dummies
  0-7645-5656-8

- Microsoft Money 2004 For Dummies
  0-7645-4195-1
- Office 2003 All-in-One Desk Reference
  For Dummies
  0-7645-3883-7
- Outlook 2003 For Dummies
  0-7645-3759-8
- PCs For Dummies
  0-7645-4074-2
- TiVo For Dummies
  0-7645-6923-6
- Upgrading and Fixing PCs For Dummies
  0-7645-1665-5
- Windows XP Timesaving Techniques
  For Dummies
  0-7645-3748-2

FOOD, HOME, GARDEN, HOBBIES, MUSIC & PETS

Feng Shui For Dummies

0-7645-5295-3

Poker For Dummies

0-7645-5232-5

Also available:

- Bass Guitar For Dummies
  0-7645-2487-9
- Diabetes Cookbook For Dummies
  0-7645-5230-9
- Gardening For Dummies *
  0-7645-5130-2
- Guitar For Dummies
  0-7645-5106-X
- Holiday Decorating For Dummies
  0-7645-2570-0
- Home Improvement All-in-One
  For Dummies
  0-7645-5680-0

- Knitting For Dummies
  0-7645-5395-X
- Piano For Dummies
  0-7645-5105-1
- Puppies For Dummies
  0-7645-5255-4
- Scrapbooking For Dummies
  0-7645-7208-3
- Senior Dogs For Dummies
  0-7645-5818-8
- Singing For Dummies
  0-7645-2475-5
- 30-Minute Meals For Dummies
  0-7645-2589-1

INTERNET & DIGITAL MEDIA

Digital Photography For Dummies

0-7645-1664-7

Starting an eBay Business For Dummies

0-7645-6924-4

Also available:

- 2005 Online Shopping Directory
  For Dummies
  0-7645-7495-7
- CD & DVD Recording For Dummies
  0-7645-5956-7
- eBay For Dummies
  0-7645-5654-1
- Fighting Spam For Dummies
  0-7645-5965-6
- Genealogy Online For Dummies
  0-7645-5964-8
- Google For Dummies
  0-7645-4420-9

- Home Recording For Musicians
  For Dummies
  0-7645-1634-5
- The Internet For Dummies
  0-7645-4173-0
- iPod & iTunes For Dummies
  0-7645-7772-7
- Preventing Identity Theft For Dummies
  0-7645-7336-5
- Pro Tools All-in-One Desk Reference
  For Dummies
  0-7645-5714-9
- Roxio Easy Media Creator For Dummies
  0-7645-7131-1

* Separate Canadian edition also available

† Separate U.K. edition also available

Available wherever books are sold. For more information or to order direct: U.S. customers visit www.dummies.com or call 1-877-762-2974.
U.K. customers visit www.wileyeurope.com or call 0800 243407. Canadian customers visit www.wiley.ca or call 1-800-567-4797.

WILEY

SPORTS, FITNESS, PARENTING, RELIGION & SPIRITUALITY

0-7645-5146-9

0-7645-5418-2

Also available:

- Adoption For Dummies
  0-7645-5488-3
- Basketball For Dummies
  0-7645-5248-1
- The Bible For Dummies
  0-7645-5296-1
- Buddhism For Dummies
  0-7645-5359-3
- Catholicism For Dummies
  0-7645-5391-7
- Hockey For Dummies
  0-7645-5228-7

- Judaism For Dummies
  0-7645-5299-6
- Martial Arts For Dummies
  0-7645-5358-5
- Pilates For Dummies
  0-7645-5397-6
- Religion For Dummies
  0-7645-5264-3
- Teaching Kids to Read For Dummies
  0-7645-4043-2
- Weight Training For Dummies
  0-7645-5168-X
- Yoga For Dummies
  0-7645-5117-5

TRAVEL

0-7645-5438-7

0-7645-5453-0

Also available:

- Alaska For Dummies
  0-7645-1761-9
- Arizona For Dummies
  0-7645-6938-4
- Cancún and the Yucatán For Dummies
  0-7645-2437-2
- Cruise Vacations For Dummies
  0-7645-6941-4
- Europe For Dummies
  0-7645-5456-5
- Ireland For Dummies
  0-7645-5455-7

- Las Vegas For Dummies
  0-7645-5448-4
- London For Dummies
  0-7645-4277-X
- New York City For Dummies
  0-7645-6945-7
- Paris For Dummies
  0-7645-5494-8
- RV Vacations For Dummies
  0-7645-5443-3
- Walt Disney World & Orlando For Dummies
  0-7645-6943-0

GRAPHICS, DESIGN & WEB DEVELOPMENT

0-7645-4345-8

0-7645-5589-8

Also available:

- Adobe Acrobat 6 PDF For Dummies
  0-7645-3760-1
- Building a Web Site For Dummies
  0-7645-7144-3
- Dreamweaver MX 2004 For Dummies
  0-7645-4342-3
- FrontPage 2003 For Dummies
  0-7645-3882-9
- HTML 4 For Dummies
  0-7645-1995-6
- Illustrator cs For Dummies
  0-7645-4084-X

- Macromedia Flash MX 2004 For Dummies
  0-7645-4358-X
- Photoshop 7 All-in-One Desk
  Reference For Dummies
  0-7645-1667-1
- Photoshop cs Timesaving Techniques
  For Dummies
  0-7645-6782-9
- PHP 5 For Dummies
  0-7645-4166-8
- PowerPoint 2003 For Dummies
  0-7645-3908-6
- QuarkXPress 6 For Dummies
  0-7645-2593-X

NETWORKING, SECURITY, PROGRAMMING & DATABASES

0-7645-6852-3

0-7645-5784-X

Also available:

- A+ Certification For Dummies
  0-7645-4187-0
- Access 2003 All-in-One Desk
  Reference For Dummies
  0-7645-3988-4
- Beginning Programming For Dummies
  0-7645-4997-9
- C For Dummies
  0-7645-7068-4
- Firewalls For Dummies
  0-7645-4048-3
- Home Networking For Dummies
  0-7645-42796

- Network Security For Dummies
  0-7645-1679-5
- Networking For Dummies
  0-7645-1677-9
- TCP/IP For Dummies
  0-7645-1760-0
- VBA For Dummies
  0-7645-3989-2
- Wireless All In-One Desk Reference
  For Dummies
  0-7645-7496-5
- Wireless Home Networking For Dummies
  0-7645-3910-8